flies for Trout

BY DICK STEWART & FARROW ALLEN

Book Design and Illustrations • Larry Largay
Photography • Dick Stewart

Published by Mountain Pond Publishing
P.O. Box 797
North Conway, NH 03860
USA

Distributed by Lyons & Burford
31 West 21 Street
New York, NY 10010
USA

Printed in the United States of America by Capital Offset Company

First Edition

ISBN 0-936644-14-1 Hardcover
ISBN 0-936644-15-X Softcover

PREFACE

For over five centuries, men and women have been trying to deceive trout. Some used natural baits to lure a trout to their hook, while others applied their wits and imagination to craft imitations of insects. Their frauds then, as now, were constructed using thread, feathers and hair. These many years later little has changed - but then again, much is different. The definition of artificial fly has been broadened to incorporate imitations of insects other than flies, as well as most other forms of aquatic life - indeed, virtually any animal form upon which fish feed.

Whether the designing of trout flies is art, craft, science, or even alchemy, we leave to the reader to decide. Fly fishers, and particularly fly tiers, are in perpetual search of their grail - that mystical combination of materials which will prove irresistible to trout. The trout fisher's aphrodisiac. Some flies have achieved a degree of success and their names are forever etched into fly-fishing history. The Royal Coachman, Mickey Finn, Adams and Muddler Minnow exemplify such successes. As with race horses, anglers have endowed their creations with names, personalizing them in perpetuity.

Other flies result from a more pragmatic approach to trout fishing. The theory is simple: understand everything about the fish, its environs, its food, and then trick that tiny fish brain by imitating that which it's programmed to eat. This more scientific approach works, and has become the basis for most modern fly tying. We not only imitate mayflies in general, but we can construct flies to represent each of their life stages, even by gender when needed, and our books and charts will generally tell us when and where these flies are to be used. The flies which result from this approach customarily bear names which describe the insects being imitated, and/or the ingredients used. Thus, we have our Green Drakes, Hexagenias, Poly Wing Spinners and Elk Hair Caddis. But even this logical method, though effective much of the time, reveals enough inconsistencies that we can only conclude there is much not yet understood concerning fish and insect behavior.

There also are other design categories: flies which are just easy to tie, flies which simply look pretty, flies strongly identified with certain locales, flies which seem to catch fish for reasons unknown, and flies bearing the names of skilled fly tiers or notable fly fishermen. Often these latter flies have had their designer's name added by vendors, to distinguish them from flies with similar names. One commonality to all flies is that they are each made with your own hands, using whatever personal skills and creativity you possess. Aside from yourself, your only critic will be the trout. The point is, there is no single approach to fly design or usage. Because of this there can be no single, all-encompassing approach to this book.

The flies we selected are important in their own right, or represent a tying style which we considered worthwhile sharing. For some readers these pages will contain too many flies, for others too few. For some we will have illustrated an excessive number of western flies, while for others the opposite will be true. We may have omitted your favorite fly, or we may have shown too many of one style for your needs. What we have presented is what we believe to be the most representative and important trout flies as we near the 21st century. We have not, however, neglected some of our roots and tradition. Fly boxes of many anglers remain filled with many hallowed fly patterns which, like an old familiar fishing vest, continue to serve the fisher well.

We hope that *Flies for Trout* will be accepted as an accurate and representative reference, for many of the flies pictured were tied by the finest tiers in American fly fishing. If any errors exist, then the responsibility for them is entirely ours and should in no way reflect on the individual fly tiers. In a few instances a fly name may be spelled, punctuated or presented in two different ways. We tried to respect the original usage whenever possible, even if it resulted in some minor inconsistencies in our listings. Also, we elected not to be too specific concerning the models of hooks to be used. With several excellent brands of hooks on the market we believe the information we provided should be sufficient to guide the fly tier toward an appropriate hook.

It is customary to use this portion of a book to express gratitude to those who made a contribution. We are so wholly indebted to so many people it's frankly impossible to single out anyone, but we particularly appreciate the free sharing of ideas and knowledge, for such a sharing of flies and ideas is like a fraternal custom, and in many ways the motivation for us to produce this book. We've been helped by scores of fellow fly tiers, and the best we can do is to call your attention to each of them as identified with the photographs. Our most heartfelt thanks to everyone who was so helpful - we really couldn't have done it without you.

One friend was not able to complete her work with us on this book. Fran Stuart, who was posthumously named Angler of the Year by *Fly Rod & Reel* magazine, had hoped to help us finish this book, but cancer intervened. Had she been able to fulfill her ambition, this book would have undoubtedly been a much better product, for it was Fran's skills and demands that made us settle for nothing less than the best we could do.

CONTENTS

All-Purpose
Dry Flies

Our classification system considers a dry fly to be "all-purpose" if it seems to have no resemblance to a specific insect. Some authorities might classify such flies as "attractor patterns," but we prefer the term all-purpose. Since the Adams has become America's most popular all-purpose dry fly, we have selected it to provide an example of the many ways in which any fly pattern might be modified. History is unclear as to what the original Adams, shown first, was intended to resemble. Clearly, it bears a similarity to some mayflies and caddisflies, and even some craneflies. In any event the Adams became the ideal candidate for tiers to modify to meet their individual preferences. Our purpose in presenting these somewhat repetitious dressings is to demonstrate how one might apply his imagination to most all of the dry-fly patterns on subsequent pages.

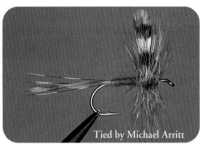
Tied by Michael Arritt

ADAMS

Hook:	Dry fly, size 10 to 20	Body:	Gray muskrat fur
Thread:	Gray or black	Wing:	Grizzly hackle tips
Tail:	Mixed grizzly and brown hackle barbs	Hackle:	Mixed grizzly and brown

Originally tied about 1920 by Leonard Halladay of Mayfield, Michigan. Named for Charles F. Adams of Lorain, Ohio, who fished it with good success on the Boardman River in Michigan.

Tied by Michael Arritt

ADAMS, DOWNWING

Hook:	Dry fly, size 10 to 20	Body:	Gray muskrat fur
Thread:	Gray or black	Wing:	Grizzly hackle tips
Tail:	Mixed grizzly and brown hackle barbs (optional)	Hackle:	Mixed grizzly and brown

Dressed with the hackle-tip wings lying back over the body, this Adams easily imitates a caddis or stonefly; in small sizes perhaps a midge.

Tied by Michael Arritt

ADAMS, FEMALE

Hook:	Dry fly, size 10 to 16	Body:	Gray muskrat fur
Thread:	Gray or black	Wing:	Grizzly hackle tips
Tail:	Mixed gray and brown hackle barbs	Hackle:	Mixed grizzly and brown
Egg sac:	Sulphur yellow fur		

Female mayflies and caddisflies can often be seen with bright yellow, green or orange egg clusters at the end of their abdomens. At times, trout seem to key on this feature and having a few flies like this, in a variety of sizes, might just save the day.

Tied by Patrick Berry

ADAMS, HAIRWING

Hook:	Dry fly, size 10 to 18	Body:	Gray muskrat fur
Thread:	Gray or black	Wing:	White calftail or calf body hair
Tail:	Moose body hair	Hackle:	Mixed grizzly and brown

Western tiers have generally preferred heavily dressed hairwing flies for their attractor patterns. It was only natural that the favorite Adams would be converted to satisfy the preferences of Rocky Mountain anglers.

Tied by Michael Arritt

ADAMS, MOOSETAIL

Hook:	Dry fly, size 10 to 20	Body:	Gray muskrat fur
Thread:	Gray or black	Wing:	Grizzly hackle tips
Tail:	A few long strands of dark moose body hair, divided to each side	Hackle:	Mixed grizzly and brown

The tail of this fly resembles that of a mayfly and results in a different silhouette than a conventionally tied Adams.

ADAMS, PARACHUTE

Hook:	Dry fly, size 10 to 18		a tiny ball of dubbed fur
Thread:	Gray or black	Body:	Gray muskrat fur
Tail:	Two small bunches of mixed grizzly	Wing:	White calftail clump
	and brown hackle barbs divided around	Hackle:	Mixed grizzly and brown

Tied by Michael Arritt

Winding the hackle on the topside of the hook, in a horizontal plane that's parallel to the shank, allows the entire body of the fly to sit on the surface and offer a truer silhouette. The white wing adds to visibility.

ADAMS, REVERSED

Hook:	Dry fly, size 10 to 16	Body:	Gray muskrat fur
Thread:	Gray or black	Wing:	Grizzly hackle tips
Tail:	Mixed grizzly and brown hackle barbs		

Tied by Michael Arritt

A reverse-dressed dry fly is not something you see every day, but it's more than a fanciful concept. Most mayfly duns float downstream head first and are usually taken that way by trout. The hackle also helps hide the hook from sight.

ADAMS, SPENT WING

Hook:	Dry fly, size 10 to 20	Body:	Gray muskrat fur
Thread:	Gray or black	Wing:	Grizzly hackle tips, tied spent
Tail:	Mixed grizzly and brown hackle barbs	Hackle:	Mixed grizzly and brown

Tied by Michael Arritt

With the current abundant supply of realistic spinner imitations, the popularity of the Spent Wing Adams has slipped from past levels. Even so, this is still one of the best searching patterns you can cast to trout since it represents various insects.

ADAMS, SWEDISH

Hook:	Swedish dry fly, size 12 to 18	Hackle:	Mixed grizzly and brown
Thread:	Gray or black	Note:	The natural orientation of this hook is
Tail:	Mixed grizzly and brown hackle barbs		with the point up. Tying the tail di-
Body:	Gray muskrat		vided helps stabilize the fly.
Wing:	Grizzly hackle tips		

Tied by Michael Arritt

This Adams is tied on a Partridge hook designed by two Swedish anglers, Nils Ericksson and Gunnar Johnson. Their primary goal was to keep the hook point from penetrating the surface of the water.

ADAMS, THORAX

Hook:	Dry fly, size 10 to 20	Wing:	Grizzly hen hackle tips, cut or burned
Thread:	Gray or black		to shape, placed toward the middle of
Tail:	Grizzly and brown hackle barbs divided		the hook shank
	around a tiny ball of dubbed fur	Hackle:	Mixed grizzly and brown, wound tho-
Body:	Gray muskrat fur		rax style, trimmed in a "V" on the bottom

Tied by Michael Arritt

Vince Marinaro introduced the thorax dun in *A Modern Dry Fly Code*. This style was to fool the wary brown trout of Pennsylvania's limestone creeks. Thorax flies present a realistic silhouette.

ADAMS, USD

Hook:	Dry fly, size 10 to 20	Wing:	Broad grizzly hen hackle tips, cut or
Thread:	Gray or black		burned to shape
Tail:	Mixed grizzly and brown hackle barbs	Hackle:	Mixed grizzly and brown tied para-
Body:	Gray muskrat fur		chute style, underneath the wing

Tied by Michael Arritt

The USD style (upside down) was introduced by Brian Clarke and John Goddard in their book, *The Trout and the Fly*. After much observation, they concluded that this style provided a truly accurate silhouette of a mayfly dun resting on its legs with its body barely suspended off the surface.

Tied by Richard Hurni

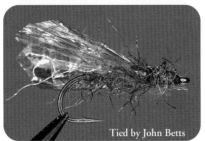

Tied by John Betts

Tied by Dick Stewart

Tied by Umpqua Feather Merchants

Tied by Walter Burr

Tied by Farrow Allen

AMY SPECIAL

Hook:	Dry fly, size 10 to 16	Body:	Fluorescent red chenille
Thread:	Black	Wing:	White calftail
Tail:	A single red hackle tip	Hackle:	Grizzly

A neat little downwing searching pattern from California's Butte Creek area, the Amy Special can be tied with other body colors to bring trout up in fast water.

BETTS GENERIC BUG

Hook:	Dry fly, size 12 to 22 (2X long for hook sizes 6 to 10)		standard Z-lon, and a small amount of brown rabbit fur
Thread:	Brown	Wing:	Zing, mottled lightly with a marking pen
Body:	Mixed brown Crinkled Z-lon, brown		

John Betts says this may be the "...best fly I've ever had, wet or dry." Tie it in any size you can manage, and fish it as a midge, mayfly, caddisfly or stonefly.

BIVISIBLE, BROWN

Hook:	Dry fly, size 10 to 16	Body:	Several brown hackles tied in at the rear
Thread:	Brown		and palmered forward tightly; in front
Tail:	Brown hackle barbs, or two brown hackle tips curving out		are several turns of white hackle.

This heavily-hackled searching pattern was developed in the East many years ago and is often tied in colors other than brown. The name "bivisible" stems from the contrasting white hackle which makes an otherwise dull-colored fly visible to the angler, as well as to the trout below.

BLACK GNAT

Hook:	Dry fly, size 12 to 20	Body:	Black fur
Thread:	Black	Wing:	Dark gray duck wing quill sections
Tail:	Black hackle barbs	Hackle:	Black

In the spring this is still one of the best all-purpose flies you can throw at native brook trout in the lakes and streams of New England. Spring, by the way, doesn't usually arrive in much of this region until June.

BURR'S BRITE

Hook:	Dry fly, size 12 to 16		hackle barbs
Thread:	Black	Body:	Fluorescent green yarn
Tail:	Light woodchuck guard hair or white	Hackle:	Grizzly

This is a radiant searching pattern that works well under overcast skies, or during the low-light periods at dawn and dusk.

COACHMAN

Hook:	Dry fly, size 10 to 18	Body:	Peacock herl
Thread:	Black	Rib:	Fine gold wire (optional)
Tag:	Flat gold tinsel (optional)	Wing:	White duck wing quill sections
Tail:	Brown hackle barbs or golden pheasant tippets	Hackle:	Coachman brown

The Coachman was first tied as a wet fly (which see) and is still more commonly tied that way. The dry fly variation usually omits the tag and the tippet tail in favor of hackle barbs for better flotation.

CRACKLEBACK

Hook: Dry fly, 2X long, size 12
Thread: Black or olive
Body: Pale yellow-olive dubbing
Shellback: Two or more peacock herls
Hackle: Dark furnace, palmered

Although Ed Story says that he only ties this fly in size 12, we've found it to be equally effective tied to size 16 or 18 when the water is low. Story describes it as "one of a series of dry woolly worm patterns."

Tied by Ed Story

DELAWARE ADAMS

Hook: Dry Fly, size 10 to 20
Thread: Gray or black
Tail: Grizzly hackle barbs
Body: Olive floss
Body hackle: Grizzly, palmered
Wing: Grizzly hackle tips
Hackle: Mixed grizzly and brown

The Delaware Adams was developed by veteran Catskill tier Walt Dette of Roscoe, New York, for the Delaware River. Because, Walt says, "someone always wants something different . . . no mater how good the original pattern is." This is a favorite fly for many anglers.

Tied by Mike Arritt

DEVIL BUG, RED

Hook: Dry fly or nymph, 1X long, size 8 to 14
Thread: White or red
Body: Red chenille
Tail, shellback and head: Natural or white deer body hair

The Devil Bug may be tied in many other colors, including one particularly popular variation tied with dark deer body hair pulled over a peacock herl body. This pattern is also known by other names, including Cooper Bug and Doodle Bug, and there are several different schools of thought regarding what this fly represents. Don't underestimate the value of this simple fly.

Tied by Dick Stewart

DISCO MOUSE

Hook: Dry fly salmon, size 4 to 12
Thread: Black
Tail: Natural dark or dyed deer or moose body hair
Body: Hair from the tail bound to the shank
with criss-cross wraps of thread
Wing: Flashabou of your choice over which is dark deer or moose body hair
Head: Butt ends from the wing pulled to the top of the hook and trimmed flat

First tied in British Columbia on the Bulkley River for steelhead, by Collin Schadrech, the Disco Mouse has earned a reputation in Alaska as a proven trout fly.

Tied by Farrow Allen

DORATO HARE'S EAR

Hook: Dry fly, size 10 to 16
Thread: Brown
Tail: Grizzly hackle barbs, short
Body: Roughly dubbed hare's ear fur
Wing: A single upright clump of woodduck
flank
Hackle: Mixed grizzly and dark ginger, trimmed flat on the bottom so the fly rides flush in the water

Bill Dorato, who introduced this fly in the late 1970s, also ties a light colored version with a bleached sandy-ginger colored hare's ear body, and a light grizzly mixed with light ginger hackle.

Tied by Mike Motyl

DOUBLE WING, LIME

Hook: Dry fly, size 6 to 18
Thread: Light green or pale yellow
Tail: White or very pale lime sparkle yarn, combed out
Tip: White floss
Rear wing: Red-brown elk hair extending over
the sparkle yarn tail
Body: Lime sparkle yarn, roughly dubbed
Body hackle: Grizzly dyed olive, trimmed flat on the top and bottom
Front wing: White calftail
Hackle: Grizzly

Gary LaFontaine designed the Double Wing series to "float very flush on the surface film" and be tied in a wide range of colors to attract fish under varying light conditions. In his book *The Dry Fly*, LaFontaine lists eleven variations.

Tied by Gary LaFontaine

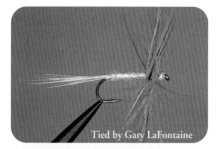

Tied by Gary LaFontaine

Tied by Farrow Allen

Tied by Farrow Allen

Tied by Dick Stewart

Tied by Bill Franke

Tied by Mike Motyl

FLAME THROWER

Hook: Dry fly, size, size 10 to 12
Thread: White
Tail: Cree hackle barbs

Body: Gray-white dubbing
Hackle: Mixed cree and fluorescent orange, tied oversize in the style of a variant

LaFontaine believes that a hot fluorescent-colored hackle wrapped together with a dull natural one enhances "the form of the fly at dusk without alarming the fish."

GOLD-RIBBED HARE'S EAR

Hook: Dry fly, size 10 to 18
Thread: Brown or gray
Tail: Brown hackle barbs
Body: Coarse hare's ear and mask fur

Rib: Fine gold wire
Wing: Dark gray goose or duck wing quill sections
Hackle: Brown

This is the dry-fly version of a fly that is most commonly tied as either a nymph or wet fly (which see). Tied as a dry, the Hare's Ear is a buggy looking thing that's a killer in small sizes.

H & L VARIANT

Hook: Dry fly, size 8 to 16
Thread: Black
Tail: White calf tail
Body: Stripped peacock quill at the rear and peacock herl at the front; if you strip off

half the herl and leave half on, you should be able to wrap the body in a single step with a single piece stem
Wing: White calftail
Hackle: Brown

Sometimes called the House & Lot, this fly is known to have been a favorite dry fly of President Eisenhower. It's still the choice of many experienced fly fishermen.

HORNBERG

Hook: Dry fly, 2X long, size 6 to 16
Thread: Black
Body: Flat silver tinsel
Wing: Yellow hackle barbs over which is a

symmetrical mallard flank feather, folded into shape, and tied tent style over the top
Hackle: Mixed grizzly and brown

This Hornberg variation (see also Hornberg Special) is tied as a dry fly, even though it may be fished either wet or dry. In Northern New England, where Hornbergs are among the best-selling dry flies, they are tied in many colors including brown, yellow and green, sometimes with a dubbed fur body.

KATMAI SLIDER

Hook: Salmon dry, turned up eye, size 2 to 6
Thread: Fluorescent orange
Tail: Dark elk or deer body hair
Body: White poly yarn

Hackle: Fairly long grizzly, wound as a collar and pulled down and back
Wing: Natural light deer body hair, with the butts trimmed short on top

Fished dead drift, it's a good fly for trout and grayling on most Alaskan rivers, but cast down and across as a "waking" fly, it's deadly.

KATTERMAN

Hook: Dry fly, size 12 to 16
Thread: Cream or white
Tail: Brown hackle barbs
Body: Peacock herl

Body hackle: Dark brown hackle, palmered heavily, but not so much that it hides or mashes down the peacock herl body
Front hackle: White

The Katterman was developed for the Catskill Mountain streams of upstate New York by Walt Dette. It combines the features of a variety of successful flies, including the Brown Bivisible and the Renegade.

KOLZER FIREFLY, YELLOW

Hook: Dry fly, size 10 or 12
Thread: Black
Tail: Natural light elk or similar
Body: Fluorescent yellow yarn in back and cream dubbing in front
Body hackle: Brown, two or three turns only
Wing: Light elk hair
Hackle: Brown

Tied using either fluorescent orange or yellow yarn, the Kolzer is an ideal fly for searching riffles and broken water in failing light. Like the Flame Thrower (which see), the Kolzer carries just the right amount of fluorescence to attract trout without frightening them.

Tied by Gary LaFontaine

MADAM X

Tail: Natural light deer body hair
Body: Fluorescent orange or yellow floss tied over the butt ends of the tail
Body hackle: Brown (optional)
Head and wing: Natural light deer body hair, tied reversed or bullethead style, with most of the deer hair pulled back on top to take more of the shape of a wing rather than a collar
Legs: White rubber hackle, tied to form an X

The Madam X was designed by Doug Swisher for fishing Montana's Bitterroot River. It has become one of the hot, new searching patterns for the Rockies and elsewhere.

Tied by Shane Stalcup

MOHAWK

Hook: Dry fly, size 10 to 14
Thread: Black
Body: White elk or deer body hair spun and trimmed flat on the bottom and like a Mohawk haircut on top
Collar: Very long, soft webby dun hackle
Note: The Mohawk is often tied two-tone, the rear ⅔ being either natural gray or dyed red, orange or green, while the front ⅓ is white.

This oddly-designed fly was originated by Gary LaFontaine's daughter, Heather, when she was 15 years old. After many years no one knows why it works, but it sure does.

Tied by Heather LaFontaine

MR. RAPIDAN

Hook: Dry fly, size 12 to 18
Thread: Tan
Tail: Dark moose hair
Body: Yellowish tan dubbing
Wing: Yellow calftail
Hackle: Mixed brown and grizzly

The Mr. Rapidan was developed for the Shenandoah Valley by Harry Murray of Edinburgh, Virginia. Murray operates a fly-fishing shop and is well known throughout the mid-Atlantic states as an authority on trout and smallmouth bass.

Tied by Harry Murray

OCCASION

Hook: Dry fly, size 14 or 16
Thread: Black
Body: Red floss covering only the front half of the hook shank
Hackle: Two cream mixed with a single cree
Wing: Tips of the two cream hackles, extending straight out over the eye of the hook

Gary LaFontaine describes this oddly conceived searching pattern as a "hanging type of fly." It sits on the surface, supported by the hackle collar, with its wings in the air pointing straight up.

Tied by Dick Stewart

RAT-FACED McDOUGAL

Hook: Dry fly, size 8 to 16
Thread: Primrose yellow
Tail: Ginger hackle barbs
Body: Natural deer body hair, spun and clipped
Wing: White bucktail
Hackle: Ginger

Harry Darbee's Rat-Faced McDougal developed from an earlier fly he called the Beaverkill Bastard and like the Beaverkill Bastard, the early Rat-Face McDougals were tied with light grizzly hackle-tip wings. Darbee tied this hairwing variation for a friend with failing eyesight, and soon it became the standard.

Tied by Larry Duckwall

Tied by Dick Surette

RIFFLE, GRIZZLY

Hook:	Dry fly, 2X long, size 8 to 16		Body:	Gray poly-dubbing or muskrat fur
Thread:	Black		Wing:	White calftail, slightly longer than usual
Tail:	White calftail		Hackle:	Grizzly

Dick Surette, founder of *Fly Tyer* magazine and author of *Trout & Salmon Fly Index*, began tying Riffle flies around 1964. Tied in several colors including gray and brown, Riffle flies all feature prominent white calftail wings and tails, making them easy to see in failing light and on a river's riffled surface.

Tied by Cathy Beck

ROYAL COACHMAN

Hook:	Dry fly, size 10 to 20		Body:	Peacock herl, red floss and peacock herl
Thread:	Black		Wing:	White duck wing quill sections
Tail:	Golden pheasant tippets		Hackle:	Dark or coachman brown

What can you say about the Royal Coachman, aside from its being the most familiar fly in the entire world, and one that has been enticing trout for over 100 years! The modern hairwing version, with white tail and wings, is more durable and commonly used.

Tied by Cathy Beck

ROYAL COACHMAN, FANWING

Hook:	Dry fly, size 10 to 14		Wing:	White duck breast feathers curving
Thread:	Black			away from one another
Tail:	Golden pheasant tippets		Hackle:	Dark or coachman brown
Body:	Peacock herl, red floss and peacock herl			

Around the turn of the century, Fredrick Halford was very involved with dry-fly design. Experimenting with different techniques and materials, he came up with the the fanwing. For many years fanwing flies were considered among the best searching patterns being fished on American waters.

Tied by Tom Travis

RENEGADE, ROYAL

Hook:	Dry fly, size 10 to 16		Rear hackle:	Brown
Thread:	Black		Body:	Peacock herl, red floss and peacock herl
Tag:	Flat gold tinsel		Front hackle:	Brown or white

This is a popular Western fly that combines features from two successful standards, the Royal Coachman and the Renegade. It may be tied and fished as either a wet fly or dry fly.

Tied by Dick Stewart

SKITTERBUG

Hook:	Dry fly, size 10 to 14		spin another equal bunch of hair with
Thread:	Black or gray		the butt ends facing forward. Trim the
Hackle:	Natural or dyed deer body hair		butts from both bunches as close as
Note:	Spin a bunch of deer body hair with the		possible, and push both bunches to-
	butt ends facing back. In front of this		gether towards the center of the hook.

In the early 1970s, Dick Stewart designed this fly as an alternative method for tying traditional skating flies, for which suitable hackle is hard to find. Under controlled line tension it literally skates on edge.

SPIDER, BADGER

Hook:	Short shank, light wire, size 12 to 16		Tail:	Badger hackle barbs
Thread:	Black		Hackle:	Badger, oversize

Spiders, with their long oversize hackles, can be deadly on still or slow-moving water. Beacause of their design, they fall to the surface very gently. They can also be skated and skittered across the surface like an escaping insect, sometimes drawing savage responses.

Tied by Dick Stewart

TRUDE, LIME

Hook:	Dry fly, size 8 to 16
Thread:	Black
Tail:	Golden pheasant tippets
Body:	Lime colored dubbing
Wing:	White calftail
Hackle:	Mixed brown and grizzly

This has been the fly of choice at the Jackson Hole One-Fly Contest, and thus has become one of the most popular Trude variations in the Rockies.

Tied by Patrick Berry

TRUDE, ROYAL

Hook:	Dry fly, size 8 to 16
Thread:	Black
Tail:	Golden pheasant tippets
Body:	Peacock herl, red floss and peacock herl
Wing:	White calftail
Hackle:	Brown

The Royal Trude is an adaptation of the original Trude, which has been a favorite for casting onto fast-water runs since it was introduced at the turn of the century. The first fly was tied at the A.S. Trude Ranch in Island Park, Idaho, as a joke, on an oversize hook. Nearly 100 years later, this "joke" is still an important pattern.

Tied by Dick Stewart

TURCK TARANTULA

Hook:	Dry fly, 2X long, size 6 to 14
Thread:	Tan
Tail:	Amherst pheasant tippets
Body:	Hares mask fur
Wing:	White calftail over which are strands of pearl crystal flash
Legs:	White rubber hackle
Collar and head:	Natural gray deer body hair, spun and trimmed, left untrimmed on top

This hot new pattern from the Rockies took first place in the 1990 Jackson Hole One-Fly Contest. It may be tied in several color variations.

Tied by Guy Turck

UGLY RUDAMUS

Hook:	Dry fly, size 8 to 14
Thread:	Yellow
Tail:	Natural elk hair
Body:	Pearl Flashabou, wrapped; front ⅓ is yellow thread
Underwing:	Sparse pearl Flashabou and mottled synthetic sheet wing material
Head and overwing:	Natural elk hair pulled back bullet head style, over the top half only
Legs:	White rubber hackle

John Foust, of Hamilton, Montana, developed the Ugly Rudamus for use on the Bitterroot River. He says it works fished dead drift, or retrieved on the surface.

Tied by Dan Bailey's Fly Shop

USUAL

Hook:	Dry fly, size 10 to 20
Thread:	Fluorescent red
Tail:	Hair from between the pads of a snow-shoe rabbit's foot
Body:	Snowshoe rabbit underfur, natural or dyed light rust
Wing:	Same as the tail, tied full, as an upright clump

The hair from a rabbit foot floats well and the fine texture provides enough subtle movement when wet to make the Usual very appealing. When it sinks at the end of a drift, fish it back wet. If you can't find a snowshoe rabbit, Betters suggests using the hair from any rabbit you can find.

Tied by Francis Betters

WRIGHT'S ROYAL

Hook:	Dry fly, 2X to 3X long, size 8 to 14
Thread:	Black or red
Rear butt:	Peacock herl
Body:	Red tying thread
Wing:	Hair from the tip of a raccoon tail, badger guard hair or light elk
Thorax:	Peacock herl
Hackle:	Cree or brown, wrapped over the thorax

Developed on Montana's Big Horn River, Wright's Royal is a fly which will produce trout anywhere in America.

Tied by Dick Stewart

All-Purpose Dry Flies

The Humpy developed as a variation of the Horner Deer Hair Fly that Jack Horner of San Francisco first tied around 1940. Several of these originals were discovered and brought to the Rockies by Pat and Sig Barnes. They were very impressed by the fish-catching qualities of this odd looking shellback dry fly, and began tying them for sale in their Montana fly shop. Not only did these Humpies and Goofus Bugs - as they were later called - catch fish, they seemed unsinkable. Even after a dozen or more trout had chewed their shellbacks to tatters, trout seemed just as eager to eat them. Since the 1940s, many variations have surfaced, but the basic shape and design remains constant. These are not your slender, quill-bodied Eastern flies, but are rugged, high floating, meaty flies perfect for fishing the faster Western rivers. Notable western fly tiers like Pat and Sig Barnes, Dan Bailey and Jack Dennis have all contributed to the refinement and popularity of the Humpy.

Tied by Dan Bailey's Fly Shop

DOUBLE HUMPY, YELLOW

Hook:	Nymph, 2X or 3X long, size 6 to 10	Overbody:	Light elk or deer body hair
Thread:	Yellow	Wing:	Light elk or deer body hair
Tail:	Light elk or deer body hair	Hackle:	Mixed grizzly and brown
Underbody:	Yellow thread or floss	Note:	Of course, almost every step is doubled

The idea for the Double Humpy seems to have come from Joe Allen, a resident guide from Jackson Hole, Wyoming. If one Humpy was good, then two Humpies on the same hook had to be better, and considering the popularity of this fly in the Rockies, he may have been right.

Tied by Umpqua Feather Merchants

FLUORESCENT GREEN HUMPY

Hook:	Dry fly, size 8 to 18		
Thread:	Yellow or light olive	Overbody:	Light elk or deer body hair
Tail:	Light elk or deer body hair	Wing:	Light elk or deer body hair
Underbody:	Fluorescent green floss	Hackle:	Dark brown

A number of floating flies with fluorescent or lime green bodies are starting to show up in the west with some regularity. The Lime Trude (which see) is an example. This new Humpy, tied as a single or a double, has been a well-received addition.

Tied by Umpqua Feather Merchants

RED HUMPY

Hook:	Dry fly, size 8 to 18	Overbody:	Dark moose or elk hair
Thread:	Red	Wing:	Dark moose or elk hair
Tail:	Dark moose or elk hair	Hackle:	Mixed grizzly and brown
Underbody:	Red thread or floss		

Sometimes called Goofus Bugs, Humpies may be tied in a wide range of colors and materials. On some of the newer variations, Jack Dennis uses a dubbed body in place of thread or floss.

Tied by Pat Barnes

ROYAL HUMPY

Hook:	Dry fly, size 8 to 18	Overbody:	Light elk or deer body hair
Thread:	Black	Wing:	White calftail
Tail:	Dark moose hair	Hackle:	Dark brown
Underbody:	Red floss		

Pat Barnes, who tied the fly illustrated, owned a shop in West Yellowstone, Montana, and was instrumental in promoting Humpy style flies beginning in the 1940s.

Tied by Umpqua Feather Merchants

YELLOW HUMPY

Hook:	Dry fly, size 8 to 18	Overbody:	Light elk or deer body hair
Thread:	Yellow	Wing:	Light elk or deer body hair
Tail:	Light elk or deer body hair	Hackle:	Mixed grizzly and brown
Underbody:	Yellow thread or floss		

The Yellow Humpy is probably the best known of the Humpy patterns.

The Irresistible is constructed almost entirely from deer body hair and is designed to present a large, highly visible silhouette rather than a slender realistic one. Most Irresistibles aren't supposed to imitate any specific food form; rather they are designed to float well in fast broken water, and look like something *irresistibly* good to eat. Joe Messinger of Morgantown, West Virginia, tied the original Irresistible in late 1930s. Messinger is best known for his unique deer-hair bass flies, like the Bucktail Frog. Many variations have appeared since Messinger tied the first fly many years ago, but they have been little more than simplified color variations. Mostly tied with hair wings, Irresistibles tied with hackle tip wings have also been popular.

IRRESISTIBLE (ORIGINAL)

Hook:	Dry fly, 1X or 2X long, size 8 to 16		over natural white deer body hair and trimmed to shape
Thread:	Black		
Tail:	Fine natural tan deer body hair	Wing:	Fine natural tan deer body hair
Body:	Dark deer body hair dyed purple, stacked	Hackle:	Purple

Tied by Joe Messinger, Jr.

This is Joe Messinger, Jr's example of his father's original Irresistible. It was first called the Deer Hair Drake and later renamed the Irresistible. Note the two-tone body.

ADAMS IRRESISTIBLE

Hook:	Dry fly 1X or 2X long, size 8 to 16	Body:	Natural gray deer body hair, spun and trimmed to shape
Thread:	Black or gray		
Tail:	Dark brown elk or deer body or moose body hair or woodchuck tail	Wing:	Grizzly hackle tips
		Hackle:	Brown and grizzly, mixed

Tied by Carl Yoshida

This is rapidly becoming one of the most popular Irresistibles in use, but then it seems that nearly any dry fly tied with a mixture of grizzly and brown hackle works like a charm.

BLUE DUN IRRESISTIBLE

Hook:	Dry fly, 1X or 2X long, size 8 to 16		trimmed to shape
Thread:	Gray or black	Wing:	Natural brown elk or deer body hair
Tail:	Natural brown elk or deer body hair	Hackle:	Medium to dark dun
Body:	Natural gray deer body hair, spun and		

Tied by George Kesel

This variation is probably the most commonly used of the Irresistible patterns.

WHITE IRRESISTIBLE

Hook:	Dry fly, 1X or 2X long, size 8 to 16	Wing:	Silver badger hackle tips. In larger sizes white bucktail or calftail are sometimes substituted
Thread:	White		
Tail:	White bucktail		
Body:	White deer body hair, spun and trimmed to shape as shown	Hackle:	Silver badger

Tied by George Kesel

This is an easy fly to see on the surface of even the most turbulent water. It's the perfect fly to tie on as the "last fly of the day" when the light is fading.

YELLOW IRRESISTIBLE

Hook:	Dry fly, 1X or 2X long, size 8 to 16		trimmed to shape
Thread:	Gray	Wing:	Grizzly hackle tips
Tail:	Natural dark elk or deer body hair	Hackle:	Mixed brown and grizzly
Body:	Yellow deer body hair, spun and		

Tied by Carl Yoshida

High floating yellow-bodied dry flies like this and the Yellow Humpy are very effective in fast water, and are most popular in the Western and Rocky Mountain states.

Few flies have made such a lasting impression on fly tying as the Wulff flies, and few individuals have been as actively involved in the development of fly fishing as Lee Wulff. If these flies were the only contribution Wulff made to modern fly fishing, they would have been enough. But Lee Wulff was a prolific writer and photographer and was instrumental in designing all sorts of fishing gear. He was also a master cinematographer who pioneered in the field of outdoor films. Throughout his life he was constantly experimenting with new fly designs, but the Wulff flies are his most enduring contribution to fly tying. The first ones were tied in 1929 during an outing with Dan Bailey, while fishing in the Adirondaks. Bailey was so impressed with Wulff's hairwing style that he developed several variations after he opened his fly shop in Livingston, Montana. The upright hairwing has become a standard that's been adopted throughout the world.

Tied by Peter Burton

ADAMS WULFF

Hook:	Dry fly, 2X long, size 8 to 18	Body:	Gray muskrat fur
Thread:	Black	Wing:	Woodchuck body guard hair
Tail:	Woodchuck body guard hair	Hackle:	Mixed brown and grizzly

Peter Burton of Middlebury, Vermont, introduced this pattern. Woodchucks are abundant in most Eastern pastureland and shouldn't be overlooked as a source of fly-tying materials. The underfur is good for dubbing and the guard hairs are used for wings and tails.

Tied by Francis Betters

AUSABLE WULFF

Hook:	Dry fly, 2X long, size 8 to 18	Body:	Australian opposum dyed rusty orange
Thread:	Fluorescent orange	Wing:	White calftail
Tail:	Woodchuck tail	Hackle:	Mixed brown and grizzly

Fran Betters is the leading fly-fishing authority on the West Branch of the Ausable River in New York's Adirondak mountains. He tied the first Ausable Wulff in 1964, and it's still considered to be one of the best fast-water patterns around.

Tied by Peter Burton

BLACK WULFF

Hook:	Dry fly, 2X long, size 8 to 18	Body:	Pink floss, lacquered
Thread:	Black	Wing:	Natural black moose body hair
Tail:	Natural black moose body hair	Hackle:	Dark furnace

Records indicate that Dan Bailey introduced this pattern in mid 1930s, shortly before he opened his fly shop in Livingston, Montana. Although it's not as commonly used as in the past, the Black Wulff was once a standard for fishing on the Yellowstone River.

Tied by Peter Burton

BLONDE WULFF

Hook:	Dry fly, 2X long, size 8 to 18	Body:	Buff tan fur
Thread:	Black	Wing:	Light elk hair
Tail:	Light elk hair	Hackle:	Cream

The Blonde Wulff was one of the early flies that resulted from the collaborative efforts of Lee Wulff and Dan Bailey. Gary LaFontaine has reported having good success fishing this fly to trout feeding on spruce moths.

Tied by Peter Burton

BROWN WULFF

Hook:	Dry fly, 2X long, size 8 to 18	Body:	Cream fur
Thread:	Black	Wing:	Brown calftail
Tail:	Brown calftail	Hackle:	Badger

The Brown Wulff, too, was a pattern that Dan Bailey helped to popularize in the 1930s and 1940s.

GRAY WULFF

Hook:	Dry fly, 2X long, size 8 to 18	Body:	Gray muskrat fur
Thread:	Black	Wing:	Brown bucktail
Tail:	Brown bucktail	Hackle:	Medium blue dun

Lee Wulff tied the first Gray Wulff sometime between 1929 and 1930. It's the earliest known pattern in the series of hairwing flies that was to follow; many years later it still stands alone as one of the best and most often used Wulffs.

Tied by Peter Burton

GRIZZLY WULFF

Hook:	Dry fly, 2X long, size 8 to 18	Body:	Yellow floss, lacquered
Thread:	Black	Wing:	Brown bucktail
Tail:	Brown bucktail	Hackle:	Mixed brown and grizzly

This is one of Dan Bailey's contributions to the Wulff series. He developed it in the mid 1930s, in the same period as the Black Wulff. It's also the only other Wulff fly tied with a floss body.

Tied by Peter Burton

MONTANA WULFF

Hook:	Dry fly, 2X long, size 8 to 16	Body:	Olive-green fur
Thread:	Black	Wing:	Red squirrel tail
Tail:	Red squirrel tail	Hackle:	Mixed brown and grizzly

Even though this fly originated in the Rockies, we first learned about it from some fly tiers in Maine where it had developed a following. They would sometimes add a few red hackle barbs to brighten up the tail.

Tied by Peter Burton

ROYAL WULFF

Hook:	Dry fly, 2X long, size 8 to 16	Hackle:	Dark brown or coachman brown
Thread:	Black	Note:	The Hairwing Royal Coachman is
Tail:	Brown bucktail		nearly identical, but features a white
Body:	Peacock herl, red floss, peacock herl		tail.
Wing:	White calftail		

The Royal Wulff is undoubtedly the most familiar of all the Wulff patterns and has fooled countless trout. It's one of the original flies that Lee Wulff tied around 1930.

Tied by Peter Burton

WERE WULFF

Hook:	Dry fly, 2X long, size 8 to 16	Body:	Hare's ear fur, roughly dubbed
Thread:	Black	Wing:	White calftail
Tail:	Brown bucktail	Hackle:	Mixed brown and grizzly

Gary LaFontaine developed this fly for the Big Hole River, with a little help from some friends. With " . . . an Adams for a mother and a Hare's Ear for a father" the Were Wulff could hardly miss the mark.

Tied by Peter Burton

WHITE WULFF

Hook:	Dry fly, 2X long, size 8 to 16	Body:	Cream colored fur
Thread:	Black	Wing:	White bucktail or calftail
Tail:	White bucktail or calftail	Hackle:	Very light badger

The White Wulff, together with the Gray and Royal Wulff, complete the group of Lee Wulff originated Wulff flies. The White Wulff was first called the Coffin May; the Gray and Royal were respectively named the Ausable Gray and Bucktail Coachman. Dan Bailey convinced Wulff to rename the flies after himself.

Tied by Peter Burton

Wet Flies

Until the mid 1900s, fly fishing in this country was done with wet flies. One glance through the many color plates of Ray Bergman's 1938 landmark edition of *Trout* easily confirms this. Some early wet flies, like the Blue Dun and the March Brown, were specifically tied to imitate insects, although it's not entirely clear if it was an emerging nymph or a drowned adult that the designer had in mind. Other flies, like the Trout Fin and Parmachene Belle of the East, or the Renegade and Chappie of the West, are American originals tied strictly as attractors. But as fishing pressure increased the trout became more selective and anglers more educated. The popularity of the wet fly diminished and has largely been replaced by a wealth of accurate imitations representing actual stages of subsurface life. Yet, because wet flies are attractive, fun to tie and easy to fish, and since trout will still smash a Silver Doctor fished down-and-across stream, wet fly angling still has its partisans.

Tied by Mark Waslick

ALDER

Hook:	Wet fly, size 10 to 16	Body:	Peacock herl
Thread:	Black	Hackle:	Black hen
Tag:	Flat gold tinsel	Wing:	Mottled turkey wing quill sections

The Alder is a very old British pattern that became a popular wet fly in this country during the early 1900s for spring fishing. It's still fished in New England with much success.

Tied by Mark Waslick

BLACK GNAT

Hook:	Wet fly, size 8 to 18	Hackle:	Black
Thread:	Black	Wing:	Dark gray goose or duck wing quill sections
Tail:	Black hackle barbs (optional)		
Body:	Black chenille, wool, or dubbing fur		

This fly is used with great success in Northeastern Canada, on lakes and ponds with good brook trout populations.

Tied by Mark Waslick

BLUE DUN

Hook:	Wet fly, size 8 to 14	Body:	Natural gray muskrat fur or similar
Thread:	Black or gray	Hackle:	Medium blue dun
Tail:	Medium blue dun hackle barbs	Wing:	Gray duck wing quill sections

We know of a fly-fishing shop manager who rates this pattern as his number one searching fly for spring trouting.

Tied by Dick Stewart

BROWN HACKLE

Hook:	Wet fly, size 10 to 16	Body:	Peacock herl
Thread:	Black	Rib:	Gold wire (optional)
Tail:	Red hackle barbs	Hackle:	Brown hen

There are many variations of the Brown Hackle, each using a different body material. Popular combinations include the Brown Hackle Silver and the Brown Hackle Yellow, using silver tinsel and yellow floss respectively. The fly pictured is often called the Brown Hackle Peacock.

Tied by Dick Talleur

CAHILL, DARK

Hook:	Wet fly, size 10 to 14	Body:	Dark gray muskrat fur or similar
Thread:	Black, gray or tan	Hackle:	Dark ginger
Tail:	Dark ginger hackle barbs or woodduck flank fibers	Wing:	Woodduck flank

In the summertime when the water is clear and low, a sparsely dressed Dark Cahill wet fly tied in size 14 or smaller can prove deadly, especially cast tight against an overhanging bank.

CAHILL, LIGHT

Hook:	Wet fly, size 8 to 16	Body:	Cream fox belly fur or similar
Thread:	Primrose or cream	Hackle:	Cream or light ginger
Tail:	Cream hackle barbs or woodduck flank fibers	Wing:	Woodduck flank

A wet Light Cahill has always been good imitation of the emergence stage of a variety of light colored mayflies.

Tied by Dick Talleur

CAREY SPECIAL

Hook:	Streamer, 3X long, size 6 to 10	Rib:	Fine gold wire (optional)
Thread:	Black	Collar:	Ringneck pheasant rump feather, tied back
Tail:	Several barbs of a ringneck pheasant rump feather (optional)	Note:	The body may be tied with chenille, floss or dubbing in any color you choose.
Body:	Peacock herl		

This big, soft hackle wet fly was developed many years ago in British Columbia where it is still commonly fished on lakes and ponds. It was named for Colonel Carey who helped design it.

Tied by Joe Howell

CHAPPIE

Hook:	Wet fly, size 6 to 10	Rib:	Orange thread or fine gold tinsel
Thread:	Orange	Hackle:	Grizzly, applied as a collar
Tail:	Grizzly hackle tips	Wing:	Matched grizzly hackles, curving out
Body:	Orange wool		

Developed as a steelhead fly in the 1940s, the Chappie has become better known as a fly for cutthroat trout. Often tied as a streamer, it's quite effective in the Pacific Northwest for sea-run fish entering coastal rivers.

Tied by Joe Howell

COACHMAN

Hook:	Wet fly, size 8 to 16	Rib:	Fine gold wire (optional)
Thread:	Black	Hackle:	Coachman brown (dark brown)
Tag:	Flat gold tinsel	Wing:	White duck wing quill sections
Body:	Peacock herl		

The Coachman has certainly withstood the test of time. It's believed that Thomas Bosworth, coachman to several British monarchs including Queen Victoria, originated this pattern in the 1830s.

Tied by Mark Waslick

COACHMAN, LEADWING

Hook:	Wet fly, size 8 to 16	Rib:	Fine gold wire (optional)
Thread:	Black	Hackle:	Coachman brown (dark brown)
Tag:	Flat gold tinsel	Wing:	Slate gray mallard wing quill sections
Body:	Peacock herl		

Many anglers find that the Leadwing Coachman in size 10 or 12 is a respectable imitation of an Isonychia mayfly nymph. It must be fished with a lot of action to imitate this fast-swimming nymph.

Tied by Mark Waslick

COACHMAN, ROYAL

Hook:	Wet fly, size 10 to 16	Hackle:	Coachman brown
Tail:	Golden pheasant tippets	Wing:	White duck wing quill sections
Body:	Peacock herl, red floss and peacock herl		

Whether tied as a wet fly or a dry fly, after over 100 years or so, the Royal Coachman remains one of the best and most popular patterns around. Try tying this fly with a wing of white calftail or marabou.

Tied by Mark Waslick

Tied by Dick Talleur

Tied by Ron Landis

Tied by Mark Waslick

Tied by Dick Stewart

Tied by Dick Stewart

Tied by Bill Thompson

COWDUNG

Hook:	Wet fly, size 8 to 14	Body:	Olive floss
Thread:	Olive	Rib:	Flat gold tinsel
Tag:	Flat gold tinsel	Hackle:	Brown
Tail:	Brown hackle barbs	Wing:	Cinnamon hen wing quill sections

The Cowdung was tied to imitate a land-bred insect that in the summer can be found swarming around fresh cow manure. Next time you find your're fishing through a meadow stretch with grazing cattle, remember the Cowdung.

FINCH

Hook:	Dry fly, size 12 to 16	Thorax:	Peacock herl
Thread:	Tan	Collar:	Several wraps of gray or white after-
Abdomen:	Crystal flash or dubbed Antron in		shaft from a partridge or hen
	whatever color desired	Hackle:	Gray or brown partridge

The Finch was developed by Ron Landis and employs a collar using after-shaft, the feather found at the base of a body hackle. This soft feather gives lifelike movement to the fly.

GINGER QUILL

			cock tail feather
Hook:	Wet fly, size 10 to 16	Hackle:	Dark ginger
Thread:	Black or gray	Wing:	Light gray duck wing quill sections
Tail:	Dark ginger hackle barbs		
Body:	Stripped or bleached quill from a pea-		

A rib of fine gold wire may be counter-wrapped to help reinforce the fragile body. Better yet, a drop of CA cement may be applied, but you'll have to wait until it dries to continue tying the fly.

GRAY HACKLE PEACOCK

Hook:	Wet fly, size 10 to 16	Body:	Peacock herl
Thread:	Black	Rib:	Fine gold wire (optional)
Tail:	Red hackle barbs	Hackle:	Grizzly

This fly can be tied with a tail of golden pheasant tippets or without a tail. Like the Brown Hackle (which see), the body material and body color may vary, while the hackle remains the same.

GRAY HACKLE RED

Hook:	Wet fly, size 10 to 16	Rib:	Oval silver tinsel with a couple of turns
Thread:	Black		at the rear of the body forming a tag
Body:	Red floss	Hackle:	Grizzly

Chose your favorite body color for this fly. We've seen it tied with black, yellow, purple and green.

GRIZZLY KING

Hook:	Wet fly, size 10 to 16	Rib:	Flat silver or gold tinsel
Thread:	Black	Hackle:	Grizzly
Tail:	Red hackle barbs	Wing:	Mallard flank
Body:	Bright green floss		

This has been a popular brook trout fly for many years in New England and Northeastern Canada. It can also be tied on a long-shank hook as a streamer, and has been a used as a wet fly for Atlantic salmon.

LEISENRING BLACK GNAT

Hook: Wet fly, size 14 to 16
Thread: Crimson or claret
Body: Two or three barbs of a crow's secondary wing feather wound over the shank, or plain black silk
Collar: Purplish black shoulder feather from a starling
Wing: Dark starling wing quill sections applied over the collar (optional)

Tied by Dick Stewart

Jim Leisenring was a noted expert on wet fly fishing and modern authorities continue to acknowledge his designs as some of the best.

LEISENRING GRAY HACKLE

Hook: Wet fly, size 12 to 14
Thread: Primrose yellow
Body: Bronze peacock herl
Rib: Fine flat gold tinsel
Collar: Gold or creamy white furnace hackle

Tied by Dick Stewart

Leisenring's Gray Hackle is considerably different from the Gray Hackle Peacock and the Gray Hackle Red (which see). Peacock herl will bleach to a rich bronze hue if exposed to direct sunlight for a period of time.

LEISENRING HARE'S EAR

Hook: Wet fly, size 12 to 14
Thread: Primrose yellow
Tail: Two or three barbs of woodduck flank
Body: English hare's ear fur
Rib: Fine flat gold tinsel
Throat: Dubbing fur picked out from the thorax
Wing: Matched segments from a woodcock secondary wing feather with noticeably light tips. Hen pheasant wing quills may be substituted.

Tied by Dick Stewart

LEISENRING IRON BLUE WINGLESS

Hook: Wet fly, size 14 to 16
Thread: Crimson or claret
Tail: Honey dun hackle barbs, sparse
Body: Dark gray mole fur, very thinly dubbed
at the rear, allowing some color from the thread to show through
Collar: Honey dun hackle

Tied by Dick Stewart

Leisenring was very specific regarding the color of the thread used for spinning dubbing. He took into account the way the body would look as the thread showed through wet, semi-transluscent dubbing.

LEISENRING TUP'S

Hook: Wet fly, size 12 to 14
Thread: Primrose yellow
Tail: Light blue or pale honey dun hackle barbs or hackle tips
Body: Rear half: Primrose yellow buttonhole twist
Front half: Yellow and claret seal fur or similar, spun on primrose yellow thread
Collar: Sparse light blue dun hen hackle

Tied by Dick Stewart

This fly is sometimes called the Tup's Indispensable and is often tied as a nymph as well as a dry fly.

MARCH BROWN

Hook: Wet fly, size 10 to 14
Thread: Brown or orange
Tail: Woodduck flank
Body: Mixed fur from a hare's mask
Rib: Yellow thread
Hackle: Partdridge, grouse or woodduck
Wing: Speckled turkey or ringneck hen pheasant wing quill sections

Tied by Mike Motyl

There's not a great deal of resemblance between the natural march brown (*Stenonema vicarium*) and this wet fly. Nevertheless, it's a buggy looking fly that definitely catches a lot of trout.

Tied by Mark Waslick

Tied by Mark Waslick

Tied by Mark Waslick

Tied by Dick Stewart

Tied by Farrow Allen

Tied by Bill Thompson

McGINTY

Hook:	Wet fly, size 8 to 14	Body:	Bands of black and yellow chenille
Thread:	Black	Hackle:	Brown
Tail:	Dyed red hackle barbs over which are barred teal flank barbs	Wing:	White tipped mallard secondary wing sections

This bumble bee pattern is a good one to carry throughout the summer. During those months of limited aquatic insect activity, bees and other terrestrials represent a significant source of food for trout.

MONTREAL

Hook:	Wet fly, size 8 to 16	Hackle:	Claret
Tail:	Claret hackle barbs	Wing:	Speckled hen or mottled turkey wing quill sections
Body:	Claret floss		
Rib:	Flat gold tinsel		

A common variation, the White-Tipped Montreal, substitutes a wing of white-tipped mallard secondary wing feathers and is sometimes even tied as a dry fly. As the name suggests, the Montreal is popular in Eastern Canada, as well as in the states that share a border with Quebec.

PARMACHENE BELLE

Hook:	Wet fly, size 8 to 14	Hackle:	Red and white, folded together and and wound as a collar
Thread:	Black		
Tail:	Red and white hackle barbs, mixed	Wing:	Married strips of duck wing quill sections: white, over which is red, and white on top
Body:	Yellow floss		
Rib:	Flat gold tinsel		

This brook trout pattern was named for Lake Parmachene in Western Maine. It's a good little fly that's worth taking the time to tie.

PARTRIDGE & GREEN

Hook:	Wet fly, size 12 to 16	Body:	Bright green silk floss
Thread:	Black	Collar:	Brown or gray partridge hackle

Soft hackle flies like this are easy to tie and tremendously useful. This one, for example, is a very acceptable imitation of an emerging green caddis pupa.

PICKET PIN

Hook:	Nymph, 2X or 3X long, size 8 to 14	Hackle:	Brown hackle tied in by the tip, palmered over the body
Thread:	Black		
Tail:	Brown hackle barbs	Wing:	Gray squirrel tail
Body:	Peacock herl	Head:	Peacock herl

The Picket Pin isn't your average wet fly. It can be retrieved like a streamer to imitate a baitfish, weighted with lead and fished like a nymph, or tied with an elk or deer hair wing and fished dry.

PROFESSOR

Hook:	Wet fly, size 8 to 16	Body:	Yellow floss
Thread:	Black	Rib:	Flat gold tinsel
Tag:	Flat gold tinsel (optional)	Hackle:	Brown
Tail:	Dyed red hackle barbs	Wing:	Mallard flank

RENEGADE

Hook:	Wet fly, size 8 to 16	Rear hackle:	Brown
Thread:	Black	Body:	Peacock herl
Tag:	Flat gold tinsel	Front hackle:	White

The Renegade developed in Idaho during in the 1930s and became a standard addition to a western anglers fly box. It's sometimes tied with dry fly hackle and fished on or just below the surface.

Tied by Dick Stewart

RENEGADE, SUPER

Hook:	Streamer, 3X or 4X long, size 4 to 10	Rear body:	Black chenille
Thread:	Black	Center hackle:	Brown
Tag:	Flat gold tinsel	Front body:	Orange chenille
Rear hackle:	Grizzly	Front hackle:	White

Ardell Jeppsen developed this Rocky Mountain favorite that's tied in any color combination you can imagine. It has rapidly become one of the most popular attractor patterns for float fishing on the South Fork of Idaho's Snake River.

Tied by Tom Travis

RIO GRANDE KING

Hook:	Wet fly, size 8 to 14	Hackle:	Yellow or brown
Thread:	Black	Wing:	White duck wing quill segments, curving out
Tail:	Yellow hackle barbs		
Body:	Black chenille		

This is the dressing for the Rio Grande King from the early 1900s. It's now more commonly dressed with a white calftail wing, but still fished wet, just below the surface.

Tied by Farrow Allen

SILVER DOCTOR

Hook:	Wet fly, size 6 to 12	Body:	Flat silver tinsel
Thread:	Red	Rib:	Silver wire
Tag:	Flat gold tinsel	Hackle:	Pale blue followed by barbs of teal flank
Tail:	Golden pheasant crest over which are a few barbs of blue kingfisher or similar	Wing:	Married narrow strips of red, blue and yellow dyed duck wing over which are strips of peacock wing, or pheasant tail
Butt:	Red wool		

This is a trout fly variation of a Scottish Atlantic salmon fly that dates back to the 1800s. With its color and flash it's always been deadly on eastern brook trout.

Tied by Mark Waslick

TROUT FIN

Hook:	Wet fly, size 4 to 12	Hackle:	Furnace
Thread:	Black	Wing:	Broad strips of dyed orange duck wing quill sections over which are narrow strips of black and white duck wing quill
Tail:	White hackle barbs		
Body:	Bright orange floss		
Rib:	Flat gold tinsel		

At one time, brook trout fins were commonly cut off and used for bait. Some "purist," or more likely some enterprising angler trying to hook his first fish, tied this fly to mimic a brookies's fin.

Tied by Dick Talleur

WOODCOCK & ORANGE

Hook:	Wet fly, size 14 or 16	Thorax:	Dark Hare's ear fur, dubbed roughly
Thread:	Brown	Collar:	Woodcock body feather
Body:	Orange silk floss		

Most soft-hackle flies are tied with only two parts, a body of colored floss and a hackle collar, usually from some small game bird or waterfowl: Partridge & Green, Snipe & Yellow, and so on. At your discretion, a dubbed thorax may be added to any of the soft-hackle patterns.

Tied by Dick Stewart

All-Purpose Nymphs

It was not until the 1940s and 1950s that nymphs became commonplace in the fly boxes of trout fishermen. Prior to then, a variety of wet flies served the function of representing a multitude of immature aquatic food forms. Studies of trout feeding habits revealed that nymphs composed a large portion of a trout's diet. Observent anglers such as Hewitt, Blades, Bergman, Quick, and many others began to promote the use of more exact imitations, and thus the nymph was "discovered." Many of the successful nymph patterns are based on general, rather than specific, design features. We do not believe these flies represent any single, particular insect form, although some of them may be classified differently in other fly listings; rather they appear to be successful because trout mistake them for a variety of possible foods. These flies, then, are most useful to the fly fisher at times when there is no surface activity, and he cannot make a specific determination as to what the fish are likely to be eating.

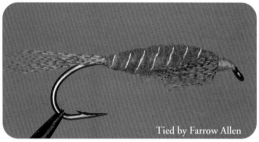
Tied by Farrow Allen

Tied by Farrow Allen

Tied by Redding Fly Shop

Tied by Farrow Allen

Tied by Gerry James

BEAVER NYMPH

Hook:	Nymph, 1X to 2X long, size 10 to 16	Body:	Medium gray beaver fur
		Rib:	Fine gold or silver wire
Thread:	Gray	Legs:	Brown speckled partridge, as a beard
Tail:	Woodduck flank feather barbs		

Beaver fur, like the fur from most other aquatic animals, makes excellent nymph bodies. It's fairly light in color, and it's easily dyed.

BIG HOLE DEMON (SILVER)

Hook:	Nymph, 3X long, size 2 to 10		tinsel
Thread:	Black	Thorax:	Black chenille
Tail:	Badger hackle tips, curving out	Legs:	Badger, palmered over the black chenille
Abdomen:	Oval silver tinsel or flat silver tinsel ribbed with oval silver	Note:	Also tied with a gold abdomen

Montana's Dan Bailey believed this to be one of the best patterns for the Big Hole River.

BIRD'S NEST

Hook:	Nymph, 2X or 3X long, Size 8 to 16	Rib:	Copper wire
		Legs:	Woodduck or dyed mallard flank tied in several sparse bunches on top and on each side
Thread:	Tan or brown		
Tail:	Brown dyed mallard or teal flank		
Abdomen:	Tannish olive blended natural and synthetic fur, picked out	Thorax:	Same as the abdomen

This generic nymph pattern from Cal Bird has become very popular in the west.

BREADCRUST

Hook:	Nymph, 1X long, size 8 to 16	Legs:	Soft grizzly hackle
Thread:	Orange or brown	Note:	The stripped hackle stem may be soaked in a diluted glycerin solution to make it less brittle.
Body:	Rusty-orange fur		
Rib:	Brown hackle stem, stripped, counter wrapped with fine gold wire (optional)		

CASUAL DRESS

Hook:	Nymph, 3X long, size 2 to 12		bing and wrapped to give the appearance of segmentation
Thread:	Black		
Tail:	Muskrat fur and guard hairs	Collar:	Muskrat fur and guard hairs, wound and teased out
Body:	Muskrat fur and guard hairs, twisted into a "noodle" of dub-	Head:	Black ostrich herl, lacquered

A good all-purpose nymph, with a great silhouette and a lot of movement. However, tied in very large sizes, Rosborough wrote, "It looks for all the world like a small drowned mouse." Tiers should try this fly using bleached and dyed muskrat.

CLOUSER SWIMMING NYMPH, GOLDEN BROWN

Hook: Nymph, lX to 3X long, size 8 to 12

Thread: Gray or tan

Underbody: Lead wire, wrapped double at the thorax

Tail: Dyed golden brown rabbit fur and guard hair around a small bunch of bronze Flashabou

Abdomen and thorax: Golden brown dubbing

Legs: A speckled brown hen saddle, wrapped over the thorax

Wingcase: Peacock herl

Tied by Bob Clouser

FLEDERMOUSE

Hook: Nymph, 3X long, size 4 to 14

Thread: Tan

Body: Blended muskrat, medium brown mink and rabbit fur, tapered and roughened

Collar: Orange-brown Australian opossum

Wingcase: Barred teal or mallard flank over which is brown widgeon flank or teal dyed brown

Rosborough says the Fledermouse ". . . never really simulates anything specific . . . but allows the fish to think it might be any number of nymphs."

Tied by Gerry James

FULLBACK

Hook: Nymph, 2X or 3X long, size 8 to 12

Thread: Black

Tail: Ringneck pheasant tail barbs

Abdomen: Peacock herl

Abdomen back: Ringneck pheasant tail barbs

Rib: Heavy black thread over the abdomen binding down the back

Thorax: Peacock herl

Wingcase: Ringneck pheasant tail barbs

Legs: Barbs from the wingcase pulled down and tied back

Tied by Kelvin McKay

GIMP

Hook: Wet fly or nymph, size 10 to 16

Thread: Black

Tail: Medium to dark soft dun hen hackle barbs

Body: Gray wool or dubbing

Wing: Two "Gimp" feathers tied flat over the body, one stacked on top of the other, extending a little beyond the bend of the hook

Legs: A collar of hen hackle, the same color used for the tail

Note: Gimp feathers are an aftershaft found under the tippets of an Amherst pheasant

Tied by Dick Stewart

GRAY SQUIRREL NYMPH

Hook: Nymph, 1X to 3X long, size 6 to 14

Thread: Gray or beige

Underbody: Lead wire along the sides of the abdomen (optional)

Tail: Gray partridge hackle barbs or gray squirrel guard hair

Abdomen: Gray squirrel body fur including guard hair

Rib: Silver oval tinsel or wire

Thorax: Same as abdomen

Wingcase: Dark turkey tail coated with vinyl cement

Legs: Picked out fur from the abdomen

Tied by Farrow Allen

HALFBACK

Hook: Nymph, 2X or 3X long, size 8 to 12

Thread: Black

Tail: Ringneck pheasant tail barbs

Abdomen: Peacock herl

Rib: Heavy black thread (optional)

Thorax: Peacock herl

Wingcase: Ringneck pheasant tail barbs

Legs: Barbs from the wingcase pulled down and tied back

Kelvin McKay, of Cowichan Fly and Tackle on Vancouver Island, describes the Halfback and Fullback (which see) as standard nymph patterns for lake fishing throughout British Columbia.

Tied by Kelvin McKay

Tied by Farrow Allen

Tied by Dick Stewart

Tied by Farrow Allen

Tied by Dick Stewart

Tied by Kaufmann's Streamborn

Tied by Farrow Allen

HARE'S EAR

Hook:	Nymph, 1X to 3X long, size 4 to 16
Thread:	Brown or gray
Tail:	Hare's mask fur with guard hairs, or woodduck flank
Abdomen and thorax:	Hare's ear and mask fur with guard hairs left in
Rib:	Oval gold tinsel
Legs:	Fur picked out of the thorax
Wingcase:	Woodduck, bronze mallard flank or a section of dark turkey wing quill tied in at the head and trimmed to extend back over the thorax, or folded over the thorax
Note:	This fly is often called the Gold Ribbed Hare's Ear.

HARE'S EAR, BEAD HEAD

Hook:	Nymph, 1X to 3X long, size 6 to 14
Thread:	Black, gray or tan
Head:	Brass bead, worked over the hook point (it may be necessary to pinch the barb down) and secured directly behind the eye
Tail:	Speckled partridge, woodduck flank or similar
Body:	Hare's ear fur
Rib:	Oval gold tinsel or wire
Legs:	Speckled partridge, woodduck, or picked out dubbing (optional)

HARE'S EAR, FLASHBACK

Hook:	Nymph, size 8 to 18
Thread:	Tan
Tail:	Partridge hackle barbs
Abdomen:	Hare's ear dubbing
Rib:	Fine oval gold tinsel
Thorax:	Hare's ear dubbing
Legs:	Fur picked out from the abdomen
Wingcase:	Pearl crystal flash

This is a very effective variation of the versatile Hare's Ear Nymph that we first saw tied by Al Troth .

HARE'S EAR, RED BROWN

Hook:	Nymph, 3X to 6X long, size 4 to 16
Thread:	Brown
Tail:	Dyed reddish brown hare's ear or mask fur with guard hair or bronze mallard flank
Abdomen and thorax:	Dyed reddish brown hare's ear and mask fur with guard hairs left in, dubbed heavily
Rib:	Oval gold tinsel
Legs:	Bronze mallard, woodduck flank or fur picked out of the thorax
Wingcase:	Bronze mallard flank or a section of dark turkey wing quill

HARE'S EAR, RUBBER LEGS

Hook:	Nymph, size 8 to 14
Thread:	Brown
Underbody:	Lead wire
Tail:	Very fine tan rubber hackles
Abdomen:	Hare's ear dubbing
Rib:	Fine oval gold tinsel
Legs:	Very fine tan rubber hackle
Wingcase:	Dark turkey wing quill segment or pheasant tail barbs, coated with vinyl cement
Thorax:	Hare's ear dubbing
Note:	Sometimes melted monofilament or small bead eyes are added.

HARE'S EAR, YELLOW

Hook:	Nymph, 1X to 3X long, size 4 to 16
Thread:	Yellow
Tail:	Dyed yellow hare's ear and mask fur with guard hairs left in, or woodduck flank
Abdomen:	Dyed yellow hare's ear and mask fur with guard hairs left in and dubbed heavily
Rib:	Oval gold tinsel
Thorax:	Same as abdomen
Legs:	Fur picked out of the thorax
Wingcase:	Woodduck or light turkey wing quill section, tied in at the head and trimmed to extend back over the thorax, or tied behind the thorax and pulled forward

LEIB'S BUG

Hook: Nymph, 2X long, size 8 to 12
Thread: Black
Underbody: Lead wire (optional)
Tail: Two goose biots dyed brown, curving outward
Body: Peacock herl

Hackle: Dark furnace, palmered over the body and trimmed on top
Rib: Fine gold wire
Legs: Two goose biots dyed brown, extending nearly to the end of the body

Tied by Joe Howell

MARTINEZ, BLACK

Hook: Nymph, 1X to 3X long, size 8 to 12
Thread: Black
Tail: Speckled guinea hackle barbs

Abdomen: Black seal fur or similar
Rib: Fine copper or gold tinsel, or wire
Wingcase: Green raffia or similar
Thorax: Black chenille

This is one of the few flies, out of the many that Don Martinez developed, that's still fairly popular. A California native, Martinez began spending his summers in West Yellowstone, Montana, in the early 1930s.

Tied by Farrow Allen

MUSKRAT NYMPH

Hook: Nymph, 3X long, size 6 to 16
Thread: Black
Body: Mixed muskrat, beaver and a small amount of rabbit fur spun into a "twisted noodle" using a

dubbing loop, wrapped to form a segmented, tapered body, picked out to make it fuzzier
Legs: Guinea hackle barbs
Head: Black ostrich herl

Polly Rosborough originally tied this to imitate a cranefly larva, but he found it is equally effective as a caddis or dark scud.

Tied by Gerry James

NEAR ENOUGH

Hook: Nymph, 3X long, size 8 to 16
Thread: Light gray
Tail: Gray mallard flank barbs
Body: Dark gray fox fur, with all the

guard hairs removed
Legs: Sparse bunches of mallard flank barbs on each side
Wingcase: Mallard flank trimmed square

This fly imitates a wide range of nymphs. ". . . when in doubt," wrote Rosborough in *Tying and Fishing the Fuzzy Nymphs*, "start off with size 8 Near Enough and work down to a size 16 if necessary, or until you find which size produces, then just fish."

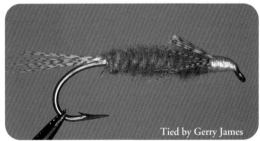

Tied by Gerry James

NONDESCRIPT

Hook: Nymph, 1X to 3X long, size 8 to 16
Thread: Brown
Tail: Fiery brown marabou
Body: Fiery brown yarn, the fuzzier the better

Rib: Bright yellow thread
Hackle: Brown saddle hackle, trimmed
Note: The hackle should be long enough for a wrap to be placed between each of the yellow ribs, and three more turns at the head.

The Rosborough's Nondescript imitates a variety of clinging and swimming nymphs.

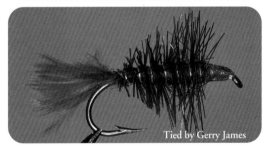

Tied by Gerry James

OTTER NYMPH

Hook: Nymph, size 10 to 16
Thread: Tan or olive
Underbody: Lead wire (optional)
Tail: Brown grouse hackle barbs, tied relatively short

Body: Otter fur, dubbed full and rough-end a little
Legs: Brown grouse hackle barbs, as a beard

Sometimes simplicity is best.

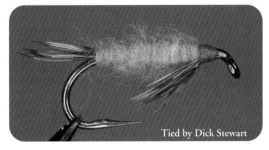

Tied by Dick Stewart

Tied by Claude Bernard

Tied by Farrow Allen

Tied by Kaufmann's Streamborn

Tied by Dick Stewart

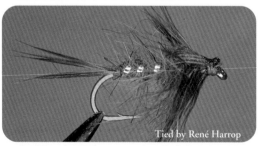

Tied by René Harrop

Tied by Jack Gartside

PHILO THORAX

Hook:	Nymph, 2X or 3X long, size 10 to 16	Abdomen:	Grouse philoplume, wrapped
Thread:	Red	Legs:	Grouse hackle applied as a collar
Tail:	Grouse hackle barbs	Note:	The abdomen may be tied in different colors, using the philoplume and grouse thorax
Thorax:	Hare's ear fur, full		

Claude Bernard guides for salmon at the Bonaventure River on Canada's Gaspé Peninsula, but this is one of his favorite nymphs when he's fishing for trout.

PRINCE

Hook:	Nymph, 1X or 2X long, size 8 to 14	Body:	Peacock herl
Thread:	Black	Rib:	Fine oval gold tinsel
Tail:	Dyed brown goose biots	Legs:	Brown hackle, wound
		Wing:	Two white goose biots

This popular fly is also known as the Brown Forked Tail. A variation called the Black Forked Tail is tied with a black biots and black ostrich herl.

SIMULATOR, PEACOCK

Hook:	4X to 6X long, size 4 to 10	Body hackle:	Dark furnace, clipped
Thread:	Claret	Legs:	Dark furnace hackle wrapped over the thorax
Underbody:	Lead wire		
Tail:	Red-brown goose biots or short bunch of brown marabou	Note:	The body of this fly is often made of brown or black dubbed fur, picked out at the thorax.
Body:	Peacock herl		

This is one of Randall Kaufmann's most versatile nymph patterns.

SOFT BODY NYMPH, OLIVE WOOLY

Hook:	Short shank, up eye, size 10 to 20		better adhesion
Thread:	Olive	Tail:	Mixed grizzly and red hackle barbs
Note:	Extended body, tied on a section of supple fly line that's been roughened with sandpaper for	Body:	Olive chenille
		Hackle:	Grizzly

Lee Wulff developed the Soft Body Nymph because he felt that most trout take a nymph tentatively, and eject it the instant they feel the stiffness of the hook

SOFT HACKLE HARE'S EAR, BROWN

Hook:	Nymph, 1X long, size 10 to 18	Thorax:	Same as the abdomen
Thread:	Brown	Legs:	Brown hen hackle folded back and applied as a collar
Tail:	Brown hen hackle barbs		
Abdomen:	Hare's mask and ear fur dyed brown	Wingcase:	Goose or turkey wing quill segment, dyed brown
Rib:	Fine flat gold tinsel		

René Harrop dresses this nymph in a variety of natural, dyed and blended colors.

SPARROW, OLIVE

Hook:	Nymph, 2X or 3X long, size 6 to 14		gray squirrel fur
Thread:	Olive	Hackle:	Several wraps of ringneck pheasant rump with the barbs extending to the end of the tail
Tail:	Reddish brown marabou from a ringneck pheasant rump		
Body:	Blended olive dyed rabbit and	Collar:	Ringneck pheasant aftershafts, wrapped

Jack Gartside's famous Sparrow is a generic fly that doesn't look like much in particular, but depending on its color, and the way it's fished, can imitate just about anything.

TEENY NYMPH

Hook:	Wet fly size 4 to 12
Thread:	Black
Underbody:	Lead wire
Body:	A large bunch of natural or dyed ringneck pheasant tail barbs, wrapped around the hook shank
Legs:	Tips of the remaining pheasant tail barbs, pulled down and back and secured under the hook
Note:	On large hooks the body (as shown) is made in equal parts with two sets of legs.

Jim Teeny originally tied this fly for trout fishing in lakes around his home in Oregon.

Tied by Teeny Nymph Company

TELLICO

Hook:	Nymph, 1X to 2X long, size 10 to 16
Thread:	Black
Tail:	Brown hackle barbs (optional)
Body:	Yellow floss, full and tapered
Rib:	Peacock herl
Shellback:	Section of ringneck pheasant tail or several peacock herls pulled over the top after the rib has been applied
Legs:	Soft brown hackle barbs, applied as a collar

Tied by Farrow Allen

THEO'S DUTCH CDC BEAD HEAD

Hook:	Nymph, size 8 to 16
Thread:	Brown
Bead head:	Appropriate size gold bead slipped over the hook point and secured behind the hook eye
Tail:	Red-brown hackle barbs
Abdomen:	Red-brown fur
Rib:	Gold wire
Wing:	Gray CDC, wrapped
Thorax:	Peacock herl

Bead Head flies have been popular in Europe for many years and are finally gaining acceptance among anglers in the U.S. The head provides weight and a bit of sparkle.

Tied by Umpqua Feather Merchants

TIMBERLINE EMERGER

Hook:	Nymph, 2X or 3X long, size 12 to 16
Thread:	Gray
Tail:	Gray marabou or aftershaft feather
Body:	Gray fur
Rib:	Fine copper wire
Legs:	Sparse soft brown hackle applied like a collar
Wing:	Two grizzly hen hackles, short
Note:	Also tied in olive and brown.

Developed by Randall Kaufmann for the High Sierra lakes that lie above timberline.

Tied by Kaufmann's Streamborn

WHITLOCK RED SQUIRREL NYMPH

Hook:	Nymph, 1X to 4X long, size 6 to 18
Thread:	Black
Tail:	Red squirrel fur or tail
Underbody:	Lead wire wrapped over the thorax
Abdomen:	Red squirrel belly, mixed with a similar colored "spikey" synthetic like Antron
Rib:	Gold or copper oval tinsel or wire
Thorax:	Dark fur from the back of the red squirrel mixed with dark Antron
Legs:	Dark speckled hen hackle or similar

Tied by Umpqua Feather Merchants

ZUG BUG

Hook:	Nymph, 1X or 2X long, size 8 to 16
Thread:	Black
Tail:	Three peacock sword feathers
Body:	Peacock herl tied full
Rib:	Oval silver tinsel
Legs:	Brown hackle applied as a collar
Wingcase:	Mallard flank, tied in at the head and trimmed to extend over the thorax

Credit for this fly goes to Cliff Zug, but as most of us know, almost anything tied with peacock herl catches fish and the more herl the better.

Tied by Farrow Allen

Mayfly Nymphs

Mayflies are the most important group of insects as far as the fly fisherman and fly tier are concerned. The history of fly fishing relates primarily to mayflies, and the various stages and species provide the foundation upon which our sport has flourished. Only a small portion of the 700 North American species are of importance to the fly fisherman, and these have been the subject of considerable research as anglers attempt to learn more about their distribution, behavior, and life cycles. Exceptions notwithstanding, the life cycle of the mayfly lasts one year, all but a day or two of which is spent underwater, first as eggs, then as larvae, commonly called nymphs. As they mature, the nymphs grow larger and become more active. This is when they assume the greatest importance to trout. Some mayflies are known by common names which are familiar to experienced trout fishermen. Other mayflies are referred to by their genus or species, using Latin names which gain in familiarity.

Tied by Farrow Allen

Tied by Farrow Allen

Tied by Michael Tucker

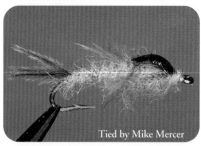
Tied by Mike Mercer

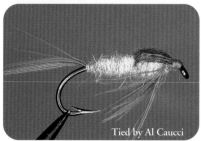
Tied by Al Caucci

A.P. MUSKRAT NYMPH

Hook: Nymph, 1X long, size 10 to 14
Thread: Gray
Underbody: Lead wire wrapped at the thorax
Tail: Dark moose hair
Abdomen: Dark muskrat fur
Rib: Gold wire or oval tinsel
Thorax: Dark muskrat fur
Wingcase: Dark moose hair
Legs: Dark moose hair, pulled back along the sides and trimmed
Head: Dark muskrat fur

This is one of a series of mayfly nymphs by André Puyans. Others include the A.P. Beaver, A.P. Olive, etc.

ATHERTON NYMPH, DARK

Hook: Nymph, 1X long, size 10 to 14
Thread: Black
Tail: Dark furnace hackle barbs
Abdomen: Blended gray muskrat and claret seal or similar
Rib: Oval gold tinsel
Wingcase: Iridescent blue kingfisher or substitute
Thorax: Same as abdomen
Legs: A collar of dark furnace hackle, trimmed top and bottom

Atherton's nymph bodies are made from blended furs of contrasting colors and textures, which contribute to giving the impression of something alive.

BAETIS NYMPH

Hook: Nymph, 3X long, size 12 to 20
Thread: Olive
Tail: Three tips of ringneck pheasant tail barbs (don't trim the butts)
Underbody: Built up olive thread wraps
Abdomen: Butt ends of the pheasant tail pulled forward over the top, overwrapped with fine clear Liqui-lace
Thorax: Peacock herl
Wingcase: Mixture of yellow, brown and green Z-lon
Legs: Z-lon from the wingcase, divided and pulled down and back, half on each side of the thorax, and trimmed

CALLIBAETIS, MERCER'S POXYBACK

Hook: Nymph, 1X to 3X long, size 14 to 18
Thread: Light olive
Tail: Three gray tips from aftershaft feathers or mini ostrich plumes
Abdomen: Creamy olive dubbing
Rib: Pearl Flashabou
Gills: Sparse gray marabou on each side, in front of the abdomen
Thorax: Same as abdomen
Wingcase: Dark turkey tail, coated with epoxy
Legs: Sparse wooduck flank or light colored grouse on the sides
Head: Same as abdomen

COMPARA-NYMPH, YELLOW-BROWN

Hook: Nymph, 1X or 2X long, size 10 to 16
Thread: Brown or gray
Tail: Light brown or ginger soft hackle barbs
Body: Blended "spectrumized" yellowish fur
Wingcase: Dark brown wing quill segment
Legs: Light brown or ginger hackle barbs, as a beard

The Compara-nymph, featuring a blend of spectrumized dubbing consisting of red, yellow, blue and white rabbit furs, may be tied to represent specific mayfly species, or as a general all-purpose mayfly imitation, like the one shown here.

FEATHER DUSTER

Hook:	Nymph, 1X to 3X long, size 10 to 16
Thread:	Brown or olive
Tail:	Partridge hackle barbs; on larger flies use barbs from a ringneck pheasant tail
Abdomen:	Natural gray ostrich herl
Rib:	Fine copper wire
Thorax:	Same as abdomen
Wingcase:	Partridge hackle barbs; on larger flies use barbs from a ringneck pheasant tail
Legs:	Pull the excess barbs from the wingcase down and back along the sides

The ostrich herl provides the illusion of moving gills, which are prominent on many mayfly nymphs.

Tied by Craig Mathews

GREEN DRAKE NYMPH (EASTERN)

Hook:	Nymph, 2X or 3X long, size 8 or 10
Thread:	Olive
Tail:	Pheasant tail barbs or small gray or brown ostrich herl tips
Abdomen:	Tannish olive fur
Rib:	Copper wire
Thorax:	Same as abdomen
Wingcase:	Dark turkey tail
Legs:	Wooduck flank tied as a beard

These burrowing nymphs live in lakes and the silted sections of rivers. They are one of the largest mayflies in the East and the nymphs, upon emergence, swim and wriggle their way to the surface.

Tied by Terry Coleman

IDA MAY

Hook:	Nymph, size 8 or 10
Thread:	Black
Tail:	Dark green grizzly hackle barbs
Abdomen and thorax:	Black fuzzy yarn or fur
Rib 1:	Peacock herl
Rib 2:	Gold wire, wrapped in the opposite direction to reinforce the peacock herl
Legs:	A grizzly hackle collar, dyed dark green

The Ida May is Charles Brooks' imitation of the nymph of the Western green drake, *Drunella grandis* (formerly *Ephemerella grandis)*. Brooks favored the rounded design because it gives the same silhouette, even when viewed from different angles as the fly twists in the current.

Tied by Craig Mathews

GREEN DRAKE, MERCER'S POXYBACK

Hook:	Nymph, 3X long, size 10 or 12
Thread:	Olive
Tail:	Three golden pheasant tail barbs
Abdomen:	Mixed olive and brown dubbing
Gills:	Filoplume, dyed olive
Abdomen back:	Dark turkey tail, coated with epoxy
Rib:	Copper wire
Thorax:	Mixed olive and brown dubbing, applied with a dubbing loop and trimmed
Legs:	Dark grouse feather tied flat over the thorax
Wingcase:	Dark turkey tail, coated with epoxy
Head:	Same as abdomen

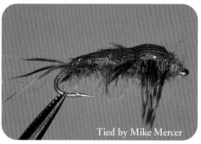
Tied by Mike Mercer

HENDRICKSON NYMPH

Hook:	Nymph, 1X or 2X long, size 12 or 14
Thread:	Brown
Tail:	Well marked woodduck flank barbs
Abdomen:	Reddish brown blended fur with a band of grayish brown fur behind the thorax
Thorax:	Reddish brown blended fur
Wingcase:	A black section of a turkey tail feather
Legs:	Brown partridge, grouse or well marked woodduck flank

The Hendricksons are usually the first mayfly hatch of major significance on Eastern trout streams. The nymphs are active swimmers as they make their way to the surface to hatch.

Tied by Barry Beck

HEX, JAY'S WIGGLE

Rear section:	
Hook:	Tied as follows, cut away the bend, attach to the front hook with a wire loop
Tail:	Small bunch of gray filoplume and a few barbs of woodduck flank
Abdomen:	Light yellow fur
Top of abdomen:	Pheasant tail segment
Rib:	Gold wire
Front section:	
Hook:	Wet fly, 1X long, size 10 or 12
Gills:	A bunch of gray filoplume on each side
Thorax:	Light yellow fur
Legs:	Two wraps of tan partridge hackle, at center and at front of thorax
Wingcase:	Dark pheasant tail segment
Eyes:	Painted black

Tied by Jay Passmore

Tied by Jeff "Bear" Andrews

Tied by Oscar Feliu

Tied by Andy Burk

Tied by the Dettes

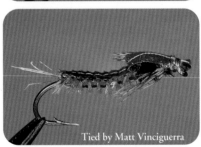

Tied by Matt Vinciguerra

Tied by Farrow Allen

HEX, JEFF'S

Hook:	Nymph, 4X long, size 6 to 12
Thread:	Tan or gray
Tail:	Gray filoplume
Abdomen and thorax:	Pale yellow sparkle yarn or dubbing
Gills:	Gray filoplume
Back:	Pheasant tail
Rib:	Gold wire
Legs and wingcase:	Grayish brown collar of pheasant or hen body

This is a relatively easy-to-tie, impressionistic imitation of a *Hexagenia* nymph. These large mayflies are common to the upper Midwest, and parts of the Northeast.

HEX, OSCAR'S

Hook:	6X long, size 6 to 10
Thread:	Orange
Tail:	Webby brown hen and ringneck pheasant tail barbs
Underbody:	Dental floss, flattened with pliers
Abdomen:	Cream sparkle yarn
Rib:	Oval gold tinsel
Gills:	A stem of filoplume tied flat over the abdomen and trimmed to a taper
Abdomen top:	Dark turkey tail, lacquered
Thorax:	Orange sparkle yarn
Legs:	Brown hackle palmered and trimmed
Wingcase:	Dark turkey tail, lacquered
Head and eyes:	Orange thread and melted monofilament

INFREQUENS, BURK'S HUNCHBACK

Hook:	Curved nymph, size 16 or 18
Thread:	Orange
Tail:	Woodduck flank barbs
Abdomen:	Rusty brown blended fur
Rib:	Yellow thread
Thorax:	Same as the abdomen
Legs:	Woodduck flank barbs on the sides
Wingcase:	Dark turkey tail or similar

Ephemerella infrequens, popularly known as the Pale Morning Dun (or PMD) is one of the most widespread mayfly hatches in the West. During summer days when they hatch, the nymphs are active around mid-morning, and swim toward the surface to emerge, usually before noon.

ISONYCHIA, DETTE

Hook:	Nymph, 3X long, size 10 or 12
Thread:	White
Underbody:	Lead wire, wrapped double over the thorax
Tail:	Ringneck cock pheasant tail barbs
Abdomen:	Gray ostrich herl over a mixture of dubbed muskrat fur and red wool
Rib:	Brown thread, counterwrapped
Thorax:	Gray muskrat fur
Legs:	Brown partridge hackle
Wingcase:	Light gray mallard wing quill section
Head:	Dark brown lacquer

Walt Dette designed this fly to imitate the *Isonychia bicolor* nymph that's common in the East.

ISONYCHIA NYMPH, MATT'S

Hook:	Nymph, 2X or 3X long, size 10 or 12, the front half bent up as shown
Thread:	Gray
Underbody:	A strip of lead on each side
Tail:	Lacquered turkey quill barbs, 3 short tails
Abdomen:	Reddish brown floss
Gills:	Light gray floss, wound over the abdomen. First place a flat toothpick along the underside. Wrap the floss, cement it on top only, then slit along the underside, freeing the toothpick and gills
Rib:	Brown floss
Back, wingcase and head:	Dark gray-brown hen body feather with a white stem
Thorax:	Peacock herl
Legs:	A few barbs of brown partridge on sides

MARCH BROWN

Hook:	Nymph, 1X or 2X long, size 8 or 10
Thread:	Brown
Tail:	Three ringneck pheasant tail barbs
Abdomen:	Blended amber and tan seal fur, or similar, dubbed full and picked out to suggest a wide, flat shape
Rib:	Brown thread
Thorax:	Same as abdomen
Wingcase:	Dark turkey tail, coated with vinyl cement
Legs:	Brown partridge hackle

The March Brown, *Stenonema vicarium*, is a large Eastern mayfly that delights anglers by hatching sporadically all day long during the late spring. The nymphs are broad and flat, and cling to rocks and boulders in fast well-oxygenated runs, crawling to slower waters close to shore to hatch.

MARCH BROWN, MULTARI

Hook: Nymph, 1X long, size 10 or 12
Thread: Brown
Tail: Three bunches of mallard flank barbs dyed dark amber, divided and lightly cemented near the tip
Abdomen: Brown seal substitute
Gills: Amber Ultra Chenille (Vernille), a section on both sides of the abdomen

Rib: Ginger colored floss and gold wire
Thorax: Same as abdomen
Legs: Three bunches of mallard flank barbs dyed dark amber
Wingcase and head: Black turkey or similar with a center stripe of ginger floss, folded over the thorax and doubled back to form the head

Tied by G. Lee Multari

MESS

Hook: Nymph, 1X long, size 6 to 12
Thread: Cream
Tail: Four brown hackle barbs, split
Body: Brown imitation seal fur
Shellback: A strip of white large-cell foam, the kind used as packaging material, cut

wide enough to overlap the body and colored with a marking pen if desired
Head: Same as body
Legs: One or two turns of brown hackle in front of which is a turn of mallard flank, tied so the barbs curve forward

The Mess can be tied in a variety of colors to look like a large clumsy mayfly nymph, trapped in the surface.

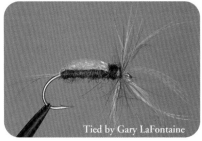

Tied by Gary LaFontaine

MOSTLY PHEASANT

Hook: Nymph, 4X to 6X long, size 4 to 14
Underbody: Weighted or unweighted Nymphorm or lead wire on the sides
Thread: Black
Tail: Pheasant tail barbs
Abdomen: Gray aftershafts, tied in by the butts and progressively wrapped forward over a base of CA cement

Top of abdomen: Pheasant "church window" feather, coated with vinyl cement and pulled forward
Rib: Oval gold tinsel or wire
Thorax: Peacock herl
Legs: Pheasant back feather
Wingcase: Pheasant "church window" feather, coated with vinyl cement

Tied by Robert Rifchen

PMD, MERCER'S POXYBACK

Hook: Nymph, 2X or 3X long, size 16 or 18
Thread: Brown
Tail: Three divided ringneck pheasant tail barbs
Abdomen: Rusty brown fur
Abdomen back: Dark turkey tail
Rib: Pearl Flashabou

Gills: Tiny bunches of light tan marabou tied on each side, in front of the abdomen
Thorax: Same as abdomen
Legs: Sparse brown partridge on each side of the thorax
Wingcase: Dark turkey tail, coated with fast-drying epoxy

Tied by Mike Mercer

PHEASANT TAIL NYMPH

Hook: Nymph, 1X long, size 12 to 20
Tail: Ringneck pheasant center tail barbs
Body: Ringneck pheasant center trail barbs, wrapped
Rib: Copper wire

Abdomen: Peacock herl
Wingcase: Ringneck pheasant tail, folded over the thorax
Legs: A few fibers from the wingcase, pulled down and tied back

The Pheasant Tail was first designed by British riverkeeper Frank Sawyer, who twisted the wire and pheasant tail around one another and wrapped them forward together, forming the abdomen and thorax.

Tied by Dick Talleur

POTAMANTHUS NYMPH

Hook: Nymph, 3X long, size 10 or 12
Thread: Brown or olive
Tail: Three ringneck pheasant tail barbs, divided
Abdomen: Blended yellow and amber seal fur and cream fox fur or similar, picked out to resemble gills
Back of abdomen: Golden pheasant tail barbs

Rib: Fine oval gold tinsel or wire
Thorax: Same as abdomen
Legs: Well-marked woodduck flank
Wingcase and head: Dark brown turkey tail, coated with vinyl cement, extending over the hook eye
Tusks: Outside barbs from the head

Tied by Farrow Allen

Tied by Andy Burk

Tied by Shane Stalcup

Tied by Farrow Allen

Tied by Gary Borger

Tied by Dan Cottrell

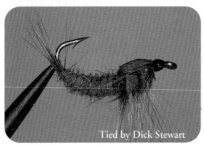

Tied by Dick Stewart

SIPHLONURUS, BURK'S BANDED

Hook:	Nymph, 3X long, size 10 to 14	Thorax:	Blended dark gray fur and Antron
Thread:	Beige or gray	Legs:	Dark partridge or mallard dyed brown,
Tail:	Three gray ostrich herl tips or similar		on either side of the thorax
Abdomen:	Blended dark gray fur and Antron	Wingcase:	Black turkey tail
	with a center band of tan dubbing	Head:	Same as thorax
Rib:	Tan thread		

This large swimming nymph is more common in the West than it is in the East.

SIPHLONURUS, STALCUP

Hook:	Nymph, 2X or 3X long, size 10 to 16	Rib:	Silver wire
Thread:	Gray	Thorax:	Same as abdomen
Tail:	Three gray ostrich plume tips or similar	Legs:	Small gray hen back feather
Gills:	Gray ostrich herl	Wingcase:	Gray poly yarn or similar
Abdomen:	Blended gray dubbing		

The *Siphlonurus* (Gray Drake) nymphs are active swimmers and should be fished with a lot of action.

STENONEMA, FLASHBACK

Hook:	Nymph, size 10 to 14	Thorax:	Same as the abdomen
Thread:	Brown or tan	Legs:	A single brown partridge feather, tied
Tail:	Brown partridge hackle barbs		flat over the thorax
Abdomen:	Blended amber and tan fur	Wingcase:	Flat silver Mylar
Rib:	Dark brown thread		

Tied with a Mylar wingcase, this is a good imitation of a pre-emergent March Brown or Light Cahill nymph.

STRIP NYMPH

Hook:	Nymph, size 6 to 12	Legs:	Rabbit body guard hair applied with a
Thread:	Tan		spinning loop and trimmed on the top
Abdomen:	Tan fur strip tied in at the tail position		and bottom
Underbody:	Lead wire	Wingcase:	Peacock herl
Thorax:	Tan dubbing		

It's a challenge to tie a fly that looks like the nymph you're trying to imitate; an even greater challenge is to tie one that mimics the way the natural moves about in the water as this one does.

SWIMMER-BURROWER

Hook:	Nymph, 3X or 4X long, size 8 to 14	Gills:	Brown ostrich herl
Thread:	Black or brown	Legs:	Dark brown braided cord, dubbed at
Underbody:	Lead wire, optional		the base (femur) with tan rabbit fur
Tail:	Three soft webby tan hackle tips	Thorax:	Same as abdomen
Abdomen:	Tan rabbit fur	Wingcase:	Gold crystal flash

Dan Cottrell designed this series of nymphs for Superfly, Inc. of Edmonton, Alberta. This pattern is also tied in golden amber, brown and olive to cover the most common colors these mayflies fall into.

TARCHER

Hook:	Curved nymph hook, size 10 to 18; the	Rib:	Fine gold or copper wire
	orientation of this fly is with the hook	Thorax:	Same as the abdomen
	point facing up	Legs:	Dark brown or black hackle
Thread:	Black	Wingcase:	Black turkey tail section, coated with
Tail:	Dark brown hackle barbs		vinyl cement
Abdomen:	Reddish brown rabbit fur		

Ken Iwamasa designed this fly to imitate how many of the non-swimming mayfly nymphs hold their bodies when drifting freely in the current.

The term emerger is one which fly fishermen have adopted to refer to aquatic insects that are in the process of changing from their immature (nymphal or pupal) form into adults. For most mayfly species, this transformation occurs at the water's surface and is a process which may take only seconds, or can require several minutes as the winged adult extricates itself from its nymphal shuck. This is a time when the insects are highly vulnerable to predation from trout. The fish are attracted by the upward movement as the nymphs swim to the surface. Some nymphs never succeed in emerging; they are imperfectly developed and cannot fly for one reason or another. These are referred to as cripples. Some experts believe that selective trout may focus on such cripples because they are easy prey, and cannot escape by taking flight. The classification of fishing flies is sometimes arbitrary, so some of the flies in this section could have easily been categorized as nymphs or as duns.

BALLOON EMERGER

Hook: Nymph, 1X long, size 10 to 16
Thread: Gray or olive
Tail: Partridge hackle barbs
Body: Tan fur

Wingcase: Gray closed cell Polycelon foam pulled over the thorax
Legs: Partridge hackle barbs

Tied by Andrew Gennaro

Gennaro's Balloon Emerger is a derivation from Charlie Brooks' Natant Nylon nymph, but it's easier to tie and more durable. Since it hangs suspended in the surface film, the fly will float forever. But do not pull the wingcase too tightly, or you will compress the air bubbles out of the foam.

CDC QUILL WING EMERGER

Hook: Dry fly, 1X long, size 12 to 18
Thread: Gray
Tail: Hen back barbs, dyed gray
Abdomen: Gray goose biot
Thorax: Gray dubbing

Wing: Gray CDC outside of which are gray duck wing quill sections, curving out
Legs: Hen back barbs, dyed gray, tied as a beard
Head: Gray thread wraps

Tied by Shane Stalcup

This is one of Shane Stalcup's favorite patterns, which he also ties with a Z-lon tail to suggest a trailing shuck.

D.A. CAHILL

Hook: Curved nymph hook, size 10 to 14
Thread: Brown
Tail: Brown Z-lon
Abdomen and thorax: Mixed amber and brown

dubbing
Wing: Tan CDC
Head: Same as body

Tied by Dave Goulet

Dave Goulet's D.A. Cahill is tied to look like an emerging *Stenonema* nymph, hanging in the surface film, struggling to split its shuck and release the dun. Since CDC feathers come from the rump of a duck, the D.A. refers to this part of the anatomy.

CAPTIVE DUN

Hook: Dry fly, size 14 to 20
Thread: Olive or tan
Tail (trailing shuck): Gray marabou or Z-lon
Body: Olive brown dubbing

Legs: Elk hair, woodduck flank or CDC barbs extending from the sides
Wingcase: Gray duck or goose wing pulled over the entire body like a shellback

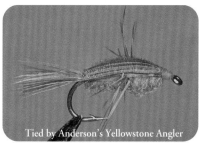
Tied by Anderson's Yellowstone Angler

This pattern was developed by René Harrop to suggest an emerging dun that has been inextricably trapped in the process of emerging.

COMPARA-EMERGER

Hook: Dry fly, size 8 to 18
Thread: Brown
Tail: Blue dun hackle barbs, divided around a ball of dubbing

Body: Blended gray spectrumized fur
Wing: Dark gray deer body hair, short
Head: Butt ends of the wing trimmed short

Tied by Blair Caucci

The size and color of the Compara-Emerger are easily varied to match any hatching mayfly. Simplicity is the hallmark of this design as it features the important ingredients in any fly: correct size, matching silhouette and proper color. Not only that, but the color has a lifelike property because it's made up of a blend of colors, much like a natural insect.

Tied by Redding Fly Shop

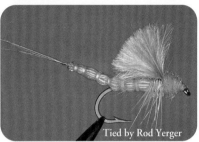

Tied by Rod Yerger

Tied by Shane Stalcup

Tied by Umpqua Feather Merchants

Tied by Gary LaFontaine

Tied by Barry Beck

DURAND'S HUNCH BACK

Hook:	Dry fly, size 14 to 18	Wing:	Light elk or deer body hair, tips pointing forward over the eye of the hook and the shorter butt ends to the rear, clipped short over the thorax
Thread:	Olive		
Tail:	Peacock sword		
Body:	Peacock sword, wrapped like herl		
Rib:	Tan thread	Legs:	Dark brown hackle, wrapped
Thorax:	Olive dubbing		

Durand's Hunch Back imitates a mayfly helplessly trapped between being a nymph and becoming a dun.

EMERGING DUN, ROD'S

Hook:	Dry fly, size 12 to 18		around the hook shank
Thread:	Gray	Hackle:	Ginger, trimmed on the top and bottom
Tail:	Three divided pheasant tail barbs		
Extended body:	Natural gray deer body hair, ribbed with gray thread and secured	Wing:	A clump of gray marabou
		Head:	Gray fur

Rod Yerger ties his emerging dun in different sizes and colors to match most any mayfly hatch. Yerger says this pattern takes fish during all stages of the hatch.

GREEN DRAKE, CDC EMERGER

Hook:	Nymph, 3X long, size 8 or 10	Thorax:	Olive dubbing
Thread:	Olive	Legs:	Brown partridge hackle on the sides
Tail:	Partridge hackle	Underwing:	Dark gray CDC fibers
Underbody:	White floss, for bulk and taper	Wing:	Blue dun Z-lon
Abdomen:	Light turkey wing biot dyed light olive	Note:	Before tying the Z-lon wing make a few more turns of olive dubbing in front of the underwing.
Rib:	Copper wire		

GREEN DRAKE, CRIPPLED DUN

Hook:	Dry fly, size 8 or 10		ward over the eye of the hook with the butt ends trimmed short
Thread:	Olive or tan		
Tail:	Ostrich plumes or marabou, dyed olive	Legs:	Grizzly hackle, dyed olive
Abdomen:	Ostrich dyed olive, wrapped over a base of olive thread	Note:	A clump of dun colored CDC fibers may be substituted for the deer hair wing.
Thorax:	Dark olive fur, tied full		
Wing:	Tan deer body hair, tips pointing for-		

HALO MAYFLY EMERGER, BROWN

Hook:	Dry fly, size 10 to 20	Halo:	White large cell foam, tied across the shank as shown
Thread:	Cream		
Tag:	Clear Antron fibers, wrapped halfway down the bend of the hook	Thorax:	Same as abdomen
		Spike:	Fluorescent orange deer body hair extending over the eye of the hook
Tail:	Brown marabou		
Abdomen:	Brown dubbing, thinly applied		

There's no telling why, but trout will pick up the Halo Emerger while passing up other patterns.

HENDRICKSON POLY-FLUFF EMERGER

Hook:	Dry fly, size 12 or 14	Legs:	Woodduck flank
Thread:	Olive	Thorax:	Same as the abdomen
Tail:	Woodduck flank	Wing:	Dark gray Z-lon
Abdomen:	Dark red-brown dubbing		

When Hendricksons emerge in the early spring, the water and air temperatures are often so low that the nymphs seem to take forever to emerge into duns. On these early spring days a good floating nymph emerger is essential.

HEXAGENIA EMERGER, LUCCA'S

Hook: Dry fly, size 6 or 8
Thread: Yellow
Extended abdomen: Creamy yellow deer body hair, secured with cross wraps of yellow thread
Tail: Untrimmed deer hair from the extended abdomen

Emerging wing: Mixed natural and yellow dyed gray deer body hair
Thorax: Creamy yellow dubbing
Wingcase: Brown turkey wing quill section dyed yellow, pulled forward over the thorax
Legs: Mixed natural and yellow dyed gray deer body hair, on each side

Tied by David Lucca

LOOP WING EMERGER, OLIVE

Hook: Dry fly, size 10 to 18, front half is bent slightly upward
Thread: Olive
Tail (trailing shuck): Clump of dun colored crinkled synthetic fiber
Abdomen: Olive brown dubbing

Thorax: Same as abdomen
Legs: Grizzly hackle dyed blue dun, wrapped over the thorax and trimmed on the top and bottom
Loop wing: Same as tail

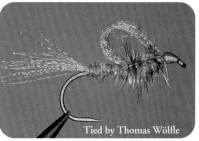

Tied by Thomas Wölfle

MARCH BROWN LOOP WING EMERGER

Hook: Dry fly, size 10 or 12
Thread: Brown
Tail: Mixed brown hackle barbs and woodduck flank
Abdomen: Creamy tan dubbing including a turn

or two underneath the tail
Thorax: Same as abdomen
Legs: Dark grizzly hackle, trimmed on the top and bottom
Looped wing: Pheasant tail, folded as shown

David Lucca can imitate most small and medium size emerging mayflies using this style in varied sizes and colors.

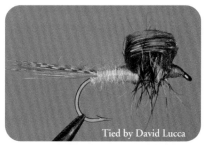

Tied by David Lucca

PMD EMERGER

Hook: Dry fly, size 16 or 18
Thread: Gray or yellow
Tail (trailing shuck): Brown to yellow Z-lon
Abdomen and thorax: Yellowish tan dubbing

Wing: Gray closed-cell foam
Legs: Two turns of gray starling hackle or similar

This Pale Morning Dun emerger is from Craig Mathews of Blue Ribbon Flies in West Yellowstone, Montana. In Mathews' and Juracek's new book *Fishing Yellowstone Hatches,* they write the PMD "is arguably the single most important insect to fly fishermen in the Yellowstone area."

Tied by Craig Mathews

PARACHUTE FLOATING NYMPH, BROWN

Hook: Dry fly, size 10 to 22
Thread: Brown
Tail: Blue dun hackle barbs
Abdomen and thorax: Mixed reddish brown

dubbing fur and sparkle yarn
Emerging wing: Mixed gray fur and sparkle yarn
Legs: Blue dun hackle, one turn wrapped parachute style around the ball of fur

Gary Borger, who designed this emerging nymph, credits the Harrops, Mike Lawson and Fred Arbona for promoting and popularizing the importance of emerger patterns.

Tied by Gary Borger

POLY-WING EMERGER

Hook: Nymph, 3X long, curved shank, size 12 to 16
Thread: Black
Tail: Ringneck pheasant tail barbs
Abdomen: Ringneck pheasant tail barbs
Rib: Copper wire
Wing: White poly yarn

Thorax: Peacock herl
Legs: Brown hackle wrapped parachute style around the poly yarn
Wingcase: A bunch of ringneck pheasant tail barbs folded forward around the poly yarn and under the brown hackle

This emerger floats with the thorax in the surface film and the abdomen submerged underwater.

Tied by Roy Richardson

Mayfly Duns

The adult mayfly, when it first hatches, is called a dun. In some species, the transformation from nymph to dun takes only seconds, and the dun flies away quickly. With other species this emergence may take several minutes, during which time the duns float upon the water's surface as their wings and bodies become prepared for flight. Collectively, the mayflies may hatch sporadically, in brief flurries, or the hatch may be massive, with large numbers of flies blanketing the water for hours. Fly fishermen dream of these hatches, for it is this dun stage that often triggers a feeding response by trout. It is the dun that was the focus of fly tying throughout much of the twentieth century. Some dun imitations are designed so that the fly bodies are in the surface film, imitating a dun not yet ready for flight - a more vulnerable dun say some experts. Other flies perch above the water supported by hackle legs; and even others are tied to resemble crippled duns, unable to fly away.

Tied by Gary Saindon

AMBIGUOUS

Hook:	Dry fly, curved shank, size 8 to 14	Tail:	Dark moose body hair
Thread:	Black	Body:	Dark brown fur
Submerged shuck:	Dubbed light brown fur sheathed with white yarn	Wing:	White bucktail or fine deer body hair
		Hackle:	Mixed grizzly and brown

Gary Saindon's Ambiguous imitates an adult mayfly trailing a submerged nymphal shuck. Like so many of the mayfly imitations, one must only change the size and color to represent other mayflies.

Tied by Farrow Allen

BEAVERKILL

Hook:	Dry fly, size 10 to 16	Rib:	Brown hackle, palmered
Thread:	Black	Wing:	Gray mallard wing quill sections
Tail:	Brown hackle barbs	Hackle:	Brown
Body:	White floss		

This is a classic dry fly from New York's Catskill region that was named after one of its best known rivers.

Tied by Jacques Juneau

BICOLOR

Hook:	Dry fly, size 10	Body:	Brown, red and black fur, well mixed
Thread:	Black	Hackle:	Dark brown in front of light ginger
Tail:	Two black moose shoulder hairs		

Designed by Juneau to imitate the adult *Isonychia bicolor* that is very common in the Northeast and which hatches during the late summer into the fall.

Tied by Chuck Allard

BLACK QUILL

Hook:	Dry fly, size 10 to 14	Body:	Stripped peacock herl
Thread:	Black	Wing:	Dark gray mallard wing quill sections
Tail:	Black hackle barbs	Hackle:	Black

The Black Quill imitates the adult *Leptophlebia* species that inhabit both fast moving and slow flowing waters.

Tied by Chuck Allard

BLUE DUN

Hook:	Dry fly, size 10 to 18	Body:	Gray fur
Thread:	Gray or black	Wing:	Gray mallard wing quill sections
Tail:	Medium blue dun hackle barbs	Hackle:	Medium blue dun

This well known and very popular mayfly pattern can be used to imitate a variety of dark mayfly duns.

BLUE QUILL

Hook: Dry fly, size 14 to 18
Thread: Gray
Tail: Medium blue dun hackle barbs

Body: Stripped peacock quill
Wing: Dark gray wing quill segments
Hackle: Medium blue dun

The Blue Quill was tied to imitate the mayfly *Paraleptophlebia adoptiva,* which emerges in the East and Midwest during the early spring, about the same time that the Hendricksons begin to appear. Other species of paraleps can be imitated with this pattern.

Tied by Chuck Allard

BLUE WING OLIVE

Hook: Dry fly, size 12 to 24
Thread: Olive
Tail: Dun hackle barbs

Body: Olive fur
Wing: Dun hackle tips
Hackle: Dun

Often referred to as a BWO, this color combination is very common among mayflies, particularly a variety of olive-bodied duns, from the tiny Baetidae to the larger Ephemerellidae families.

Tied by Farrow Allen

BLUE WING OLIVE, CDC BIOT DUN

Hook: Dry fly, size 14 to 24
Thread: Olive
Tail: Dun hackle barbs, divided
Body: Goose biot, dyed olive
Thorax: Olive dubbing

Wing: Dun CDC fibers
Legs: A few barbs of woodduck flank on
         each side
Head: Olive dubbing

Stalcup's CDC Biot Duns lend themselves to imitating many of the smaller adult mayflies.

Tied by Shane Stalcup

BLUE WING OLIVE, LOOP WING PARADUN

Hook: Dry fly, size 12 to 16
Thread: Olive
Tail: Blue dun hackle barbs
Abdomen: Stripped hackle quill, dyed olive
Thorax: Olive dubbing

Wing: Two blue dun hackles, trimmed close
         to the center shaft so only a stubble of
         barbs remains, and tied in a loop as
         shown
Hackle: Grizzly dyed olive, parachute style

The double loop wings offer a broad shape and a prominent silhouette. On smaller flies, a single loop wing should be sufficient.

Tied by Chuck Allard

BORCHER SPECIAL

Hook: Dry fly, size 10 to 18
Thread: Black
Tail: Mahogany ringneck pheasant tail barbs
Body: Two or three long mottled turkey wing

quill barbs, wrapped
Wing: Blue dun hackle tips or cut wings
Hackle: Brown and grizzly

The Borcher Special is an popular pattern originated in Michigan.

Tied by Terry Coleman

BROWN DRAKE

Hook: Dry fly, size 10 or 12
Thread: Tan
Tail: Dark moose hair
Body: Yellow-tan dubbing

Rib: Yellow floss
Wing: Light brown elk
Hackle: Mixed grizzly and grizzly dyed yellow

The large brown drake or chocolate drake *(Ephemera simulans)* is a fairly widespread species found in the East and as far west as the Rockies.

Tied by Terry Coleman

Tied by Kaufmann's Streamborn

BROWN DRAKE, EXTENDED BODY PARADRAKE

Hook: Dry fly, size 8 or 10
Thread: Yellow
Tail: Three black moose hairs
Wing: Natural tan elk hair, tied as an upright clump
Extended body: Golden brown elk or deer body

hair, tied reversed to form a bullethead, pulled around the upright wing and secured with cross wraps of the yellow tying thread
Hackle: Grizzly, dyed tan to yellow

This fly is designed to imitate the adult *Ephemera simulans* that's present in many areas.

Tied by Larry Duckwall

CAHILL, LIGHT (FLICK)

Hook: Dry Fly, sizes 12 or 14
Thread: Primrose or cream
Tail: Light ginger or cream hackle barbs

Body: Cream fox belly fur
Wing: W   Woodduck flank
Hackle: Light ginger or cream hackle barbs

Writing in his classic 1969 edition of *The New Streamside Guide*, Art Flick wrote, "To date I have never met a fisherman who had fished any stream where trout could not be taken on this fly."

Tied by Chuck Allard

CAHILL, LIGHT PARACHUTE

Hook: Dry fly, size 12 to 20
Thread: Primrose yellow or cream
Tail: Ginger or cream
Body: Creamy yellow dubbing

Wing: Upright clump of white calftail, calfbody hair or similar
Hackle: Ginger or cream, tied parachute style

This variation of the tradional Light Cahill (above) floats like all parachute hackled flies, right in the surface film. The white wing is also more visible in riffled water where most species of these mayflies are found.

Tied by Barry Beck

CAHILL QUILL

Hook: Dry fly, size 10 to 16
Thread: Cream or primrose
Tail: Cream or light ginger

Body: Stripped peacock quill
Wing: Woodduck flank
Hackle: Cream or light ginger

In a few areas of the country the Cahill Quill is still a popular imitation of the different *Stenonema* or *Stenacron* species, particularly when a slender silhouette is in order. Like all the Light Cahill patterns, the Cahill Quill is also tied in a range of sizes to match a variety of small, light-colored mayflies.

Tied by Anderson's Yellowstone Angler

CALLIBAETIS, GULPER SPECIAL

Hook: Dry fly, size 14 to 18
Tail: Grizzly or dun hackle barbs, or the two mixed
Body: Tannish gray dubbing
Wing: Cream or white poly yarn, tied upright

Hackle: Grizzly tied parachute
Note: Troth ties the Gulper Special with a black wing for dark overcast days and an orange wing for fishing around foamy back eddies.

The Gulper is a fly style, and this is Al Troth's imitation of the prolific *Callibaetis* mayfly dun common to many western lakes where the trout cruise around audibly gulping mayflies.

Tied by Kaufmann's Streamborn

CALLIBAETIS, THORAX

Hook: Dry fly, size 14 to 18
Thread: Tan
Tail: Blue dun hackle barbs or Micro Fibetts, divided
Body: Gray to tannish gray dubbing

Wing: Mottled brown hen or partridge tied upright
Hackle: Grizzly, tied thorax style, trimmed on the bottom to form a "V"

This is a very common mayfly in the Western and Rocky Mountain states. They are restricted mainly to lakes and ponds, though some are found in slow moving spring creeks.

COMPARA-DUN

Hook:	Dry fly, size 10 to 20	Body:	Blended spectrumized rabbit fur
Thread:	Dark brown	Wing:	Dark deer body hair tied in a 180° arc
Tail:	Divided dark dun hackle barbs		on top of the hook

The Compara-dun was developed in the mid 1960s by Al Caucci and utilized some of the features of Fran Betters' famous Haystack (which see). Unlike the Haystack, which is tied in just a few colors, Compara-duns are part of a larger system for imitating a wide range of mayflies. This style of fly has become widely accepted.

Tied by Al Caucci

COMPARA-DUN, UPSIDE DOWN

Hook:	Dry fly, size 10 to 18		divided
Thread:	Cream or light olive	Body:	Olive Fuzzy Foam
Tail:	Brown Nylon bristles or Micro Fibetts,	Wing:	Gray Z-lon

Betts' upside down Compara-dun helps keep the hook from picking up debris and weeds in waters where that presents a problem. It also keeps the hook from hanging intrusively below the surface. Betts borrowed the basic construction ideas from the standard Compara-dun(above)

Tied by John Betts

COMPARA-DUN, Z-LON

Hook:	Dry fly, size 10 to 18		tapered
Thread:	White	Thorax:	Mixed crinkled and regular olive Z-lon,
Tail:	Dun colored Nylon bristles or Micro		cut into short pieces and dubbed
	Fibetts, divided	Wing:	Dun Z-lon
Abdomen: Olive rabbit fur, thinly dubbed and			

This and the preceding Upside Down all-synthetic Compara-dun were tied by John Betts, who sometimes substitutes a piece of ginger or brown-gold Z-lon for the tail to imitate a trailing shuck.

Tied by John Betts

CREAM VARIANT (FLICK)

Hook:	Dry fly, short shank, size 12	Body:	Stem of a cream hackle with the barbs
Thread:	Primrose yellow		stripped off, tied in by the tip
Tail:	Cream hackle barbs	Hackle:	Cream hackle, tied oversize

The Cream Variant in Art Flick's *Streamside Guide* was tied to imitate the mayfly *Potamanthus distinctus,* often referred to as the yellow may. These duns are a common summer sight at dusk on many northeastern trout waters.

Tied by Larry Duckwall

DUN VARIANT (FLICK)

Hook:	Dry fly, short shank, size 12		stripped off
Tail:	Dark dun hackle barbs	Hackle:	Dark dun, tied oversize
Body:	A brown hackle stem with the barbs		

Designed to imitate the adult *Isonychia bicolor*. The bicolor nymph is more available than the dun because the dun does not emerge in the water. Like a stonefly, the nymph crawls out of the water, and the adult emerges on dry ground. Nonetheless, when it's windy or the water is high, large numbers of *bicolor* adults end up on the water.

Tied by Larry Duckwall

DUN VARIANT, SMALL (FLICK)

Hook:	Dry fly, size 16 or 18	Body:	Olive yarn mixed with a little gray
Thread:	Olive		muskrat fur
Tail:	Dark dun hackle barbs	Hackle:	Dark dun

Designed to imitate the *Ephemerella attenuata*, a small olive-bodied fly that hatches in the late spring and early summer. This is a good fly for imitating many of the smaller blue wing olives, but for the larger imitations the addition of a wing helps make the fly more visible to the angler as well as more convincing to the trout.

Tied by Larry Duckwall

Tied by George Kesel

Tied by Barry Beck

Tied by Larry Duckwall

Tied by Larry Duckwall

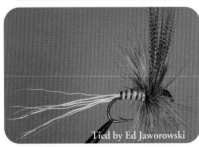

Tied by Ed Jaworowski

Tied by James Bowen

FLUORESCENT WING DUN, LIGHT

Hook:	Dry fly, size 10 to 20	Body:	Cream fur
Thread:	Primrose yellow	Wing:	Fluorescent orange hackle tips
Tail:	Light ginger hackle barbs	Hackle:	Light ginger

George Harvey, the legendary fly-fishing instructor from Penn State, began tying dry flies with fluorescent wings so that he could see them better as, with age, his visual acuity began to fail. What he discovered was that the fluorescent colored wings made little difference whatsoever to the trout, but helped him immensely.

GINGER QUILL

Hook:	Dry fly, size 12 to 18	Wing:	Very light gray mallard wing quill sections
Thread:	Primrose yellow, gray or black		
Tail:	Light ginger hackle barbs	Hackle:	Light ginger
Body:	Stripped peacock quill		

This is an established pattern that imitates many different light colored mayflies, depending on how large or small you choose to tie it

GRAY FOX (FLICK)

Hook:	Dry Fly, size 12	Body:	Light fawn-colored red fox fur
Thread:	Primrose yellow	Wing:	Mallard flank
Tail:	Light ginger hackle barbs	Hackle:	Mixed light grizzly and light ginger

Art Flick's Gray Fox is tied to imitate the *Stenonema fuscum* that emerges on rivers in the East around the same time as the March Brown, *S. vicarium* (which see). Both insects are very similar in appearance and habits, although the Gray Fox is slightly smaller and usually begins emerging a week or so later than the March Brown.

GRAY FOX VARIANT (FLICK)

Hook:	Dry fly, size 10 or 12		stem, tied in by the tip
Thread:	Primrose yellow	Hackle:	Mixed light ginger, dark ginger and
Tail:	Ginger hackle barbs		grizzly, tied oversize
Body:	Cream or light ginger stripped hackle		

Art Flick designed the Gray Fox Variant for fishing to the eastern Green Drake hatch. It has proven itself to be a very high floating, searching pattern for trout hiding in rapids and pocket water.

GREEN DRAKE, EASTERN (JAWOROWSKI)

Hook:	Dry fly, size 10		fullness instead of a single divided flank feather
Thread:	Olive		
Tail:	Bleached elk hair, long	Hackle:	Mixed heavily barred grizzly, light ginger and dyed insect green
Body:	Mixed tan colored red fox fur and natural kapok		
Rib:	Dark brown cotton thread	Note:	Apply some dubbing between and in front the wings before the hackles are wound, in order to bulk up the thorax.
Wing:	Two woodduck flank feathers for extra		

GREEN DRAKE, WESTERN (BOWEN)

Hook:	Dry fly, size 10 or 12	Rib:	Yellow floss
Thread:	Olive	Legs:	Deer body hair dyed light olive or yellow
Tail:	Three strands of black FisHair		
Abdomen:	Yellow poly yarn wrapped back along the hook shank, up the black FisHair tail and back again	Wing:	Gray poly yarn
		Thorax and head:	Olive poly dubbing
		Eyes:	Melted monofilament
Back:	Green or olive poly yarn		

James Bowen's fly imitates a freshly emerged Green Drake dun, which Bowen describes as "compact and bulky," and nearly chartreuse in color.

GREEN DRAKE, WESTERN (LEMPKE)

Hook: Dry fly size 10
Thread: Olive
Tail: Three strands of dark monofilament
Egg sac: Peacock herl
Abdomen: A piece of monofilament is secured to the hook shank. Dark olive-green floss is wrapped back along the shank, up the tail and back again
Rib: Yellow rod wrapping thread
Thorax: Peacock herl
Wing: Dark gray duck wing quill sections, cut to shape and lightly cemented
Hackle: Mixed natural and dyed yellow grizzly, trimmed on the bottom

Tied by Bing Lempke

GREEN DRAKE, WESTERN EXTENDED BODY

Hook: Dry fly, size 8 or 10
Thread: Olive
Tail: Three black moose hairs
Wing: Black or gray elk hair, tied as an upright clump
Extended body: Golden olive or olive elk or deer body hair, tied reversed to form a bullethead, pulled around the upright wing, secured with wraps of olive tying thread
Hackle: Grizzly, dyed yellow, tied parachute style

Tied by Kaufmann's Streamborn

GREEN DRAKE, WESTERN, LAWSON'S

Hook: Dry fly, size 8 or 10
Thread: Olive
Tail: Three black moose hairs
Wing: Natural tan elk hair, tied as an upright clump
Extended body: Olive elk hair, tied reversed to form a bullethead, pulled around the upright wing, secured with wraps of olive tying thread
Hackle: Grizzly, dyed olive, tied parachute style

Mike Lawson took the Swisher-Richard's Paradrake style and modified it by adding the bullethead that did not exist in the original pattern.

Tied by Redding Fly Shop

HENDRICKSON (FLICK)

Hook: Dry Fly, size 12
Thread: Primrose yellow
Tail: Medium blue dun hackle barbs
Body: Pinkish urine-burned red fox belly fur
Wing: Woodduck flank
Hackle: Medium blue dun hackle barbs

The Art Flick version and Roy Steenrod's original imitation of the female *Ephemerella subvaria*, are almost identical. No one has ever seen much need to change the pattern. If you can't find authentic urine-burned fox fur, it's O.K. because Steenrod tied Hendricksons with ordinary fawn fox belly fur.

Tied by Larry Duckwall

HENDRICKSON, DARK

Hook: Dry fly, size 10 to 18
Thread: Black or gray
Tail: Medium to dark blue dun hackle barbs
Body: Gray muskrat fur
Wing: Woodduck flank
Hackle: Medium to dark blue dun

Not all mayflies of the same species always look the same. Regarding the wing color of natural Hendrickson duns, Art Flick wrote in *The New Streamside Guide*, "There is considerable variation in the shade in the various specimens that I have collected." Today we know he might have actually been seeing more than a single *Ephemerella* species.

Tied by Terry Coleman

HENDRICKSON THORAX DUN

Hook: Dry fly, size 12 or 14
Thread: Dark olive or gray
Tails: Blue dun hackle barbs, divided
Abdomen: Mixed gray, tan and pinkish dubbing
Wing: Dark gray hen back tips, tied upright
Thorax: Same as abdomen, built up around and in front of the wings
Hackle: Blue dun tied thorax style

Vince Marinaro introduced the Thorax Dun in his 1950 publication of *A Modern Dry Fly Code*. His intent was to design a fly that floated flush in the surface film and had an overwhelming wing silhouette for the trout to key on.

Tied by Barry Beck

Tied by John Betts

Tied by David Lucca

Tied by David Lucca

Tied by Redding Fly Shop

Tied by Mike Motyl

Tied by Del Mazza

HEXAGENIA (BETTS)

Hook: Dry fly, straight eye, size 10 or 12
Abdomen: Tan, gold and yellow poly-yarn
Tails: Lacquered brown sewing thread
Thorax: Rabbit fur appropriately colored with marking pens
Hackle: One brownish yellow badger tied in by the tip, wound forward over the thorax, and trimmed on the bottom
Wing: A single piece of heavy plastic bag, sanded with emery paper to reduce the glare, and cut to shape
Note: A small loop of poly yarn behind the wing will help support it.

HEXAGENIA, CLIPPED DEER HAIR COMPARA-DUN

Hook: Dry fly, straight eye, size 4 to 8
Thread: Cream or primrose yellow
Tail: Divided ginger elk hair or similar
Body: Creamy yellow deer body hair, spun and clipped to shape
Wing: Natural gray deer body hair, tied upright in the compara-dun style
Note: Don't tie the butt ends of the wing down, but let them flare and clip them to conform with the shape of the body.

David Lucca lives and fishes in the Midwest where the *Hexagenia limbata* is abundant. His Clipped Deer Hair Compara-dun floats well and is suited for imitating larger mayflies.

HEXAGENIA, EXTENDED BODY DEER HAIR

Hook: Dry fly, size 4 to 8
Thread: Yellow
Extended body: Creamy yellow deer body hair over which is peacock herl
Tail: Untrimmed deer hair tips from the extended body with peacock herl over
Rib: Yellow rod wrapping thread
Wing: Deer or elk hair dyed olive-yellow
Hackle: Mixed brown, natural grizzly and grizzly dyed yellow

HEXAGENIA PARADUN

Hook: Dry fly, up eye salmon, size 6 or 8
Thread: Yellow
Body: Yellow elk or deer body hair, secured with wraps of yellow tying thread, extending a little beyond the bend of the hook
Body hackle: Light ginger, palmered forward over the part of the abdomen that's secured around the hook shank
Tail: Yellow hair from the abdomen
Wing: Elk hair, dyed yellow and tied as an upright clump
Hackle: Grizzly, dyed yellow, tied parachute style

HOUSATONIC QUILL

Hook: Dry fly, size 12 to 16
Thread: Cream or primrose yellow
Tail: Natural light badger or dyed light dun badger hackle barbs
Body: Stripped peacock herl
Wing: Wooduck flank
Hackle: Natural light badger or dyed light dun badger hackle barbs

This is a fly that's been around for many years. It was named for one of Connecticut's most notable trout rivers, the Housatonic, which offers some excellent trophy brown trout fishing.

ISONYCHIA DUN, HEN WING

Hook: Dry fly, size 10 to 14
Thread: Brown
Tail: Grizzly hackle barbs dyed medium dun
Body: A stripped stem of a Rhode Island Red neck hackle, dyed chestnut brown, wrapped and lacquered
Hackle: Grizzly dyed medium dun
Wing: Very light colored grizzly hen hackle tips

"I prefer dyed grizzly for all my (dry) flies," writes Del Mazza, "because the natural flecking imitates the natural insect more closely." The hackle point wings also provide a more visible silhouette.

IWAMASA DUN, OLIVE

Hook:	Dry fly, size 12 to 18	Legs:	Light elk hair, tied as a bunch and
Thread:	Olive		divided equally
Tail:	Dun hackle barbs, with a wrap of thread	Body:	Olive dubbing
	underneath to keep the barbs splayed	Wing:	Gray hen back, trimmed to shape

Iwamasa's Duns look so real that it can be hard to find your fly among the naturals. Imitative flies such as this are often best on flat, calm water.

Tied by Dick Stewart

LADY BEAVERKILL

Hook:	Dry fly, size 12 or 14	Body:	Light gray muskrat fur
Thread:	Light gray	Wing:	Light dun hen hackle tips
Tail:	Grizzly hackle barbs dyed light dun	Hackle:	Bleached Grizzly
Egg sac:	Yellow fur		

This is Del Mazza's variation of the Lady Beaverkill, which has been a standard imitation of the female egg-laying *Ephemerella subvaria* for well over half a century.

Tied by Del Mazza

LITTLE MARRYATT

Hook:	Dry fly, size 12 to 18	Body:	Pale yellow dubbing
Thread:	Primrose yellow	Wing:	Light blue dun hackle tips
Tail:	Light ginger hackle barbs	Hackle:	Light ginger

This is a lovely old pattern that was designed to imitate one of several sulphur colored duns that emerge on eastern rivers in the evenings during the summer.

Tied by Chuck Allard

LOOP WING DUN, RED-BROWN

Hook:	Dry fly, size 16 to 24		the bottom
Thread:	Brown	Wing:	Mallard flank barbs, looped
Tail:	Dun hackle barbs	Note:	Once the large loop is formed and
Body:	Red-brown dubbing		loosely secured, smaller concentric
Hackle:	Wrapped "X" style forward and back,		loops are made by pulling some of the
	over a dubbed thorax, and trimmed on		individual mallard tips.

Gary Borger's Loop Wing Dun has "a strong dun silhouette with a minimum of weight."

Tied by Gary Borger

MARCH BROWN, AMERICAN (FLICK)

Hook:	Dry fly, size 10 or 12	Wing:	Heavily-marked woodduck flank with
Thread:	Orange		a brownish cast
Tail:	Ginger hackle barbs	Hackle:	Dark grizzly and dark ginger grizzly
Body:	Light fawn colored fox fur		variant

The American March Brown, *Stenonema vicarium*, with its strikingly dark veined wings, tends to emerge sporadically throughout the day. The dun is large and clumsy and struggles on the surface as it tries to take off. All this activity attracts the attention of trout on the lookout for the faltering duns.

Tied by Larry Duckwall

PALE MORNING DUN (PMD)

Hook:	Dry fly, size 16 or 18	Body:	Sulpur-yellow dubbing
Thread:	Primrose yellow	Wing:	Very pale gray duck wing quill sections
Tail:	Pale blue dun hackle barbs	Hackle:	Pale blue dun

This is the traditionally tied quill-wing version of the prolific PMD.

Tied by René Harrop

Tied by René Harrop

Tied by René Harrop

Tied by René Harrop

Tied by Dick Stewart

Tied by Kaufmann's Streamborn

Tied by Larry Duckwall

PALE MORNING DUN, HAIRWING, NO HACKLE

Hook: Dry fly, size 16 or 18
Thread: Yellow
Tail: Medium blue dun hackle barbs, divided
Body: Sulphur yellow dubbing

Wing: Fine elk hair, dyed blue dun
Head: Elk hair butts, clipped short
Note: If you can find it, Harrop suggests using dyed "yearling elk" for the wing

PALE MORNING DUN, NO HACKLE

Hook: Dry fly, size 16 or 18
Thread: Yellow
Tail: Medium blue dun hackle barbs, divided
Body: Pale sulphur yellow fur

Wing: Pale gray duck quill segments, tied in the Swisher/Richards style
Note: René Harrop ties a double-wing variation which is known as a Sidewinder.

This style was introduced for fishing to selective feeders in slow water by Carl Richards and Doug Swisher in their in 1971 book, *Selective Trout*.

PALE MORNING DUN, TAILWATER DUN

Hook: Dry fly, size 16 or 18
Thread: Yellow
Tail: Medium blue dun hackle barbs, divided
Body: Pale sulphur yellow dubbing

Wing: Two CDC feathers, curving away from each other, with the stem ends pulled back along the sides to help balance and float the fly, while giving the impression of legs

René Harrop's tailwater design places much of the CDC wing material into actual contact with the water to provide maximum floatation. Trout that live in tailwater runs are often very selective.

PALE MORNING DUN, THORAX

Hook: Dry fly, size 16 or 18
Thread: Yellow
Tail: Pale blue dun hackle barbs
Body: Sulphur yellow dubbing
Wing: Barbs of a turkey body feather dyed pale blue dun and tied as a clump
Hackle: Pale blue dun, tied thorax style

Note: After the wing is secured in an upright position, and before the hackle is wound, continue to dub over the thorax behind and in front of the wing. The hackle is wound in an "X" pattern, crossing in front and behind the wing, then trimmed in a "V" on the bottom.

PARACHUTE, DUN-BROWN

Hook: Dry fly size 12 to 20
Thread: Brown
Tail: Dun nylon bristles, Micro Fibetts or hackle barbs
Body: Dark brown dubbing
Wing: Pair of turkey body feather tips, dyed dun

Hackle: Dun hackle wound around the base of the wings
Note: After the wings have been secured, and before the hackle is wound, bring the dubbing up in front of the wing and build up the thorax.

QUILL GORDON (FLICK)

Hook: Dry fly, size 12 or 14
Thread: Primrose yellow
Tail: Medium blue dun hackle barbs

Body: Stripped or bleached peacock eye quill
Wing: Woodduck flank
Hackle: Medium blue dun

There is probably no other fly pattern that better illustrates the style and aesthetics of the traditional Catskill dry fly. The slender quill body is complemented by the delicate woodduck wings and sparse dun hackle. Not only that, but this fly has become an American standard, found in the boxes of most fly fishermen.

QUILL GORDON (MAZZA)

Hook: Dry Fly, size 12 to 20
Thread: Gray
Tail: Grizzly hackle barbs dyed medium blue dun
Body: Stripped peacock quill, lacquered
Wing: Woodduck flank

Hackle: Grizzly dyed medium blue dun
Note: In order to protect the fragile peacock herl body, Mazza coats it with lacquer. Others may chose to counter wrap the body with very fine gold wire.

Del Mazza's version substitutes dyed grizzly in place of the natural dun.

Tied by Del Mazza

QUILL GORDON (ORIGINAL)

Hook: Dry fly, size 10 or 12
Thread: Brown
Tail: Medium blue dun hackle barbs
Body: Stripped peacock herl

Rib: Gold wire, counter-wrapped
Hackle: Medium blue dun
Wing: Woodduck flank, a clump set in front of the hackle

Ed Leonard, author of *Flies*, tied this Quill Gordon as it might have looked had it been tied by its originator, Theodore Gordon. Unlike most contemporary versions that imitate the *Epeorus pleuralis*, Gordon's version was more of a generic mayfly pattern.

Tied by J. Edson Leonard

RED QUILL (FLICK)

Hook: Dry fly, size 12
Thread: Black or gray
Tail: Medium blue dun hackle barbs
Body: Stripped stem of a Rhode Island red

rooster, tied in by the tip
Wing: Woodduck flank
Hackle: Medium blue dun

The Red Quill was designed by Art Flick to represent the male Hendrickson, *Ephemerella subvaria*. It appears that Art Flick may have been the first tier to use a stripped hackle quill for the body.

Tied by Larry Duckwall

SPARKLE DUN, SULPHUR

Hook: Dry fly, size 16 to 20
Thread: Primrose yellow
Tail (trailing shuck): Brown Z-lon
Body: Sulphur yellow dubbing

Wing: Fine gray elk or deer body hair, tied upright and fanned out like a Compara-dun

This fly was developed by Craig Mathews and John Juracek of Blue Ribbon Flies. Z-lon has the right amount of "sparkle" to imitate the shimmer of a trailing nymphal shuck.

Tied by Craig Mathews

SULPHUR DUN (FOX)

Hook: Dry fly, size 16 or 18
Thread: Primrose yellow
Tail: Very pale blue dun hackle barbs

Body: Cream fur
Wing: Cream hackle tips
Hackle: Very pale blue dun

Charles Fox is the author of *The Wonderful World of Trout* and *Rising Trout*. This is his imitation of the important eastern mayfly *Ephemerella dorothea*, or pale evening dun.

Tied by George Kesel

SULPHUR DUN (HARVEY)

Hook: Dry fly, size 16 or 18
Thread: Primrose yellow
Tail: Cream hackle barbs

Body: Cream fur
Wing: Cream hackle tips
Hackle: Two cream and one dyed orange, mixed

This pattern was designed by George Harvey, Penn State fishing instructor and author of *Techniques of Trout Fishing and Fly Tying*. Harvey found that even though the naturals appeared to be all pale yellow, imitations which contained some orange seemed to outperform the plain yellow patterns.

Tied by George Kesel

Tied by Del Mazza

Tied by George Kesel

Tied by Umpqua Feather Merchants

Tied by Dick Stewart

Tied by Dick Stewart

Tied by Mike Motyl

SULPHUR DUN, PARACHUTE (MAZZA)

Hook: Dry fly, size 14 to 18
Thread: Yellow
Tail: Bleached grizzly hackle barbs divided around a ball of dubbed yellow fur
Abdomen: A stripped stem of a white neck hackle, dyed sulphur yellow and lacquered
Wing: Bleached coastal deer body hair
Thorax: Sulphur yellow fur
Hackle: Bleached grizzly, wound parachute style

Del Mazza's variation was designed for maximum visibility during the low light conditions encountered at dusk when the dorotheas are most abundant.

SULPHUR DUN (SHENK)

Hook: Dry fly, size 16 or 18
Thread: Primrose yellow
Tail: Cream hackle barbs
Abdomen: Cream fur
Thorax: Orange fur
Hackle: Mixed buff, light ginger and cream

This pattern for the Sulphur was designed by Ed Shenk of Carlisle, Pennsylvania, who is best known for having originated the Letort Hopper and Cricket (both of which see).

TRANSITION DUN

Hook: Dry fly, size 12 to 18
Thread: Primrose yellow or light olive
Tail: Light tan Z-lon
Shuck: Blended brown fur or dubbing, teased out so some extends back over the Z-lon
Wing: Light olive Z-lon over which is light blue dun CDC, both angled back slightly
Body: Light olive fur or dubbing, in front and behind the wing

This pattern, from the Harrops, represents a light colored dun struggling to free itself from its darker nymphal shuck. The fly may be dressed in sizes and colors to match any insect you choose to imitate.

TRICO DUN

Hook: Dry fly size 20 to 24
Tail: Dun colored nylon bristles or Micro Fibetts
Body: Black dubbing
Wing: Translucent poly sheet, folded and trimmed into the shape of a pair of wings
Hackle: Black
Note: To form the wing use any of the thin, clear, flexible plastic materials. You should experiment and use your imagination; any type of synthetic sheet can be cut into the shape of a wing.

TWO FEATHER FLY

Hook: Dry fly, size 12 to 18
Thread: Tan or cream
Tail, abdomen and wing: Mallard flank feather, dyed or natural
Hackle: Medium dun

Begin by stroking the barbs away from the tip; leave a few barbs for the tail. Cut away the center leaving a few divided barbs forming the tail. Hold the remaining barbs together and tie everything down about midway on the hook shank. Take the rest of the feather that's facing forward, cut away the center stem, and secure the barbs upright, into divided wings, and add hackle. This fly is also called a Hatchmaster.

WHITE FLY DUN

Hook: Dry fly, size 14 or 16
Thread: White
Tail: Sparse woodduck flank barbs
Abdomen: Fluorescent white nylon yarn
Thorax: White snowshoe rabbit foot fur
Wing: Short bunch of white snowshoe rabbit foot fur, over which are two white hackle tips, curving out and back slightly

This is Mike Motyl's imitation of the *Ephron leukon* (or white fly) dun that often emerges in staggering numbers. The duns molt quickly, and the spinner falls develop before the emergence is completely over, making it necessary to carry both dun and the spinner imitations.

After hatching, mayflies undergo one final transformation into sexually mature adults. The duns moult and the resulting stage, called a spinner, is usually distinct with a thinner body, larger eyes, and clearer wings. Anglers often encounter swarms of mating spinners hovering above the water. This stage is the final one in the life of a mayfly, for after mating and the depositing of eggs, the spinner falls to the water's surface to die. "Spinner falls" can happen quickly, almost all at once, or may last for hours. The dying spinners sometimes carry one or both wings upright, or their wings may be fully extended to each side, awash in the surface film. The latter are called "spent wing" spinners, and most imitations feature this type of wing, but the well-prepared angler will carry both upright-wing and spent-wing spinners is his fly box.

BENT-BODY SPINNER, BROWN

Hook: Swimming nymph, size 10 to 16
Thread: Brown
Tail: Light dun hackle barbs, divided
Abdomen: Mahogany brown dubbing
Wing: Blue dun hackle barbs, tied spent
Thorax: Same as the abdomen, built up in front and around the wings

Bill Thompson, who owns Mountain Anglers, a fly shop in Ossipee, New Hampshire, ties many of his spinner imitations on a "Swimming Nymph" hook, to represent the curved body position commonly observed on some of the larger mayfly spinners.

Tied by Bill Thompson

BIOT CDC SPINNER, RUSTY

Hook: Dry fly, size 14 to 20
Thread: Orange
Tail: Blue dun hackle barbs, divided
Abdomen: Light ginger goose biot
Wing: White CDC over which is sparse light blue dun Z-lon
Thorax: Rusty brown dubbing, built up around the spent wings

The goose biot body is particularly effective for smaller spinners. It maintains a slim body silhouette and provides distinct segmentation.

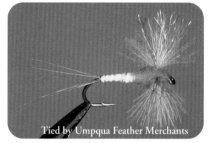
Tied by Umpqua Feather Merchants

BLUE WING OLIVE, CRYSTAL WING SPINNER

Hook: Dry fly, size 14 to 20
Thread: Olive
Tail: Dun hackle barbs, nylon bristles or Micro Fibetts, divided
Body: Olive dubbing
Wing: Pearl crystal flash tied spent

This pattern is easily adapted to most spinner imitations. The wing can be tied with all crystal flash as shown, or some combination of crystal flash and natural hair or hackle.

Tied by Farrow Allen

CALLIBAETIS, BIOT CDC SPINNER

Hook: Dry fly, size 12 to 16
Thread: Tan
Tail: Pale blue dun hackle barbs, divided
Abdomen: Stripped goose biot dyed light to creamy tan
Wing: White to light blue dun CDC over which is sparse brown Z-lon
Thorax: Tan dubbing

CDC, Cul de Canard, feathers are found around the oil producing glands of a duck. It is the product of this anal gland that keeps a duck's feathers waterproof. Natural CDC feathers are rich in this oil and perfect for winging spinners and duns.

Tied by Redding Fly Shop

CLEAR WING SPINNER, BROWN

Hook: Dry fly, size 10 to 22
Thread: Brown
Tail: Medium blue dun hackle barbs, divided
Body: Brown dubbing
Wing: Clear Antron yarn fibers

Gary LaFontaine ties the Clear Wing Spinner in a wide range of body colors to match a variety of mayfly spinners. His experiences suggest that this is one of his most consistent producers.

Tied by Gary LaFontaine

Tied by the Dettes

Tied by Ed Jaworowski

Tied by Al Caucci

Tied by Del Mazza

Tied by Dick Stewart

Tied by John Betts

COFFIN FLY (DETTE)

Hook: Dry fly, long shank, size 12 or 14
Thread: Black
Tail: Three black and white peccary hairs, divided
Underbody: White poly yarn
Body: White saddle hackle with the barbs trimmed to a short stubble, wrapped over the white poly yarn. The wraps should not be touching one another
Rib: White 3/0 thread, counterwrapped over the trimmed hackle
Wing: Divided segments of well-marked teal flank, curving out
Hackle: Golden badger

COFFIN FLY (JAWOROSKI)

Hook: Dry fly, size 10
Thread: White
Tail: Three stripped black hackle stems. These are also the foundation over which the extended body is wrapped
Body: Coarse white dubbing fur mixed with natural kapok, spun very tightly and dubbed down the stripped hackle and back up onto the hook
Rib: White thread
Wing: Very dark brown to black bucktail, tied half or fully spent
Hackle: Grizzly, trimmed in a "V" on the bottom

COMPARA-SPINNER

Hook: Dry fly, size 10 to 20
Thread: Brown
Tail: Medium blue dun hackle barbs, divided around a ball of dubbed fur
Abdomen: Rusty colored blended spectrumized dubbing fur
Thorax: Same as abdomen
Wing: Grizzly hackle, wound then trimmed on the top and bottom to form a spent wing
Note: Before the hackle is wound, dub over the thorax with your blended fur mix, then wind the hackle over the dubbed thorax

COMPARA-SPINNER, HAIR HACKLE WING (COFFIN FLY)

Hook: 4X long size 10 to 14
Thread: White
Tail: Black coastal deer body hair divided around a ball of white dubbed fur
Abdomen: White fur
Wing: Black coastal deer, tied spent
Thorax: Black fur
Hackle: Bleached and natural grizzly, wound over the thorax and trimmed on the bottom
Head: White fur

Del Mazza says this is his "favorite dressing for the Green Drake Spinner," and credits Bob Nastasi for originating the idea.

EXTENDED FOAM MAGIC WING SPINNER

Hook: Dry fly, size 14 to 18
Thread: Brown or white
Extended abdomen: Small section of large cell foam, the type used as packaging material
Body: Large cell foam, wrapped over the hook
shank
Wing: White Magic Wing or bridal organza fibers
Note: The abdomen, thorax and wings may be colored with marking pens to match the coloration of the naturals if desired

This type of foam floats well and has the right translucency for imitating the nearly transparent spinners.

GREEN DRAKE SPINNER (BETTS)

Hook: Dry fly, straight eye, size 10 or 12
Thread: White
Abdomen: Cream poly-yarn with an orange-yellow egg sac fused on
Tails: Three dun colored nylon bristles
Wing: Nylon bristles "tie dyed" gray and black for a mottled look
Legs: Three strands of dark olive sewing thread
Thorax: A mixture of crinkled and straight Z-Lon and dark green rabbit fur

This is a most realistic imitation of the Eastern Green Drake Spinner.

HACKLE TIP SPINNER

Hook: Dry fly, size 12 to 20
Thread: Brown
Tail: Dun colored nylon bristles, Micro Fibetts or hackle barbs, divided
Abdomen: Rusty gray dubbing

Wing: Medium blue dun hackle tips, spent
Thorax: Same as abdomen
Hackle: Medium blue dun wrapped over the dubbed thorax, behind and in front of the wings

Hackle tip spinners can be tied in all sizes and colors to match the naturals on the water. A heavy-hackled spinner works best in faster, broken water.

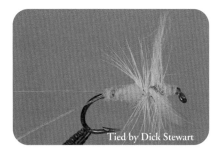
Tied by Dick Stewart

HEN WING SPINNER, RUSTY

Hook: Dry fly, size 10 to 18
Thread: Brown or orange
Tail: Medium blue dun hackle barbs

Body: Rusty reddish brown fur
Wing: Light blue dun hen hackle tips

Hen wing spinners present a very convincing silhouette to trout cruising the shallows, looking for an easy meal. The drawback is that the hen hackle wings are very absorbent, and the fly sinks easily in anything but the most quiet water.

Tied by Farrow Allen

HENDRICKSON HACKLE WING SPINNER

Hook: Dry fly, straight eye, size 10 to 14
Thread: Brown
Tail: Medium blue dun hackle tips, divided
Abdomen: Reddish brown dubbing
Wing: Grizzly, or grizzly dyed light blue dun,

wrapped and trimmed on the top and bottom
Thorax: Same as the abdomen, but built up around, between and in front of the hackle wings

Female Hendricksons drop their eggs from above. Inevitably, some insects fall to the surface with their sulphur colored eggs still attached. These can be imitated by adding a ball of yellow fur

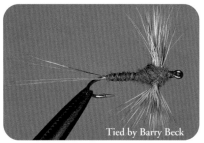
Tied by Barry Beck

HENDRICKSON PARACHUTE SPINNER

Hook: Dry fly, 2X long, size 12 to 16
Thread: Brown
Hackle post: Elk mane
Tail: Dark brown hackle barbs, divided around a dubbed ball of mahogany fur
Abdomen: A stripped stem of a Rhode Island red

neck hackle, dyed chestnut brown and lacquered
Thorax: Mixed claret and brown fur
Wing: Bleached grizzly hackle, tied parachute style and trimmed front and back to form the spent wing

Del Mazza designed this spinner with its unique parachute spent wing.

Tied by Del Mazza

HEX, ANTI-

Hook: Dry fly, long shank, size 6 or 8 (tied backwards with the tail extending over the hook eye)
Thread: Black or brown

Wing: White calftail
Body: Natural light brown deer body hair
Rib: Black thread
Tail: Natural light brown deer body hair tips

Most *Hexagenia* spinners float downstream head first, so trout, naturally facing upstream, take them head first. Hook-ups improved tremendously after Ron Reinhold began tying the Anti-Hex imitations backwards, with the head of the fly over the barb of the hook, and fished them downstream.

Tied by Ron Reinhold

HEXAGENIA SPINNER, EXTENDED DEER HAIR BODY

Hook: Dry fly, size 6 or 8
Thread: Yellow
Extended abdomen: Creamy yellow elk or deer body hair
Rib: Yellow rod wrapping thread, "X" wrapped to hold the deer hair together and secure the abdomen to the hook
Tail: Untrimmed hair from the extended

abdomen
Thorax: Yellow dubbing
Wing: Creamy yellow elk or deer body hair over which is yellow crystal flash, darkened slightly on top with a yellow marking pen
Wingcase: Yellow closed-cell foam

Tied by David Lucca

Mayfly Spinners

Tied by David Lucca

Tied by Dick Stewart

Tied by Dick Stewart

Tied by Farrow Allen

Tied by Craig Mathews

Tied by Jan Weido

HEX SPINNER, LUCCA'S FOAM

Hook: Dry fly, size 6 to 10
Thread: Yellow
Tail: Dark brown moose or elk hair
Extended abdomen: Strip of yellow closed-cell foam, folded around an underbody of moose hair (part of which becomes the tail) and secured with "X" wraps of heavy yellow thread

Wing: Natural deer body hair
Thorax: Strip of yellow closed-cell foam, wrapped
Back: Dark turkey wing quill section, lacquered
Note: When the fly is finished, the extended abdomen may be colored appropriately with marking pens.

MIRUS SPINNER

Hook: Dry fly, long shank, size 10
Thread: Brown
Tail: Brown nylon bristles, Micro Fibetts or hackle barbs
Abdomen: Yellow dubbing
Rib: Stripped brown hackle stem

Thorax: Same as abdomen, but fuller
Wing: Brown CDC to the rear, grizzly hackle wrapped over the thorax and trimmed on the top and bottom
Back: Brown foam pulled over the thorax and grizzly hackle wing

Found on Stewart's home river, *Siphlonurus mirus* is distinguished by its chocolate brown hind wings

POLY WING SPINNER

Hook: Dry fly, size 14 to 20
Thread: Light olive
Tail: Light blue dun nylon bristles or Micro Fibetts, divided

Abdomen: Creamy yellow blended fur
Wing: Medium blue dun polypropylene yarn
Thorax: Same as abdomen, built up around and in front of the wings

Although there are many new synthetic wing materials on the market today being used on spinners, polypropylene yarn is still effective and easy to come by. It's best used on smaller flies, size 14 to 20.

QUILL BODY SPINNER

Hook: Dry fly, 1X long, size 12 to 18
Tail: Light blue dun nylon bristles or Micro Fibetts
Body: Stripped saddle hackle, bleached pea-

cock herl or similar
Wing: Grizzly hackle, wrapped and trimmed on the top and bottom

This is not a great floater, and is sometimes difficult to see on fast water towards evening when spinner falls most often occur. But on calm water this delicate, slender-bodied fly is quite effective.

SPARKLE SPINNER, MAHOGANY

Hook: Dry fly, size 14 to 18
Thread: Gray
Tail: Dun hackle barbs, divided around a tiny ball of reddish brown dubbing

Body: Reddish brown dubbing
Wing: Light dun Z-lon, tied spent

SUNDOWN SPINNER, BROWN

Hook: Dry fly, size 10 to 16
Thread: Brown
Tail: Medium blue dun nylon bristles or Micro Fibetts, divided
Body: Rusty brown dubbing

Wing: White crinkled Z-lon
Wing marker: Yellow or white closed-cell foam, folded over the wing like you would a wingcase on a nymph

Jan Weido developed this spinner on Connecticut's Housatonic river to solve the problem of seeing the fly in fading daylight. The foam, of course, helps the fly stay afloat as well.

TRICO, DOUBLE

Hook: Dry fly, 2X long, size 14 or 16
Thread: Black
Tail: Dun hackle barbs, divided
Bodies: Black dubbing
Wings: White poly yarn or Z-lon

This is basically what it appears to be, two tiny flies tied on a single hook. This provides a more appetizing mouthful for a hungry trout and allows the angler to use a larger, stronger hook.

Tied by George Kesel

TRICO, FEMALE

Hook: Dry fly, straight or up eye, size 20 to 24
Thread: Black or white
Tail: Light blue dun hackle barbs, divided
Abdomen: White thread or dubbing
Wing: White poly yarn or Z-lon
Thorax: Black dubbing

The spinners of this mayfly return to the water within a few hours of hatching. If the wind is calm and they don't get blown away from the water, thousands of these tiny spinners can blanket the surface of the river. In these very small sizes, straight-eye hooks are often used because down-eye hooks reduce the effective gape, making the hook more difficult to set.

Tied by George Kesel

TRICO, MALE

Hook: Dry fly, straight or up eye, size 20 to 26
Thread: Black
Tail: Light blue dun hackle barbs, divided
Body: Black dubbing
Wing: White poly yarn or Z-lon
Head: Black

As the *Tricorythodes* spinners begin to fall to the water shortly after mating, larger trout may key in and feed exclusively on either the black males or the white females. Although the tricos are so small that the difference between males and females may seem unimportant to us, it can be of critical importance to feeding trout.

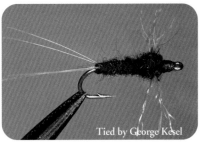

Tied by George Kesel

WHITE FLY SPINNER

Hook: Dry fly, size 10 or 12
Thread: White
Tail: White hackle tips, stripped
Body: Fluorescent white nylon yarn, single
ply wrapped to give the impression of segmentation
Wing: Pale gray Z-lon or poly yarn, tied spent
Thorax: Snowshoe rabbit fur from the foot

This imitation of the *Ephron* (commonly called the white fly) spinner was designed by Mike Motyl of Enfield, Connecticut. Motyl says the snowshoe rabbit fur provides superior flotation and a buggy outline, and the fluorescent white abdomen is easy to see at dusk.

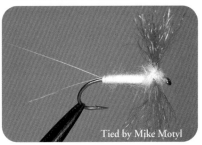

Tied by Mike Motyl

Z-LON SPINNER, OLIVE

Hook: Dry fly, straight eye, size 10 to 20
Thread: Olive
Tail: Dun hackle barbs, divided
Body: Blended olive fur, dubbed very thinly
Wing: Light colored Z-lon, tied "Compara-style" and colored with a marking pen if desired

This is a style for tying mayfly spinner imitations. Size and color may be changed to replicate any hatch, and the wing position simulates both upwing and downwing spinners.

Tied by John Betts

ZING-WING SPINNER, GRAY

Hook: Dry fly, straight eye, size 10 to 20
Thread: Dark gray
Tails: Dun colored monofilament, fused into the core of the abdomen
Abdomen: 30lb. to 40lb. braided Dacron fishing
line, colored gray with waterproof marking pens
Legs: Dun colored Z-lon
Wing: Zing wing material
Thorax: Gray dubbing

John Betts, America's master of flies made from synthetic materials, shows here how a realistic mayfly spinner can be tied. Zing wing material is commonly available packaging tape which is also sold in fly-tying specialty shops.

Tied by John Betts

Caddisfly Larvae

Fly fishermen categorize caddisfly (sometimes called sedge) larvae into two groups: The "case-building caddis" lives in a protective case it constructs using sticks, leaves, sand or gravel, whereas the "free-living caddis" range about underwater without benefit of any such protection or camouflage. Some case-builders attach themselves to rocks or logs, while others carry their cases about as they search for food. Their head, legs, and sometimes a small portion of their body, extend from the case opening. Trout ingest these immature insects, case and all, whenever the opportunity presents itself. Both cased caddis and free-living caddis will, from time to time, allow themselves to drift freely with the current. The most prevalent form of drift occurs just after sunset, and again before sunrise. At these times the larvae are particularly vulnerable and the trout will readily accept a good imitation.

Tied by Dick Stewart

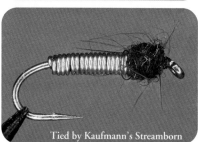
Tied by Kaufmann's Streamborn

Tied by Dan Bailey's Fly Shop

Tied by Gary LaFontaine

Tied by Kaufmann's Streamborn

BRACHYCENTRUS LARVA

Hook:	Nymph, 1X long, size 12 to 16
Thread:	Black
Underbody:	Two strips of flat Twiston lead (the kind that comes in the little matchbook) trimmed into a long triangle and secured on each side of the hook shank to form the geometric foundation for the Brachycentrus' case
Case:	Four or 5 bleached (stripped) peacock herls, wrapped over the lead foundation and cemented
Legs:	One turn of dark brown or black hackle

Ken Iwamasa designed the dressing for this distinctive, but common, caddis larva.

BRASSIE

Hook:	Wet fly or nymph, 1X or 2X long, size 12 to 20
Thread:	Black
Abdomen:	Copper or brass wire, the diameter of which is in proportion to the hook size
Head:	Black to gray fur, picked out a little
Note:	On larger flies a tapered underbody of floss may be applied

This deceptively simple nymph was developed in the Southwest, and is now fished all over. It sinks like a rock and is deadly on rivers with a lot of caddis. It's also commonly tied in gold or red.

BUCKSKIN CADDIS NYMPH

Hook:	Wet fly, size 12 to 18
Abdomen:	A strip of natural cream colored buckskin, or a similar suede leather
Legs:	Several wraps of black hackle
Head:	Black thread, built up

Buckskin, along with other natural and synthetic hides, is sold in a variety of colors and produces nearly indestructible segmented bodies that absorb water and keep the fly down.

CADDIS LARVA, OLIVE-BROWN

Hook:	Curved nymph hook, size 10 to 20
Thread:	Primrose yellow or brown
Underbody:	Lead wire (optional)
Abdomen:	Olive fur or synthetic dubbing
Head:	Dark brown fur or synthetic dubbing
Legs:	Partridge or woodduck barbs

Gary LaFontaine uses this basic design and ties it in many colors and sizes to imitate a variety of free-living caddis larvae.

CASED CADDIS, HAZEL

Hook:	6X long, size 8 to 12
Thread:	Black
Underbody:	Lead wire
Case:	Peacock herl
Hackle:	Brown, clipped short
Rib:	Copper wire, counter-wrapped
Body:	A band of cream or pale gray fur
Head:	Black fur

John Hazel designed this fly to be fished along the bottom, to imitate a caddis caught in the current, or simply drifting.

CASED CADDIS, TUCKER

Hook: Nymph, 2X or 3X long, size 10 to 16
Thread: Black
Underbody: Lead wire (optional)
Case: Blended black, olive and brown fur, or
           a similar blend of furs designed to look
           like the debris that a case-building cad-
           dis might collect from the bottom to
           construct its home
Rib: Fine gold wire
Body: Bright green Liqui Lace
Head: Black lacquered Liqui Lace
Legs: Black Z-lon

Tied by Michael Tucker

CASED CADDIS LARVA, LaFONTAINE

Hook: Dry fly, long shank or standard length,
           size 12 to 16; the front half of the shank
           may be bent up at a 45 degree angle
Thread: Brown
Weight: Lead wire over the rear of the shank
Case: Grouse body feather or similar, wrapped
           over yellow thread and trimmed to
           shape
Body: Pale yellow dubbing or chenille
Legs: Dark brown or gray grouse hackle barbs

This is Gary LaFontaine's imitation of a case-building caddis larva peeking out of its case. An older fly, the Strawman, was tied with a clipped hackle body and may have given LaFontaine the idea for this fly.

Tied by Gary LaFontaine

OSCAR'S RHYACOPHILA NYMPH

Hook: Curved nymph, size 10 to 14
Thread: Black
Underbody: Dubbed light gray rabbit fur, ta-
           pered
Abdomen: Chartreuse Larva Lace
Legs: Dark deer hair tips
Head: Black rabbit fur

An effective imitation of one of the most common of the free-living caddisflies. Tied with Larva Lace, Oscar Feliu's fly is very realistic .

Tied by Oscar Feliu

PEEKING CADDIS

Hook: Nymph, size 8 to 16
Thread: Black
Case: Dark dirty-looking gray hare's ear fur,
           or a similar blend
Rib: Fine gold or copper wire
Body: Olive fur
Legs: Speckled brown partridge or similar
Head: Black ostrich herl

This fly was developed by George Anderson of the Yellowstone Angler, to imitate a partially exposed caddis larva "peeking" from its case. It may be tied in colors which match the caddis that are common in your area.

Tied by Kaufmann's Streamborn

CADDIS, CASED SAND

Hook: Nymph, 1X or 2X long, size 8 to 14
Thread: Brown or black
Underbody: Neutral colored yarn or chenille
Case: Coarse sand
Body: Brown fur or similar to imitate the larva
           sticking out of the case
Legs: Brown partridge
Note: To build the case, saturate the under-
           body with epoxy and bury it in some
           sand. When the cement has set, pull the
           hook out, scrape off any loose sand,
           lacquer over the case to help hold the
           sand in place and tie the rest of the fly

Tied by Dick Stewart

SKUNK HAIR CADDIS

Hook: Nymph, 1X or 2X long, size 6 to 12
Thread: Black
Underbody: Lead wire (optional)
Body: A bunch of black and white skunk tail
           hairs tied in by the black tips, wrapped
           forward and saturated with lacquer (af-
           ter each wrap, untwist the bunch so the
           body lies flat and the individual hairs
           are parallel)
Rib: Copper wire
Legs: One turn of soft black hackle

Charlie Brooks, in his book *Nymph Fishing for Larger Trout,* says the Skunk Hair Caddis ". . . is the best cased-caddis imitation I know of."

Tied by Craig Mathews

Caddisfly Pupae

Once mature, caddisfly larvae seal themselves away for a few weeks while they change into pupae. During this time wings develop and legs and antennae lengthen. Once the pupae are ready to hatch, they vacate their protection and swim to the surface, buoyed by air which has been gathered within the pupal shuck. At the water's surface the pupal shuck splits open, and the winged adult caddisfly quickly becomes airborne. All of this activity takes very little time as most species are quite active swimmers. The fly fisherman may witness trout slashing or splashing at the surface as they try to chase down a meal. While many soft-hackle wet flies are acceptable representations of caddis pupae, the more exact imitations which have developed are included in the following patterns.

Tied by Kaufmann's Streamborn

Tied by Gerry James

Tied by Gary LaFontaine

Tied by Gary LaFontaine

Tied by Robert Rifchin

CDC CADDIS EMERGER, OLIVE

Hook: Nymph, size 12 to 18
Thread: Olive
Tail: Olive Z-lon
Abdomen: Olive dubbing
Rib: Copper wire
Wing: Dark gray CDC feather over which is light dun Z-lon
Antennae: Barbs of woodduck flank
Legs: Brown partridge
Head: Dark brown dubbing

This is a good, simple representation of an emerging caddisfly as its wings begin to unfold.

DARK CADDIS EMERGENT

Hook: Wet fly or nymph, 1X long, size 6 or 8
Thread: Black
Abdomen: Pale orange yarn
Rib: Orange 3/0 thread
Legs and wing: Dark furnace hackle on each side
Head: Black ostrich
Note: To make the legs and wing, Rosborough wraps about four turns of long furnace hackle in front of the abdomen and trim the top and bottom barbs

Polly Rosborough suggests fishing his Emergent Caddis with "fast two-inch jerks" just below the surface, during a hatch of large *Dicosmoecus* caddis.

DEEP SPARKLE PUPA, BROWN-YELLOW

Hook: Dry fly, size 12 to 18
Thread: Primrose yellow
Underbody: Lead wire
Underbody: Gold or russet colored Antron yarn mixed with brown fur and dubbed
Overbody: Russet or gold Antron yarn, combed
out, tied in at the bend, separated and pulled forward in two steps, one bunch over and one bunch under the hook
Legs: Grouse, partridge or woodduck barbs tied on the sides
Head: Brown fur

The sheath of Antron (sparkle yarn) traps air bubbles providing a glisten similar to the natural pupa.

EMERGENT SPARKLE PUPA, ORANGE

Hook: Dry fly, size 12 to 18
Thread: Primrose yellow
Tail: Orange Antron yarn
Underbody: Orange Antron yarn mixed with rusty orange fur and dubbed
Overbody: Orange Antron yarn, combed out,
tied in at the bend, separated and pulled forward in two steps, one bunch over and one under the hook
Wing: Natural light deer body hair
Head: Yellow thread

Suspended in the surface film, with trailing air bubbles, this fly is both an imitator and an attractor.

KRYSTAL FLASH CADDIS PUPA

Hook: Curved shank nymph, size 8 to 16
Thread: Brown
Abdomen: Pearl Krystal Flash
Legs: Brown partridge hackle
Head: Brown fur
Note: The Krystal Flash body is made by tying short ½ inch to ¾ inch bunches of Krystal Flash along the shank, as you
might tie in bunches of deer body hair if you were making a bass bug. "The finished mess," say the originator, "will look like flared deer hair," and should be trimmed to shape in the same way you trim deer hair. Combine the colors as you would in traditional fur-bodied caddisflies.

LATEX CADDIS PUPA

Hook: Nymph, size 10 to 16
Thread: Dark brown or black
Abdomen: A strip cut from a sheet of cream colored latex, applied with slightly overlapping wraps to form a tapered shape

Wings: Gray duck quill sections, coated with vinyl cement
Head: Black-brown seal fur or similar
Legs and antennae: Fur from the thorax, picked out

Latex strips make great looking abdomens on pupa and larva imitations. You can color the bodies at your tying desk, or tie them all cream colored and carry a selection of marking pens in your vest.

Tied by Farrow Allen

MERCER'S OLIVE Z-WING CADDIS

Hook: Curved nymph, short shank, size 12 to 16
Thread: Black
Underbody: Lead wire
Abdomen: Blended olive dubbing

Shellback: Dark brown turkey wing or similar
Rib: Chartreuse thread
Wing: Ginger Z-lon
Head: Peacock herl

Mike Mercer of the Fly Shop in Redding, California, designed this caddis pupa. He ties it in several different colors and sizes to imitate a range of natural caddis pupae.

Tied by Mike Mercer

OCTOBER EMERGER

Hook: Nymph, 3X long, size 4 to 8
Thread: Orange
Body: Orange dubbing
Rib: Pearl Flashabou
Wing: Two small bunches of gray marabou,

one on each side
Legs: One wrap of grouse or dark brown partridge hackle
Head: Gray dubbed marabou, or ostrich

The giant orange caddis is a very large, and extremely important species of the genus *Dicosmoecus*, which is found from the Rockies westward to the Pacific. It hatches from September to late October.

Tied by Mike Mercer

R.A.M. CADDIS

Hook: Wet fly, size 10 to 14
Thread: Black or olive
Underbody: Lead wire
Abdomen: Olive floss
Rib: Gold or silver wire
Legs: One or two turns of white hen hackle

Head: Dark brown fur or thread, built up
Note: An unweighted emerging variation is dressed on a light wire hook without the wire. Spun brown deer body hair, trimmed short, replaces the fur or thread head.

Ross A. Merigold (R.A.M.) developed this for Montana's Madison River, where it's a steady producer.

Tied by Ray Cotnoir

SLOW WATER PUPA

Hook: Nymph, 3X long, size 12 to 18
Thread: Black
Abdomen: Creamy tan fur, dubbed in a "rope" that accentuates the segmentation
Rib: Fine gold wire

Legs: 4 to 6 barbs of partridge hackle
Wings: Gray goose wing quill sections
Head: Mixture of black and brown seal fur and hare's ear dubbing or similar
Antennae: 2 wodduck flank barbs

This is an easy fly to tie, and realistic enough to fool even the most selective slow-water trout.

Tied by René Harrop

WINGED BIOT EMERGER

Hook: Curved nymph, size 12 to 18
Thread: Black
Body: Hare's ear dubbing or similar
Rib: Goose or turkey biot, dyed brown

Wing: Grizzly hackle tips
Legs: Gray or brown partridge hackle
Head: Black marabou, dubbed

Dave Hall, a knowledgeable guide on Oregon's North Umpqua River, developed this emerging pupa which he ties in different colors to match the various caddisflies he encounters while fishing.

Tied by Dave Hall

Caddisfly Adults

We've noticed that many fly fishermen tend to be somewhat confused by the behavior of caddisflies. Large numbers of insects might be observed on streamside vegetation, or concentrations are seen flying upriver in the evenings. The angler may see lots of insects, but no feeding activity by trout. Conversely, the trout may be splashing actively, but there are few caddisflies to be seen. Close observation will reveal that frequently the adult caddisflies are away from the water and unavailable to trout. Unlike mayflies, caddisfly adults live about a month after hatching, so large quantities may accumulate at streamside. They may return to the river on a sporadic basis to drink, and in the evening they migrate upstream, but they are mainly unavailable to trout except for when they hatch, and again when the females return to deposit their eggs. Egg laying can cause a lot of commotion as caddisflies may splat upon the waters surface, or may dive underwater.

Tied by Dick Stewart

AFTERNOON DELIGHT

Hook:	Dry fly, size 12 to 16	Body:	Light olive dubbing
Thread:	Tan	Front wing:	Light elk hair
Tail:	Olive Antron or Z-lon	Note:	The two wings should be trimmed to
Rear wing:	Light elk hair		form small heads

Scott Ross of Livingston, Montana, ties this fly to imitate a pair of adult caddisflies. It's supposed to look like an easy mouthful of several small flies.

Tied by Dick Stewart

ALDER FLY

Hook:	Dry fly, size 12		turn dark brownish olive when wet
Thread:	Olive	Wing:	Fine dark deer body hair
Body:	Spectrumized blended fur, designed to	Head:	Butt ends of the wing clipped short

In parts of New England the caddisfly species *Macronema zebratum*, or zebra caddis, is often called the alder fly. This locally common name causes this caddisfly to be confused with the dark, smoky-gray member of the dobsonfly family which is also called an alderfly. Stewart's imitation is based on the Compara Caddis design, and matches the natural in size and color.

Tied by Farrow Allen

BUCK CADDIS, DARK

Hook:	Dry fly, size 8 to 14	Body hackle:	Dark brown furnace
Tail:	Dark brown hackle barbs	Wing:	Dark deer body hair
Body:	Rusty orange dubbing		

This is a high-floating fly that's hard to sink, and is perfect for fishing in very fast-moving water. Obviously, it can be tied in any colors as needed.

Tied by Farrow Allen

BUCKTAIL CADDIS, YELLOW

Hook:	Dry fly, 2X long, size 10 to 16	Rib:	Brown hackle
Thread:	Brown	Wing:	Brown bucktail cut from near the base
Tail:	Short brown hackle barbs		of the tail
Body:	Yellow poly yarn or dubbing	Hackle:	Brown

The Bucktail Caddis is commonly tied in several colors, especially orange, and is best suited to imitating the larger naturals.

CDC ADULT QUILL WING CADDIS

Hook:	Dry fly, size 14 to 20	Wing:	Gray CDC feather outside of which are
Thread:	Gray		two gray duck wing quill sections
Body:	Gray goose biot	Head:	Gray dubbing
Legs:	Sparse woodduck flank or similar, two	Antennae:	Gray Micro-Fibetts
	or three barbs per side		

Shane Stalcup's biot-bodied adult caddis is an excellent pattern for slow water.

Tied by Shane Stalcup

CHUCK CADDIS

Hook:	Dry fly, size 12 to 18	Wing:	Guard hair from the back of a wood-
Thread:	Gray		chuck
Body:	Dark gray dubbing	Hackle:	Mixed brown and grizzly

Eric Leiser developed this all-purpose caddis imitation to be dressed with varied body colors to match different naturals. Woodchuck hair is often overlooked as a fly-tying material, and rarely available through fly-tying shops, yet it's ideal for making caddis wings.

Tied by Eric Leiser

COLORADO KING

Hook:	Dry fly, size 12 to 16		yellow rabbit fur
Thread:	Black or yellow	Body:	Yellow rabbit fur
Tail:	Two peccary bristles or dark moose	Hackle:	Grizzly, palmered over the body
	hairs divided around a dubbed ball of	Wing:	Light elk hair

The Colorado King was developed about 1970 by George Bodmer of Colorado Springs, Colorado. It is the standard around which many hair wing caddisfly imitations were developed.

Tied by Bill Franke

COMPARA CADDIS

Hook:	Dry fly, size 12 to 18	Wing:	Fine deer body hair
Thread:	Neutral cream or gray	Head:	Butt ends of the wing trimmed short
Body:	Blended spectrumized rabbit fur		

Al Caucci and Bob Nastasi have been as successful imitating caddisflies with a Compara Caddis as they have imitating mayflies with a Compara Dun. The body is a mix of red, yellow, blue and white fur, which, in combination, can produce any color needed.

Tied by Blair Caucci

D.A. CADDIS

Hook:	Curved shank, size 12 to 20	Wing:	Black deer body hair, around which is
Thread:	Brown		a sparse collar of gray CDC feather
Tail or trailing shuck:	Tan Z-lon	Head:	Same as the body
Body:	Reddish brown blended fur		

Dave Goulet, of the Classic & Custom Fly Shop in New Hartford, Connecticut, spent a few years working out the design of the D.A. patterns. All are tied on a curved shank hook to place the rear end of the fly underwater, giving the impression of an adult struggling out of its pupal skin.

Tied by Dave Goulet

DANCING CADDIS, OLIVE

Hook:	Dry fly, straight eye or Swedish dry fly,	Hackle:	Medium blue dun, trimmed on the
	or salmon dry, size 10 to 18		bottom
Thread:	Olive	Note:	The orientation of this fly is with the
Body:	Pale olive dubbing, very thin		hook point up
Wing:	Natural elk or deer body hair		

Gary LaFontaine introduced this uniquely constructed, upside-down pattern, in his distinguished 1981 book *Caddisflies*.

Tied by Gary LaFontaine

DELTA WING CADDIS

Hook:	Dry fly, size 12 to 18		delta wing
Body:	Grayish tan fur or poly dubbing	Hackle:	Mixed grizzly and brown, clipped on
Wing:	Grizzly hackle tips tied flat, spent and		the top and bottom

This style of fly is designed to float flush in the surface film, like a spent caddisfly adult. Tie it in whatever colors match the naturals you want to imitate.

Tied by Farrow Allen

Tied by Gary LaFontaine

Tied by Craig Mathews

Tied by Farrow Allen

Tied by Farrow Allen

Tied by Larry Duckwall

Tied by Terry Coleman

DIVING CADDIS, GINGER

Hook: Dry fly, size 12 to 18
Thread: Primrose yellow
Body: Amber colored Antron, or Antron mixed with fur and dubbed
Wing: Dun hackle barbs over which is clear Antron
Hackle: Brown, tied very sparse
Note: Gary LaFontaine lists 15 color variations of this pattern in *Caddisflies*.

LaFontaine designed the Diving Caddis to imitate an egg-bearing female, diving below the surface to deposit her eggs.

EGG-LAYING CADDIS

Hook: Dry fly, size 12 to 18
Body: Bright green dubbing
Wing: Light elk over which is a collar of dark grouse or similar, trimmed away from the bottom
Antennae: Two long barbs of pheasant tail
Note: Golden yellow and olive are good colors for the body of this fly

This pattern, like the Diving Caddis, represents a female caddis diving underwater to lay her fertilized eggs. It can also be fished dead drift imitating a spent caddis, awash in the surface.

ELK HAIR CADDIS, TAN

Hook: Dry fly, size 12 to 18
Thread: Tan
Body: Hare's ear dubbing
Hackle: Medium to dark brown
Rib: Fine gold wire
Wing: Light elk hair
Head: Butt ends of the wing clipped short
Note: Tie the wire in at the back and the hackle in front of the body; wind the hackle back to where the wire was tied in and secure the hackle by wrapping the wire forward

This Al Troth fly is durable, convincing, and easily adapts to imitating caddis of all colors and sizes.

ELK HAIR CADDIS, OLIVE NO HACKLE

Hook: Dry Fly, standard or 1X short, size 12 to 18
Thread: Olive
Body: Olive dubbing
Wing: Light elk hair
Head: Butt ends of the wing clipped short

This is a variation that Al Troth likes for fishing in clear ponds and spring creeks.

EVERYBODY'S CADDIS, DARK

Hook: Dry fly, size 12 to 18
Thread: Black
Body: Gray dubbing
Wing: Dark elk mane, tied flat over the body
Hackle: Medium blue dun, clipped on the bottom
Antennae: Stripped stems of the same dun hackle
Note: Be sure to try and find elk mane for the wing because elk body hair will flare too much.

Larry Duckwall designed this caddis fly for everybody. It's generally tied like this, or with a light body and bleached elk mane wing, in whatever color you choose.

FLUTTERING CADDIS

Hook: Dry fly, size 12 to 18
Body: Gray muskrat fur
Wing: Dun hackle barbs or mink tail hair
Hackle: Rusty dun
Note: Because stiff hackle barbs of adequate length are difficult to find, mink tail is usually the better choice, although hackle barbs were originally used.

Leonard Wright introduced this fly in his book, *Fishing the Dry Fly as a Living Insect*. Wright observed that caddis adults frequently skittered upstream before becoming airborne. The Fluttering Caddis was designed to be fished to imitate that action. Any colors may be used.

GIANT ORANGE CADDIS

Hook: Salmon, turned-up eye, light wire, size 2 to 6
Thread: Fluorescent orange
Butt: Fluorescent orange floss or dubbing
Wing: Natural brown deer body hair applied in 4 to 6 sections along the rear ⅔ of the hook shank (the last bunch of hair should be applied after the hackle has been wrapped and trimmed)
Body: Fluorescent orange yarn wrapped between the wing sections
Hackle: Dark coachman brown
Antennae: Orange nylon bristles

Tied by Kent Bulfinch

GODDARD CADDIS

Hook: Dry fly; size 10 to 16
Thread: Gray or black
Body: Natural deer body hair, spun and trimmed into the shape of a winged adult caddisfly
Antennae: Two stems of a brown hackle with the barbs stripped
Hackle: Brown
Note: A small loop of fur may be spun in at the back as a first step and pulled forward underneath and tied off as a final step if desired. This step is generally omitted.

Introduced by English angler John Goddard in *The Trout and the Fly,* coauthored with John Clarke.

Tied by Farrow Allen

HATCHING CADDIS

Hook: Dry fly, long shank, size 8 to 18
Thread: Brown
Abdomen: Olive brown blended fur
Rib: Oval gold tinsel
Wing: Natural rabbit or hare's mask guard hair
Thorax: Same as abdomen
Legs: Two turns of gray partridge dyed dark brown
Wingcase: A section of goose shoulder dyed brown or nylon raffia
Note: The rabbit hair wing and partridge hackle are divided by pulling the wingcase forward over the thorax and separating them into equal parts, left and right.

Tied by David Wotten

HEMINGWAY CADDIS

Hook: Dry fly, size 12 to 18
Thread: Olive
Body: Olive dubbing
Rib: Light blue dun hackle
Wing: Woodduck flank tied flat over the body, over which are a pair of gray mallard wing quill segments, curving out
Thorax: Peacock herl
Hackle: Light blue dun

This was developed as a variation of the Henryville Special (which see), which seemed "too brown" to imitate certain caddis encountered. It was later named for Jack Hemingway, who fished it often.

Tied by Dick Talleur

HENRYVILLE SPECIAL

Hook: Dry fly, size 12 to 18
Thread: Olive
Body: Light olive fur or floss
Rib: Grizzly hackle with barbs slightly less than the hook gape or trimmed
Wing: Sparse woodduck flank over which are matched sections of natural goose or mallard wing quill, tied tent shape
Hackle: Dark ginger or grizzly dyed brown, optionally trimmed even with the hook point
Head: Brown

Del Mazza trims the rib and hackle "to enable the fly to land right side up on every cast."

Tied by Del Mazza

KING'S RIVER CADDIS

Hook: Dry fly, size 10 to 16
Thread: Brown
Body: Tan raccoon fur or similar
Wing: Dark mottled turkey, coated with vinyl cement and V-notched, tied tent shape
Hackle: Brown

The King's River Caddis was developed in the 1950s by Wayne "Buz" Buszek for a tailwater fishery on the King's River near Fresno, California. Buszek, who ran a fly shop in Visalia, California, was so highly admired that the Federation of Fly Fishers called their annual award for fly-tying excellence, The Buz Buszek Memorial Award .

Tied by Mike Motyl

Tied by Louis Tanguay

Tied by Kelvin McKay

Tied by Kent Bulfinch

Tied by Del Mazza

Tied by Dan Bailey's Fly Shop

Tied by Craig Mathews

L.T. CADDIS

Hook:	Dry fly, size 10 to 14	Hackle:	Grizzly
Thread:	Tan	Head:	Natural light deer body hair, spun and trimmed to shape
Body:	Several golden pheasant tail barbs, wrapped	Note:	Tanguay suggests that you spin and trim the deer hair head first, and then go back and tie the rest of the fly.
Rib:	Fine gold wire, counter wrapped		
Wing:	Very fine dark deer body hair or bucktail		

The L.T. Caddis is effective imitating some of the larger caddisflies that emerge in lakes.

MIKULAK SEDGE

Hook:	Nymph, 2X or 3X long, size 8 or 10		along the hook shank
Thread:	Black	Body:	Olive or tan fur
Tail:	Tan elk	Hackle:	Brown, clipped on the bottom
Wing:	Three successive bunches elk hair tied	Head:	Butt ends of the front wing, clipped

Designed as an imitation of the "... giant traveling sedges" that are found in great numbers on many trout lakes in British Columbia. It was named for its inventor, Arthur Mikulak, of Calgary, Alberta.

OCTOBER CADDIS

Hook:	Salmon, dry fly, size 6		yarn or dubbing
Thread:	Black	Wing:	Red squirrel tail, divided, pointing over the eye
Tail:	Golden pheasant crest or calftail dyed yellow	Hackle:	Sparse brown or furnace, wound behind the wing
Body:	Yellowish orange or fluorescent orange		

This fly was developed by Bill Bakke, a director at Oregon Trout. When fished downstream on the surface, the wings make the fly "waffle" back and forth, like a caddis struggling on the surface.

PARACHUTE CADDIS, MAZZA

Hook:	Dry fly, size 14 to 20		tent style
Thread:	Light tan	Hackle post:	Butt ends of the deer hair wing
Abdomen:	Apple green fur	Thorax:	Same as the abdomen
Wing:	Bleached coastal deer body hair tied	Hackle:	Bleached grizzly

Del Mazza borrowed the idea for this fly from Tom Rosenbauer, whom he credits for introducing the idea of a parachute-hackled caddis. Mazza says, "this fly can be dressed in many colors and sizes to imitate all caddis species."

PARTRIDGE CADDIS, SPENT

Hook:	Dry fly, size 12 to 18	Thorax:	Peacock herl
Thread:	Olive	Hackle:	Mixed brown and grizzly, wound through the thorax and clipped on the top and bottom
Abdomen:	Olive fur		
Wing:	Barbs of partridge hackle tied flat and spread out		

This fly from Sheralee Lawson utilizes speckled, multicolored, partridge body feathers to imitate the wing colors of many natural caddisflies.

PAUL'S CADDIS

Hook:	Dry fly, size 14 to 20		is a piece of synthetic mottled wing fabric, trimmed to shape and "V" notched
Thread:	Cream		
Body:	Hare's ear dubbing, roughened	Head:	Hare's ear dubbing, roughened
Wing:	Very sparse deer or elk hair over which		

Craig Mathews describes Paul Brown's caddis as having "enough correctness in its outline" to represent an emerger, an adult or an egglaying adult caddis.

PEACOCK CADDIS

Hook:	Dry fly, size 12 to 18	Rib:	Copper wire
Thread:	Black or gray	Wing:	Very fine texture brown deer hair
Body:	Peacock herl	Hackle:	Mixed brown and grizzly

Originated in Idaho, the Peacock Caddis has proven to be a reliable fly on fast, broken water.

Tied by Dan Bailey's Fly Shop

PHEASANT CADDIS, GARTSIDE

Hook:	Dry fly, up or down eye, size 12 to 16	Wing:	Ringneck cock pheasant throat feather, reinforced with spar varnish or similar
Thread:	Brown		
Body:	Brown fur or Antron dubbing		
Rib:	Furnace or brown hackle, clipped slightly shorter than the hook gape	Hackle:	Furnace, or dyed brown grizzly or badger

Jack Gartside's wing design gives this fly a very crisp, realistic silhouette.

Tied by Jack Gartside

POLY WING CADDIS, OLIVE

Hook:	Dry fly, size 10 to 22		trimmed on the top and bottom
Thread:	Yellow or light olive	Wing:	Gray poly yarn
Body:	Olive fur	Head:	Butt ends of the gray poly yarn, trimmed short
Hackle:	Medium blue dun, tied thorax style and		

Gary Borger derived this fly from the design of Al Troth's Elk Hair Caddis. In very small sizes, poly yarn is easier to work with, and it is also available in more colors than elk hair.

Tied by Farrow Allen

RACKLEHANE VARIANT, TAN

Hook:	Dry fly, size 10 to 18		over the rear ⅔ of the shank
Thread:	Brown	Wing:	Mixed brown and light tan poly yarn
Body:	Mixed brown and light tan poly yarn, twisted in a dubbing loop, and wrapped	Head:	Same as body

The Racklelhane Variant was developed in Sweden by Kenneth Bostrom, who kept the fly a secret because he was ashamed of its shabby appearance, though it was his most effective caddis imitation.

Tied by Zubair Moghal

SACO CADDIS, LIGHT

Hook:	Dry fly, size 14	Rib:	Grizzly hackle, palmered over the body
Thread:	Tan	Wing:	Natural light brown deer body hair
Egg sac:	Bright apple green dubbing	Hackle:	Dark ginger
Body:	Tan fur		

Dick Stewart tied this egg-laying female caddis imitation for use on his home water, the Saco River in New Hampshire.

Tied by Dick Stewart

SCHROEDER'S PARACHUTE CADDIS

Hook:	Dry fly, size 12 to 18	Wing:	A strip of mottled turkey wing coated with vinyl cement, clipped in a "V" and tied tent wing style
Thread:	Dark brown or gray		
Hackle post wing:	White calftail		
Body:	Dark hare's ear fur	Hackle:	Grizzly

This design from Ed Schroeder produces a very convincing caddis imitation that's easy for the angler to see in broken water. The hackle post serves as an effective visual aid on this otherwise dark fly.

Tied by Redding Fly Shop

Tied by the Dettes

Tied by Gary Saindon

Tied by René Harrop

Tied by John Gierich

Tied by Craig Mathews

Tied by Edwin Logue

SHAD FLY

Hook:	Dry fly, size 12 to 18	Body:	Dark blue dun hackle, wrapped and trimmed
Thread:	Black		
Egg sac:	Medium olive hackle, wrapped and trimmed	Wing:	Partridge body feather, tied flat on top
		Hackle:	Medium blue dun and brown, mixed

This fly imitates the egg-bearing female *Brachycentrus* that hatches in the Catskills in the spring, about the time that shad run up the Delaware River to spawn. This important hatch has always been overshadowed by the popular Quill Gordon and Hendrickson hatches that occur at the same time.

SHUCKSPIECE

Hook:	Dry fly, long shank, size 10 to 14	Shuck:	Olive poly yarn or similar
Thread:	Black	Wing:	Fine light colored deer body hair
Body:	Olive yarn, or furry foam	Hackle:	Grizzly
Rib:	Dark olive thread		

Gary Saindon introduced the Shuckspiece in the mid 1980s. It's basically a Bucktail Caddis (which see), tied with a trailing nymphal shuck, and without a palmered hackle, insuring that the fly sits low and the shuck stays in the water.

SLOW WATER ADULT CADDIS, HARROP

Hook:	Dry fly, size 12 to 18	Underwing: Sparse elk hair
Thread:	Black	Wing: Two speckled hen back feather tips, reinforced with a drop of vinyl cement applied at the base of each feather
Body:	Olive fur	
Hackle:	Grizzly, 4 to 5 turns in the center of the body, clipped in a "V" at the bottom	Antennae: Stems of the wing feathers, stripped

Harrop's Slow Water Caddis works best on flat waters, where more realistic imitations are needed to fool selective trout.

SLOW WATER CADDIS, GIERICH

Hook:	Dry fly, size 12 to 18	trimmed in a "V", tied tent style, curving over the body
Thread:	Primrose yellow	
Body:	Light olive fur	Hackle: Dark ginger clipped top and bottom
Wing:	Mottled light brown turkey wing quill segment, coated with vinyl cement and	Antennae: Two dark ginger hackle tips, stripped of their barbs

This Slow Water Caddis from John Gierich is tied in both light and dark versions.

SPENT SPARKLE CADDIS

Hook:	Dry fly, size 14 to 20	Wing:	Gray Z-lon
Thread:	Tan	Head:	Hare's ear fur
Body:	Tan Antron dubbing		

The Spent Sparkle Caddis has been a reliable fly for imitating spent caddis adults on the rivers in the Yellowstone area. The beauty of this fly may lie in its simplicity and, naturally, it can be tied to match different species of caddisflies.

SUPER BUG

Hook:	Dry fly, size 12 to 16	Hackle:	Light blue dun palmered over the body
Thread:	Black	Wing:	Natural light colored deer body hair
Tail:	Dark deer body hair, tied short and about halfway down the bend	Head:	Butt ends of the wing, clipped short
Body:	Green peacock herl	Note:	Use the greenest peacock herl you can find

Edwin Logue's Super Bug imitates several green-bodied caddisflies that are common from east to west; this fly has proved to be a good searching pattern that the trout seem to like.

TIED DOWN CADDIS, ORANGE

Hook: Dry fly or nymph, 1X or 2X long, size 8 to 14
Thread: Orange
Tail: Brown deer body hair
Body: Orange poly yarn, Antron dubbing or similar
Hackle: Brown
Rib: Gold wire (optional)
Shellback: Brown deer body hair

This is a popular fly in Oregon and was sent by Joe Howell, who runs the Blue Heron Fly Shop on Oregon's famous North Umpqua River. It is tied in other colors and fished either wet or dry.

Tied by Joe Howell

TRIPLE A

Hook: Dry fly, size 10 to 12
Thread: Black
Body: Peacock herl
Hackle: Brown, trim the barbs to about the length of the hook gape or slightly longer before palmering over the body
Wing: Well marked natural deer body hair
Antennae: Black porcupine hairs, tied high on the head so they won't interfere with the eye when tying the fly to the leader

This was designed to imitate the eastern "alder fly" adult, actually a caddis, *Macronema zebratum*. Goudie believes the extra long antennae are important in deceiving fussy trout.

Tied by Dayton Goudie

VERMONT HARE'S EAR CADDIS

Hook: Dry fly, 12 to 20
Thread: Tan
Body: Hare's ear dubbing, tied full
Hackle: Mixed grizzly and brown

This is a great generic caddisfly imitation that has taken fish well beyond the borders of Vermont. A good friend, Bob Hoar, moved from Vermont to West Yellowstone, Montana, and fished Vermont Hare's Ear throughout the Rockies with great success. At the end of a natural drift let it swing around waking on the surface, then pull it under and fish it back wet.

Tied by Gene Leibhaber

W.B. CADDIS

Hook: Dry fly, size 12 to 18
Thread: Brown
Body: Tan poly dubbing
Wing: Brown feather from the throat of a drake mallard, tied curving down and around the top of the body
Hackle: Brown, one turn

Ed Reif of Eddie's Fly Shop in Bangor, Maine, says that "the W.B. Caddis is probably the best all-around searching pattern I have ever used." It can be fished dead drift, or pulled under like an egg-laying adult.

Tied by Ed Reif

WHITE TOP DEER HAIR CADDIS

Hook: Dry fly, size 12 to 18
Thread: Black
Body: Gray fur
Hackle: Mixed grizzly and dyed dun
Wing: Natural dark elk or deer body hair over which is white deer body hair
Head: Butt ends of the wing trimmed short

This is little more than a dark variation of Al Troth's Elk Hair Caddis (which see), with a pinch of white deer hair on top to improve visibility for the angler.

Tied by Farrow Allen

X CADDIS

Hook: Dry fly, size 12 to 18
Tail: Gold Z-lon
Body: Olive Antron dubbing
Wing: Natural deer body hair
Head: Butt ends of the wing clipped short

The X Caddis has established itself as an effective imitation of an adult caddis trailing a nymphal shuck. It was developed in West Yellowstone, Montana, by Craig Mathews and John Juracek of the Blue Ribbon Fly Shop.

Tied by Craig Mathews

Stonefly Nymphs

There is not a time of year when you can't use stonefly nymphs to catch trout, and that's one of the reasons for their great appeal to fishermen. As youngsters we used to capture stonefly nymphs and use them for bait. Today, we imitate these nymphs with fur and feather, and present our frauds right at the bottom of rivers and streams - and they do catch trout. Stonefly nymphs may live as long as three years in the water before they hatch into winged adults. This means that at any given moment there are a variety of stoneflies present in the stream, with each year's brood being a different size. Trout become habituated to feeding on these stonefly nymphs, and they'll take an imitation when it's properly presented. Also, just prior to hatching, stonefly nymphs commonly migrate into the shallows. This movement exposes them to the trout, and fishing a nymph at this time can be deadly. Because stonefly nymphs prefer fast, well oxygenated water, we usually weight our imitations to get them down to the rocky stream bottom.

Tied by Farrow Allen

Tied by John Betts

Tied by Joe Howell

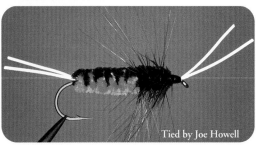
Tied by Joe Howell

Tied by Montana's Master Angler

ALBINO STONE

Hook:	Nymph, 3X to 4X long, size 4 to 12; bent as shown (optional)	Rib:	Transparent swannudaze
		Thorax:	Same as abdomen
Underbody:	Lead wire on each side	Legs:	Light grizzly trimmed top and bottom
Thread:	White		
Tail:	Teal flank barbs	Wingcase and head: Pale mottled turkey
Abdomen:	Off-white seal fur or similar	Antennae:	Mottled turkey biot

Nymphs which have recently molted can be nearly white, and very desirable to trout.

BETT'S BLACK STONEFLY NYMPH

Hook:	Nymph, Straight eye, 4X to 6X long, size 4 to 10	Abdomen:	Black latex, wrapped
		Eyes:	Black glass beads on monofilament
Tail:	Black 12lb. braided Dacron		
Underbody:	Furry foam wrapped over three parallel strips of lead wire secured to the top of the hook	Thorax:	Brown Furry Foam
		Antennae:	Black 12lb. braided Dacron
		Wingcases:	Tyvek paper, colored black, trimmed to shape and applied in layers
Legs:	Black 30lb. braided Dacron, untwisted at the base		

BIRD'S STONEFLY NYMPH

Hook:	Nymph, 2X to 4X long, size 4 to 12	Thorax:	Peacock herl
		Legs:	Dark furnace hackle palmered over the thorax
Thread:	Orange		
Tail:	Brown goose biots	Wingcase: A piece of clear plastic, pulled forward over the thorax
Abdomen:	Brown fur		
Rib:	Orange thread		

Also tied in a light variation with yellow thread and a gray abdomen

BITCH CREEK

Hook:	Nymph, 2X to 4X long; size 4 to 12	Abdomen:	Woven orange and black chenille
Thread:	Black	Thorax:	Black chenille
Underbody:	Lead wire	Legs:	Furnace or brown hackle
Tail:	White rubber hackle	Antennae:	White rubber hackle

The Bitch Creek nymph has been a popular stonefly imitation in the Rocky Mountains since the early 1960s.

BOX CANYON STONE

Hook:	Nymph, 4X to 6X long, bent down slightly as shown, size 2 to 10	Abdomen: Fuzzy black yarn, twisted tightly to look segmented
		Thorax:	Black fuzzy yarn, built up
Thread:	Black	Legs:	Furnace hackle, palmered through the thorax
Tail:	Dark brown dyed goose biots		

This easy-to-tie stonefly nymph is a popular imitation for Western anglers during the "Salmon Fly" hatch.

BROOKS' MONTANA STONE

Hook: Nymph, 3X or 4X long, size 4 to 8
Thread: Black
Underbody: Lead wire
Tail: Six barbs of crow or raven wing quill or similar
Abdomen: Black fuzzy yarn
Rib: Copper wire
Thorax: Black fuzzy yarn
Legs: Two wraps of mixed natural grizzly and a grizzly hackle dyed dark brown. Strip away the inside barbs of both hackles and wind them together
Gills: Gray ostrich herl wrapped next to the two grizzly hackles

Tied by Craig Mathews

BROOKS' YELLOW STONE

Hook: Nymph, 3X to 4X long, size 4 to 10
Thread: Brown
Underbody: Lead wire
Tail: Cinnamon turkey wing quill barbs
Abdomen: Brown yarn with a yellow cast
Rib 1: Gold yarn tied in at the front of the abdomen, wrapped backward then forward
Rib 2: Gold wire
Thorax: Same as abdomen
Legs: Two wraps of a natural grizzly and a grizzly hackle dyed dark brown. Strip the inside barbs of both hackles and wind together
Gills: Gray or white ostrich herl

Tied by Craig Mathews

BROWN STONE, RUBBER LEGS

Hook: Nymph, 3X long, size 8 to 12
Thread: Brown
Tail: Two strips of fine white rubber hackle
Abdomen: Chocolate brown and tan yarn, woven so the brown is on top and the tan underneath
Legs: Fine white rubber hackle, the first pair tied behind the thorax and the second pair in front
Thorax: Hare's ear fur, dubbed full and picked out

Developed by George Anderson of the Yellowstone Angler in Livingston, Montana.

Tied by Anderson's Yellowstone Angler

CATSKILL CURLER

Hook: Nymph, 3X long, size 6 to 12
Underbody: Strips of lead wire
Tail: Two peccary hairs
Abdomen: Long barbs of dark brown turkey tail, twisted with brown thread
Thorax: Ostrich herl dyed tan, twisted with brown thread
Wingcase and head: Dark brown turkey tail section, coated with vinyl cement, and folded over the thorax and eye of the hook
Legs: Mottled ringneck hen pheasant tail, tied on the sides in three sections
Eyes: Painted black

Tied by Matt Vinciguerra

EASTERN YELLOW STONEFLY

Hook: Nymph, 3X long, size 6 to 10; bent as shown (optional)
Thread: Yellow
Underbody: Strips of lead wire
Tail: Two woodduck flank barbs
Abdomen: A mixture of yellow, amber and cream fur
Rib: Golden yellow floss and gold wire
Thorax: Same as the abdomen, but heavier and picked out
Legs: Ginger grizzly trimmed on the top and bottom
Wingcase and head: Mottled turkey wing quill, well lacquered and folded forward and back as shown
Antennae: Mottled turkey wing biots

Tied by Farrow Allen

GIRDLE BUG

Hook: Nymph, 3X or 4X long, size 2 to 12
Thread: Black
Tail: Two strips of white rubber hackle
Legs: Three pairs of white rubber hackle
Body: Black chenille
Note: Girdle Bugs can be tied in different color combinations of chenille and rubber hackle.

The Girdle Bug has been around for a long time. It's an easy-to-tie, popular Western nymph that's still a reliable pattern for many anglers.

Tied by Shane Stalcup

Trout
63

Tied by Kaufmann's Streamborn

Tied by Kaufmann's Streamborn

Tied by Joe Howell

Tied by John Betts

Tied by Gerry James

Tied by Mike Mercer

KAUFMANN BLACK STONE

Hook: 6X long, size 2 to 10
Thread: Black
Underbody: Lead wire
Tail: Black goose biots
Abdomen: Black fur mixed with small amounts of purple, claret, brown, blue, orange and amber Antron or seal substitute
Rib: Transparent black Swannundaze
Thorax: Same as abdomen
Wingcase: Three dark mottled turkey tail sections, lacquered, cut to a "V" shape and applied in three sections with dubbing in between
Head: Same as thorax
Antennae: Black goose biots

MATT'S FUR

Hook: 6X long, size 6 to 12
Thread: Brown
Tail: Woodduck flank or dyed mallard
Abdomen: Mixed cream angora and brown otter fur
Rib: Oval gold tinsel or wire
Thorax: Same as abdomen
Wingcase: Woodduck flank or dyed mallard
Legs: Tips of the woodduck barbs from the wingcase pulled down and back on each side

MONTANA

Hook: Nymph, 3X long, size 4 to 12
Thread: Black
Underbody: Lead wire (optional)
Tail: Divided black goose biots or black hackle barbs
Abdomen: Black chenille
Thorax: Yellow chenille
Legs: About three wraps of black hackle over the thorax
Wingcase: Black chenille

The Montana was designed to suggest, rather than imitate accurately, a large Western black stonefly nymph. In fast water it's still an effective pattern.

PHOTOCOPY STONEFLY

Hook: 6X long, size 2 to 10
Thread: Yellow
Underbody: Yellow Furry Foam or similar
Overbody: Photocopied stonefly nymph, secured with wraps of yellow tying thread
Note: Select an image that you want to reproduce. Using a yellow marking pen on a piece of Avery 6725 coated plastic photocopy paper, color the area where you want the image to reproduce, and run the copier. Once the image has dried and won't smear, cut it out and tie it onto the built up underbody.

POLLY'S GOLDEN STONE

Hook: Nymph, 2X or 3X long, size 4 or 6
Thread: Light golden brown
Tail: Teal flank, dyed golden yellow
Abdomen and thorax: Gold yarn
Back: Teal flank, dyed golden yellow
Rib: Dark yellow buttonhole twist or heavy rod-wrapping thread
Wingcase: Brown and tan colored teal neck feather or similar
Legs: Teal flank dyed golden yellow, on the sides

This is Polly Rosborough's imitation of the Western gold-colored *Acroneuria* nymph.

RUBBERLEGS

Hook: Nymph, 4X long, size 2 to 10
Thread: Black
Underbody: Lead wire
Tail: Two strips of black rubber hackle
Legs: Three pairs of black rubber hackle, evenly spaced along the upper part of the body, tied in the area of the thorax
Body: Black chenille
Antennae: Strips of black rubber hackle
Note: The Rubberlegs can be tied in many different colors.

Although the Rubberlegs and the Girdle Bug (which see) are virtually the same, some Western fly authorities maintain that the Rubberlegs is usually tied larger than the Girdle Bug and is always heavily weighted.

SUPERFLY SWANNUNDAZE STONEFLY NYMPH

Hook: 6X long, size 2 to 10
Thread: Brown
Underbody: Lead wire (optional) and
           brown poly yarn for bulk
Tail: Brown goose biots, divided
           around a ball of brown rabbit fur
Abdomen: Brown rabbit fur

Rib: Transparent brown Swan-
           nundaze
Legs: Tan cord, dubbed at the base
           (femur) with brown rabbit fur
Thorax: Brown rabbit fur
Gills: Tufts of orange yarn
Antennae: Tan cord

Tied by Dan Cottrell

TED'S STONEFLY

Hook: Nymph, 3X long, size 6 to 12
Thread: Black
Tail: Two brown goose biots
Abdomen: Brown chenille

Thorax: Orange chenille
Legs: Very dark brown or black hackle
Wingcase: Brown chenille

Credit for this fly goes to outdoor writer Ted Trueblood. Although the dressing is very similar to the Montana (which see), on some waters the brown and orange works better than the black and yellow of the Montana.

Tied by Umpqua Feather Merchants

TERRIBLE TROTH

Hook: 6X long, size 2 to 6
Thread: Black
Tail: Black goose biots
Underbody: Lead wire overwrapped with
           black or brown chenille to pro-
           vide bulk and shape
Legs: Three pairs of dark brown dyed
           hackles with the barbs trimmed

close to the stem, bent at the
joints, coated with vinyl cement
and secured on top
Abdomen and thorax: Mixed black and
           brown seal fur or substitute,
           teased and trimmed on the top
           and bottom
Antennae: Black goose biots

Tied by Farrow Allen

WHITLOCK BLACK STONE

Hook: Salmon, size 4 to 10
Thread: Black
Tail: Dyed black monofilament, di-
           vided around a ball of brown
           sparkle dubbing
Abdomen: Black sparkle dubbing
Back: Black nylon raffia
Rib: Copper wire

Thorax: Brown sparkle dubbing
Head: Black sparkle dubbing
Legs: Dark grouse or hen feather tied
           flat over the thorax
Wingcase and top of head: Black nylon
           raffia
Antennae: Dyed black monofilament

Tied by Umpqua Feather Merchants

YUK BUG, BROWN

Hook: Nymph, 3X or 4X long, size 2
           to 8
Thread: Black
Underbody: Lead wire

Tail: Red or gray squirrel tail
Legs: White rubber hackle
Body: Brown chenille
Hackle: Grizzly, palmered

Tied by Jeff Currier

YUK BUG, PEPPERONI

Hook: Nymph, 3X or 4X long, size 2
           to 8
Thread: Black
Underbody: Lead wire
Tail: Red or gray squirrel tail

Legs: White rubber hackle
Body: Black and orange chenille as
           shown
Hackle: Brown, palmered

The Peppeoni variation of the Yuk Bug comes from the Jackson, Wyoming area. Like the Montana, Ted's Stonefly, and the Bitch Creek (all of which see), the two-color effect serves to imitate several large, dark, stonefly nymphs.

Tied by Jeff Currier

Stonefly Dries

Larger species of stoneflies crawl out of the water to hatch into winged adults. In fact, it's a common sight to find the empty nymphal shucks on streamside rocks and vegetation. Not all of the newly hatched adults manage to stay out of the water, however, as these awkward and clumsy fliers can sometimes be found on the water's surface during a major hatching period. Later on, when it's time for the females to oviposit, fishermen will witness flights during which the stoneflies splat upon the water and actively struggle as they release the fertile eggs. This activity can bring on some exciting surface feeding, often by large trout, and a good floating stonefly should be part of the fly fisherman's array of imitations. Smaller species, such as the little yellow and little green stoneflies, are often abundant. Tied on hooks ranging from size 12 to size 16, these mini-stones can be important to both the eastern and western angler. In fact, on a few occasions we've seen a heavy flotilla of little stones that lasted for an hour or so. These concentrations seemed to move every fish in the river.

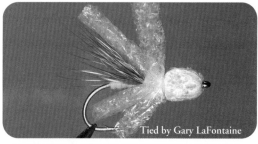

Tied by Gary LaFontaine

Tied by Joe Howell

Tied by Dick Stewart

Tied by Lee Clark

Tied by Farrow Allen

AIR HEAD

Hook: Dry fly, size 8 to 16
Abdomen: Bright green dyed mink fur or similar
Wing: Light elk hair tied downwing style
Thorax: Same as abdomen
Head and collar: White foam strips, reversed

Note: To make the head, cut four to six thin strips of white foam, the spongy kind that's used in padded envelopes. Tie them facing forward, then pull them back and tie them off to form a bullethead. Tied in a variety of colors to match the naturals.

BIRD'S STONEFLY

Hook: Dry fly, long shank, size 4 to 8
Thread: Orange
Tail: Two dark peccary bristles
Abdomen: Burnt orange floss
Rib: Two or three sections of dark furnace hackle, clipped short

Wing: Natural brown bucktail
Thorax: Burnt orange floss
Hackle: Dark furnace wrapped in front of the wing, trimmed on the top and bottom
Antennae: Two dark peccary bristles

This classic imitation of a giant black stonefly was originated many years ago by Cal Bird.

BROWN OWL

Hook: Streamer, 6X long, size 6 to 10
Thread: Dark gray or brown
Body: Oval gold
Collar: Sparse brown bucktail from the rump area, extending a little beyond the back of the hook
Wing: Teal flank, tent style to the back of the hook
Hackle: Soft, brownish grizzly, wrapped like a collar, trimmed on the top

The Brown Owl was tied by Bob Broad to be fished in the surface film, imitating a helpless adult stonefly struggling on the surface.

CLARK'S STONEFLY

Hook: Nymph, 3X long, size 8 or 10
Thread: Orange
Body: Flat gold tinsel
Wing: Gold and rust colored polypropylene macrame yarn, combed out and blended together, over which is natural dark deer body hair
Hackle: Brown, fairly sparse and trimmed in a "V" on the bottom so the fly will ride flush in the film

Clark says his pattern can be modified to represent an adult caddis or grasshopper.

EARLY BLACK STONEFLY

Hook: Dry fly, size 12 to 16
Body: Black dubbing
Legs: Black hackle, wound over the thorax and trimmed on the top and bottom
Wing: Two black hen hackles, coated with vinyl cement, stroked to shape and tied on top, slightly to the sides but overlapping

In the late winter or early spring, these tiny black stoneflies are quite active on days when the sun is shining brightly and water temperatures rise to 40 degrees or better. It is not uncommon to see snow-covered banks littered with the adults.

FLUTTERING ORANGE STONE

Hook: Dry fly, size 2 to 6
Thread: Orange
Body: Orange poly yarn, twisted and doubled, extending a little beyond the bend of the hook
Wing: Light elk hair applied in two steps: a long bunch over which is a shorter bunch, about half the length of the first
Hackle: Brown, heavy
Antennae: Stripped hackle stems dyed orange
Note: Also tied in yellow. Some find that the poly yarn tail is less likely to foul the hook if it is doubled, but not twisted.

Tied by Dan Bailey's Fly Shop

FOAM STONE

Hook: Dry fly, long shank, size 4 to 10
Thread: Orange
Body: Orange closed-cell foam ribbed with orange thread
Wing: Natural elk hair
Head and collar: Elk hair dyed brown and tied reversed to form a bullethead
Note: The foam body is built on a straight pin using a strip of foam that's folded in half and segmented with orange thread, then slipped off the pin and threaded onto the hook as shown.

Tied by Joe Howell

GOLDEN STONE RUBBER LEGS

Hook: Dry fly, long shank, size 6 to 10
Body: Elk or deer body hair dyed orange-yellow
Rib: Yellow thread, wrapped criss-cross
Tail: Tip ends of the hair used to form the body
Wing: Gray deer body hair
Head and collar: Gray deer body hair tied reversed to form a bullethead; the collar should be trimmed on the bottom
Legs: Gray rubber hackle

Tied by Dan Bailey's Fly Shop

HENRY'S FORK GOLDEN STONE

Hook: Dry fly, long shank, size 6 to 10
Thread: Yellow
Tail: Elk hair bleached or dyed yellow
Body: Yellow poly dubbing
Rib: Brown hackle, trimmed
Wing: Natural elk hair
Head and collar: Elk hair bleached or dyed yellow, tied reversed to form a bullethead; the collar at the bottom should be trimmed
Note: The body is often reverse-tied elk hair which is tied back along the shank then folded forward and secured with "X" wraps.

Tied by Umpqua Feather Merchants

JUG HEAD

Hook: Nymph, 3X long, size 2 to 8
Thread: Orange
Tail: Dark moose hair
Body: Orange yarn
Rib: Furnace hackle, clipped short
Wing: Red squirrel tail
Collar: Tan antelope hair extending over the top of the body and cut short
Head: Tan elk hair, spun and trimmed as shown

The Jughead was designed by Betty Hoyt and popularized by Pat Barnes at his West Yellowstone fly shop.

Tied by Tom Travis

LITTLE YELLOW STONEFLY

Hook: Nymph, 3X long, size 12
Thread: Light yellow
Tail: Small bunch of red hackle barbs, clipped short to suggest an egg sac, over which is a larger bunch of honey dun hackle barbs
Body: Sulphur colored yarn
Rib: Light yellow thread
Wing: Synthetic clear wing
Legs: Pale cree or honey dun hackle

This is Polly Rosborough's imitation of the female adult yellow stonefly. It should be fished submerged in the surface film.

Tied by Gerry James

Tied By David Lucca

Tied by Montana's Master Angler

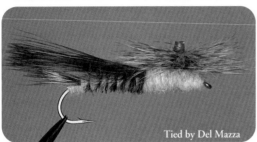

Tied by Del Mazza

Tied by Rainy Riding

Tied by Ron Brown

Tied by Kaufmann's Streamborn

LUCCA'S YELLOW FUR COAT FOAM STONE

Hook:	Dry fly, long shank, size 4 to 10	Body:	Yellow fur dubbed over the foam
Thread:	Yellow	Wing:	Natural elk or deer body hair
Underbody:	Yellow closed-cell foam secured around the shank	Hackle:	Mixed dark and light ginger
		Antennae:	Peccary, moose hair or similar

This represents an interesting technique, masking a foam underbody with natural fur to achieve a traditional looking fly with exceptional floating properties.

MacSALMON

Hook:	Dry fly, long shank, size 2 to 8	Head and collar:	Deer body hair dyed chocolate brown, spun and trimmed to shape
Thread:	Orange and black		
Extended body:	Braided orange macrame cord, fused with a flame	Note:	The fused macrame cord is threaded on the hook like a worm, cemented and tied. Also can be tied with a reversed bullethead and with rubber legs.
Underwing:	Mottled gray synthetic Fly Film, tied tent style		
Wing:	Light elk hair, slightly longer than the underwing		

PARACHUTE STONEFLY

Hook:	6X long shank, size 8 to 12		medium dun, clipped flush on the top and bottom
Thread:	Yellow		
Tail:	Coastal deer body hair, flared over a ball of dubbed sulfur fur	Wing:	Elk mane
		Hackle post:	Butts of the elk mane wing
Abdomen:	Golden yellow fur	Thorax:	Golden yellow fur
Body hackle:	Two grizzly hackles dyed	Hackle:	Natural and bleached grizzly

This is Del Mazza's imitation of the Eastern *Pteronarcys* adult stonefly.

RAINY'S STONEFLY

Hook:	Dry fly, long shank, size 2 to 10	Rib:	Dark furnace hackle, trimmed
Thread:	Orange	Wing:	Pearl crystal flash over which is light elk hair
Tail:	Natural light elk hair		
Body:	Orange Float Foam, cut to shape	Hackle:	Brown, tied full

Rainy Riding distributes Float Foam, a cylindrical closed-cell foam that's available in a number of colors and diameters. It's easy to work with and well suited to tying ants, crickets, hoppers, inchworms and more.

RON'S STONEFLY

Hook:	Dry Fly, 4X to 6X long, size 4 to 8	Rib:	Fluorescent orange, counter-wrapped
Thread:	Fluorescent orange	Wing:	Mixed black and light stiff moose hair or elk hair
Tail:	Moose body hair		
Abdomen:	Black closed-cell foam, wound on	Legs:	Two pairs of black goose biots
		Thorax and head:	Black fur
Body hackle:	Black, trimmed	Antennae:	Black peccary bristles or similar

SEDUCER

Hook:	Dry fly, long shank, size 6 to 16		a piece of dark dun Fly Film (thin, flexible, transluscent plastic), trimmed to shape and tied flat over the body
Thread:	Fluorescent orange		
Tail:	Black moose hair		
Abdomen:	Fluorescent orange dubbing		
Body hackle:	Brown or dark furnace, clipped on top	Thorax:	Same as abdomen
		Hackle:	Grizzly, over the thorax
Rib:	Fine gold wire	Note:	Tied in a wide range of colors, including yellow and black.
Wing:	Sparse crystal flash over which is		

SILHOUETTE STONE, LIGHT

Hook:	Dry fly, long shank, size 6 to 10	Underwing:	Bleached elk hair
Thread:	Orange	Hackle:	Light ginger, tied full but short
Tail:	Bleached elk hair	Wing:	Light ginger nylon raffia, tied down in front of and behind the hackle
Body:	Gold colored dubbing, over which is a piece of dark brown nylon raffia		
Rib:	Light ginger hackle, trimmed	Antennae:	Light gray rubber hackle

Tied by Joe Howell

SOFA PILLOW, IMPROVED

Hook:	Dry fly, long shank, size 4 to 10	Body hackle:	Brown
Thread:	Black or orange	Rib:	Gold wire (optional)
Tail:	Natural elk hair	Wing:	Natural elk hair
Body:	Orange poly yarn or dubbing	Hackle:	Brown, tied full

The original Sofa Pillow can be traced back to the 1940s, and to Pat Barnes and his wife, who were both fly tiers and owned a shop in West Yellowstone, Montana. This is a popular variation.

Tied by Farrow Allen

SPRING STONE

Hook:	Dry fly, size 14 to 18	Wing:	Center tip of a mallard flank feather, coated with vinyl cement and tied flat over the body
Thread:	Black		
Tail:	Black moose mane or bear hair divided	Hackle:	Grizzly, dun or black
Body:	Black fur	Antennae:	Black moose or bear hair

On sunny, late winter days, it is not uncommon along freestone rivers to find the air filled with small black stonefly adults.

Tied by John Yashinski

STIMULATOR, YELLOW

Hook:	Dry fly, 3X long, size 6 to 14	Rib:	Fine gold wire (optional)
Thread:	Orange	Wing:	Natural elk or deer body hair
Tail:	Natural elk or deer body hair	Thorax:	Orange to amber dubbing
Abdomen:	Yellow dubbing	Front hackle:	Same as body hackle, wrapped over the thorax
Body hackle:	Grizzly or badger		

This is one of Randall Kaufmann's most popular patterns that began as an imitation of an adult stonefly. It's tied in a variety of colors and sizes.

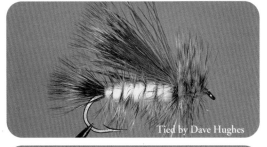
Tied by Dave Hughes

YELLOW SALLY

Hook:	Dry fly, long shank, size 14 to 18		top
Thread:	Primrose yellow	Wing:	Pale gray duck wing quill section, coated with vinyl cement and tied flat over the body
Tail:	Pale chartreuse-yellow deer body hair		
Body:	Sulphur colored dubbing	Hackle:	Creamy white, trimmed on top
Body hackle:	Creamy white, trimmed on		

During the summer, little yellow and little green stoneflies are a common sight at dusk.

Tied by Farrow Allen

YELLOW SALLY, HENRY'S FORK

Hook:	Dry fly, size 14 or 16		hair
Thread:	Yellow	Thorax:	Same as abdomen
Abdomen:	Sulphur colored dubbing	Legs:	Three turns of blue dun hackle, trimmed on the top and bottom
Wing:	Fine light colored deer body		

This is Mike Lawson's imitation for several species of small yellow stoneflies. Any fly designed for the Henry's Fork has to be able to deceive some fussy trout.

Tied by Umpqua Feather Merchants

Midges

Compared to mayflies, caddisflies and stoneflies, fly fishermen know very little about the huge group of insects known as midges. These are members of the order Diptera, or two-winged flies, and for convenience we've included mosquitoes in this section. There are well over two thousand species of midges. These represent such an enormous diversity of size, color, behavior, locale and other characteristics that anglers have not attempted to deal at the level of genera, much less species. The larval and pupal forms are aquatic, whereas the adults are mostly terrestrial. Some species prefer the bottoms of lakes, others inhabit rapids. Some crawl among vegetation, others swim freely in open water. Some have gills, others utilize breathing tubes. Some are tiny, down to 2mm, others grow quite large, to 20mm (about ¾ inch) long. Colors range from white to black, and include red, yellow, brown, green, olive and purple. All these differences aside, hatching midges, suspended at or in the surface film, present a great challenge to anglers, who should carry an assortment of midges in different sizes and colors.

Tied by Umpqua Feather Merchants

BIOT MIDGE, BLACK

Hook: Dry fly, straight eye, size 16 to 26
Thread: Black
Abdomen: Black goose biot wrapped over black
          thread
Thorax: Peacock herl
Gills: One turn of light colored hackle or
          CDC

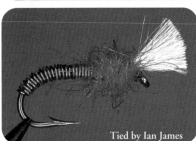

Tied by Ian James

COPPER BUZZER, ORANGE

Hook: Wet fly, size 12 to 18
Thread: Black
Abdomen: Copper wire
Thorax: Orange seal fur or substitute
Head: A piece of white floss clipped square and
          flared slightly

Ian James of Guelph, Ontario, ties the Copper Buzzer with either a black or orange fur thorax, and describes both variations as "effective chironomid imitations with British and Scottish origins." In Great Britain, midge imitations are commonly called "buzzers."

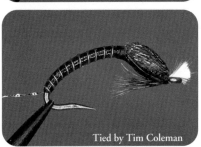

Tied by Tim Coleman

CRYSTAL CHIRONOMID

Hook: Curved nymph, size 16 to 24
Thread: Black
Tail (air bubble): Single strand of silver crystal
          flash, two or three times the length of
          the body
Abdomen and thorax: Black tying thread
Rib: Fine silver wire; lacquer the entire ab-
          domen and thorax after wrapping the
          silver wire
Wingcase: Ringneck pheasant tail fibers
Gills: White marabou
Legs: Grouse hackle barbs (optional)

Tim Coleman says the trailing silver crystal flash makes this fly more effective.

Tied by Joe Howell

DIAMOND LAKE AIR BUBBLE MIDGE

Hook: Dry fly, size 12 to 18
Thread: Black
Tail (air bubble): Several strands of pearl crystal
          flash and a clear glass bead
Body: Black tying thread
Rib: Yellow tying thread
Hackle: Grizzly, about four turns
Note: To make the air bubble, tie two or three
          knots in the crystal flash, cement them,
          and while the cement is still wet, slide
          the glass bead over the knotted section
          and carefully jam the knots inside the
          bead.

Tied by Kaufmann's Streamborn

FLASHABOU CHIRONOMID

Hook: Nymph, 1X long, size 14 to 18
Thread: White
Tail: White Z-Lon or Antron, cut off short
Underbody: Red Flashabou (olive and pearl
          Flashabou are also popular colors)
Abdomen: Clear Larva Lace or Body Glass
          wrapped over the Flashabou
Note: When tying very small flies, you may
          want to overwrap the Flashabou with
          fine monofilament.

This pattern is best fished in still water with a hand twist retrieve, or it is fished dead-drift in moving water. Chironomidae is the largest family of the midges.

FLOATING MIDGE, BLACK

Hook: Curved nymph, short shank, size 6 to 22
Thread: White
Abdomen: Black Liqua Lace
Rib: One strand of green Kreinik Metallic Flash

Antennae: White CDC
Thorax: Peacock herl outside of which are two strips of white closed cell foam pulled forward on each side, cemented and sprinkled with pearl glitter before it dries

Tied by Michael Tucker

Tucker ties and fishes his floating midge in many colors, and as large as size six.

MOSQUITO PUPA

Hook: Nymph, 1X or 2X long, size 14 to 20
Thread: Black or olive
Tail: Soft grizzly hackle barbs, short
Abdomen: Stripped peacock herl
Thorax: Peacock herl
Rib: Fine gold or copper wire, wrapped over the abdomen and thorax

Wings: Grizzly hen hackle tips, short
Gills: Soft grizzly hackle barbs, extending over the head
Note: If you're careful and strip off the right amount of herl, you can complete the abdomen and thorax from the same stem

Tied by Kaufmann's Streamborn

RED MIDGE PUPA

Hook: Nymph, 1X to 3X long, size 10 to 16; the orientation of this fly is with the head of the pupa at the rear of the hook
Thread: Bright red
Head: Several turns of black ostrich herl

Hackle: Three turns of dry fly quality grizzly, concave side facing the head
Abdomen: Bright red yarn
Rib: Bright red thread

Tied by Gerry James

Polly Rosborough ties all his midge pupa in this reversed style. Black, gray, red and tan are his favorite colors.

SERENDIPITY, OLIVE

Hook: Curved nymph, short shank, size 14 to 22
Thread: Olive
Body: Olive Z-lon twisted into a rope and

wrapped tightly
Head: Natural deer body hair, spun and trimmed to form a collar on top and small head in front

Tied by Craig Mathews

The Olive Serendipity came to us from Craig Mathews of Blue Ribbon Flies. In Mathews and Juracek's book, *Fishing Yellowstone Hatches*, they say the Serendipity has ". . . proven to be the most productive nymph to be fished on the Madison in years."

SERENDIPITY, RED

Hook: Nymph, 1X or 2X long, size 14 to 22
Thread: Black or gray
Body: Red Z-lon twisted into a rope and wrapped tightly

Head: Natural deer body hair, spun and trimmed to form a collar on top and small head in front

Tied by Kaufmann's Streamborn

Red is a common color for several species of Chironomid pupae, so it's only natural to tie the Serendipity in this color. Many tiers are also beginning to use variations of the Serendipity to imitate emerging caddis pupae.

SUSPENDER MIDGE

Hook: Nymph, 1X long, size 14 to 22
Thread: Brown
Tail: Piece of clear or white packaging foam
Abdomen: Pearl Flashabou over brown tying

thread
Thorax: Peacock herl
Head: Same as the tail

Tied by Dick Stewart

This fly is designed to hang in the surface film, like a partially emerged midge resting for awhile before trying to struggle free. The foam helps keep the fly suspended, and offers the impression of the half-emerged adult.

Tied by Dick Stewart

Tied by Shane Stalcup

Tied by Kaufmann's Streamborn

Tied by Kaufmann's Streamborn

Tied by Gary Saindon

Tied by Dick Stewart

BLACK HERL MIDGE

Hook:	Dry fly, size 18 to 26	Body:	Black ostrich herl
Thread:	Black	Note:	Tied in brown, gray and yellow.
Tail:	Black hackle barbs		

Ed Koch, author of *Fishing the Midge*, tied the first Black Herl Midge on the banks of one of his favorite streams in central Pennsylvania, to match a hatch of tiny black flies. This simple little fly saved the day for Koch, who has used this design as a standard pattern.

CDC ADULT MIDGE

Hook:	Dry fly, size 16 to 26		Z-lon
Thread:	Black	Note:	Stalcup say that a few barbs of black
Abdomen:	Natural gray goose biot		CDC may be included underneath the
Wing:	Natural gray CDC over which is white		wing to imitate legs.

The addition of a few fibers of white Z-lon, on top of the gray CDC wing, makes this fly to see a lot easier to see on the water.

CALIFORNIA MOSQUITO

Hook:	Dry fly, size 12 to 20	Rib:	White thread
Thread:	Black	Wing:	Grizzly hackle tips, either curving in or
Tail:	Grizzly or dyed bright red hackle barbs		out from one another
Body:	Black floss, tapered	Hackle:	Grizzly

The California Mosquito, with it's downwing construction, is fairly representative of a natural mosquito. Since the early 1960s, it's been a good fly for the mountain lakes of the high Sierras.

CLUSTER MIDGE

Hook:	Dry fly, size 12 to 18	Hackle:	Grizzly, palmered
Thread:	Black	Rib:	Fine gold wire
Body:	Peacock herl	Wing:	White CDC

This is basically a Griffith's Gnat (which see) that René Harrop provided with a white wing, to give greater visibility to the angler, which is always an issue when fishing small dark flies. It is designed to represent a cluster of insects.

DEPARTING DIPTERA

Hook:	Dry fly, size 12 to 18	Body:	Reddish brown to black fur
Thread:	Black	Wing:	Fine deer hair, sparse
Shuck:	Clear or white poly yarn or similar	Hackle:	Dark dun, sparse

Gary Saindon tied the Departing Diptera to imitate the adult insect trying to escape the nymphal shuck, when it's "half pupa and half adult."

GRIFFITH'S GNAT

Hook:	Dry fly, size 14 to 22	Hackle:	Grizzly, palmered through the herl body
Thread:	Black	Rib:	Fine gold wire (optional)
Body:	Peacock herl		

This fly was developed by George Griffith, who is credited with helping found Trout Unlimited. The Griffith's Gnat has become an established standard throughout the country. It's easier see on the water than many other micro patterns, and is readily taken by trout in a variety of situations.

OLIVE GRIZZLY MIDGE

Hook: Dry fly, size 18 to 26
Thread: Olive
Tail: Grizzly hackle barbs
Body: Olive dubbing or thread
Hackle: Grizzly

This is basically a traditional, wingless, variant style dry fly tied in small sizes in a variety of colors, and simply called a midge because of its small size. True midges are downwing insects, but are still fairly well imitated with this type of fly as long as the color and size match the natural.

Tied by Dick Stewart

MIGHTY MYSTERY MIDGE

Hook: Dry fly, size 18 to 26
Thread: White
Body: Black synthetic yarn, or whatever color
best matches the natural you want to imitate
Wing: Clear, white or gray poly yarn

Originally this fly was dressed by Ken Parkany with a wing of white or gray deer body hair, but Gennaro says poly yarn makes a more natural looking imitation that fishes well wet or dry. It's quite easy to use this design and tie yourself a good selection of midges in various sizes and colors.

Tied by Andrew Gennaro

MOSQUITO

Hook: Dry fly, size 12 to 20
Thread: Black or gray
Tail: Grizzly hackle barbs
Body: Dark and light moose mane, wrapped
together
Wing: Grizzly hackle tips
Hackle: Grizzly

This Mosquito pattern has been around for a long time and withstood the arrival of many more accurately conceived exact imitations. Nonetheless, it's a good summertime dry fly that continues to take a lot of trout.

Tied by Umpqua Feather Merchants

PALOMINO MIDGE, RED

Hook: Dry fly or curved nymph, short shank, size 16 to 26
Thread: Dark red or brown
Extended abdomen: Reddish brown New Dub or Ultra Chenille
Thorax: Reddish brown dubbing
Wingcase: White Z-lon, including a short section extending over the eye of the hook, imitating a partially emerged adult
Note: When the abdomen has been secured , touch the rear with an exposed flame and it will melt into a tapered end.

The extended body Palomino style can be used to create all manner of nymphs and dry flies.

Tied by Farrow Allen

REAL MOSQUITO

Hook: Dry fly, size 12 to 18
Thread: Black
Body: Black tying thread, very thin
Rib: Stripped grizzly hackle stem
Wing: Two matched gray CDC tips tied downwing. Over this are two black
CDC tips with the butt ends divided by "X" wraps of black dubbing so they extend from the thorax like short spent wings. Finally cut away the black center stems and take a couple of turns of dubbing at the head of the fly.

This is a good pattern which imitates a variety of adult midges, as well as mosquitoes.

Tied by Kaufmann's Streamborn

STILLBORN MIDGE

Hook: Dry fly, size 14 to 22
Thread: Black
Tail (trailing shuck): Single piece of pearl flashabou
Abdomen: Stripped peacock herl
Rib: Fine gold wire (optional)
Wing: Dun hackle tips, tied spent and angled back like a delta wing
Thorax: Hare's ear fur or similar
Hackle: Dun, wrapped sparsely over the thorax in front of the wing

This fly was designed by Dick Stewart to represent an emerged adult, unable to detach itself from its translucent nymphal shuck.

Tied by Dick Stewart

Crane Flies

Crane flies are largest members of the order Diptera, or two-winged insects. The larvae are large, measuring from one to three inches in length, providing trout with a sizeable mouthful. Craig Mathews and John Juracek, in their book *Fly Patterns of Yellowstone*, describe the giant crane fly larvae as looking like "olive link sausages." Although a number of crane fly species exist in the East, and from time to time can produce good fishing in certain rivers, overall these flies are more abundant in the West, particularly in the Rockies. They are a diversified group of insects that inhabit a variety of water types including freestone creeks and, more commonly, the silt and decaying organic matter of quieter waters.

Tied by Dan Bailey's Fly Shop

CRANEFLY LARVA, CREAM

Hook:	Nymph, 2X or 3X long, size 6 to 14	Rib:	Clear Larva Lace, Swannundaze or monofilament
Tail (gills):	Pale gray CDC or fine marabou		
Underbody:	Lead wire (optional)	Head:	Gray fur or yarn
Abdomen:	Cream-tan to gray yarn or dubbing		

Tied down to size 14, this is an effective imitation of a cranefly larva that's known in the West as the summer cranefly. It's most prevalent in cold spring-fed ponds, and the slower sections of some rivers.

Tied by George Kesel

GANGLE-LEGS

Hook:	Dry fly, size 10 to 18		spent
Thread:	Brown	Note:	The parachute hackle is wound around a base formed by the its own stem. After it's been wrapped and trimmed, the remaining stem should be folded forward and tied off with thread wraps. This will hold it in place.
Body:	Ruddy tan dubbing		
Hackle:	Grizzly, a spade type neck hackle with extra long barbs, wrapped sparse, parachute style and trimmed in front in a "V"		
Wing:	Grizzly hackle tips, either upright or		

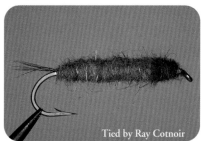

Tied by Ray Cotnoir

GIANT CRANE FLY LARVA

Hook:	Nymph, 3X to 4X long, size 2 to 10	Body:	Mixed dark olive with gold colored rabbit fur
Thread:	Olive		
Tail (gills):	Dark brown pheasant tail barbs	Rib:	Gold wire
Underbody:	Lead wire, overwrapped with olive yarn to help build up the bulk	Head:	Dark brown fur

This large fly was developed at Blue Ribbon Flies in West Yellowstone, Montana, to imitate a huge two-inch long olive crane fly larva that's common in the Rockies.

Tied by Terry Ruane

PARADEER

Hook:	Dry fly, size 8 to 14 (the front ⅓ of the hook is bent down slightly		tied to the shank and secured in an upright position perpendicular to the hook shank, like the wing on a parachute fly. The hair is then "teased" down and pressed flat with the thumb and secured with a few criss-cross wraps.
Thread:	Olive		
Butt:	Fluorescent red or green thread		
Body:	Olive thread		
Wing/Hackle:	Fine deer body hair. The hair is		

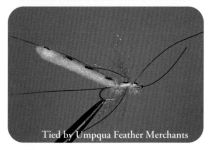

Tied by Umpqua Feather Merchants

STALCUP'S CRANE FLY, TAN

Hook:	Dry fly, size 12 or 14	Wings:	Cream colored Z-lon, tied spent
Thread:	Tan	Thorax:	Tan Furry Foam
Extended abdomen:	Narrow strip of tan foam; leave enough foam to later pull forward for the head and back	Back and head:	Excess foam from the abdomen pulled forward like a wingcase and tied off to form the head
Legs:	Monofilament, appropriately colored	Note:	Add markings with a waterproof pen.

Damselfly nymphs can be found in virtually all lakes and ponds, and in the slow-moving sections of many rivers. Although damselflies can be significant to the Eastern trout fisherman, they are generally more abundant in Western waters. The nymph is easily identified by its long skinny abdomen, short thorax, and wide head with large protruding eyes. The three broad leaf-shaped tails at the end of its abdomen are actually breathing gills, which are also used to propel it like a minnow. Damselfy nymphs are active swimmers, even if they don't have much stamina. They usually wiggle and swim for a foot or two, rest, then continue. This is how they travel toward the shallows before emerging. They swim near the water surface, so trout feeding on them can often be seen. If the nymph reaches the shore, it crawls out of the water to emerge. The freshly emerged adult is a light tan and soon darkens to brown. Mature adult males turn electric blue, green or red while the females remain dull colored. Being weak fliers they are easily blown into the water by the wind, where they become easy pickings for trout.

ADULT DAMSEL

Hook: Dry fly, size 8 to 12
Thread: Olive
Extended abdomen: Clear braided monofiliment leader butt material, colored as needed and sealed on the end with CA cement

or a match to resist unravelling
Wings: White calftail
Eyes: Black beads connected by monofilament
Thorax and head: Olive dubbing
Wingcase: Olive poly yarn or similar

To match the colors of the natural insects, the Adult Damsel is commonly tied in tan, pale yellow, brown, blue or bright green.

Tied by Dan Bailey's Fly Shop

A.K.'S SWIMMING DAMSEL

Hook: Swimming nymph, size 10 or 12
Tail: A small bunch of light olive ostrich herl tips
Abdomen: Olive poly dubbing
Rib: Fine copper wire

Eyes: Black beads
Thorax: Olive poly dubbing
Wingcase: Gray nylon raffia
Legs: Grizzly hen hackle barbs dyed olive

The unique shape of the hook on which A.K. Best ties his imitation helps to make it look alive when it's being retrieved.

Tied by Umpqua Feather Merchants

BLUE ADULT DAMSEL

Hook: Dry fly, size 8 to 10
Thread: Black
Extended abdomen: Blue closed-cell (Polycelon) foam secured around a base of 25 lb. stiff monofilament with "X" wraps of black thread

Wings: Black bucktail tied delta wing style
Abdomen: Blue rabbit fur
Eyes: Black beads on 25 lb. monofilament
Wingcase: Blue closed-cell foam
Head: Blue closed-cell foam folded back over the eyes

Tied by Karl Svendsen

BRAIDED BUTT DAMSEL, BLUE

Hook: Dry fly, 10 or 12
Thread: Blue
Extended abdomen: Braided monofilament leader butt material, dyed blue and black as shown
Abdomen: Blue dubbing
Wingcase and hackle post: A loop of blue acrylic yarn

Wing: Blue dun hackle, parachute style
Head: Blue yarn from the wingcase, tied off and trimmed to extend over the head
Note: To make the wing, take 5 or 6 turns of hackle around the yarn loop, separate the barbs in front, to one side or the other and pull the loop forward, tie down and trim the head.

Tied by Gary Borger

BROOKS' GREEN DAMSEL

Hook: Nymph, size 6 to 10
Thread: Black or olive
Tail: Three peacock sword tips
Abdomen: Green fur or yarn

Rib: Oval gold tinsel
Abdomen: Green fur or yarn
Legs: Three turns of green dyed grizzly hackle over the thorax

Charles Brooks also used to tie this damselfly nymph in tan, olive and gray.

Tied by Craig Mathews

Damselflies

Tied by Andy Burk

Tied by Andy Burk

Tied by Umpqua Feather Merchants

Tied by John Shewey

Tied by Farrow Allen

Tied by Thomas Woelfle

BURK'S BLUE DAMSEL

Hook: Dry fly, straight eye, size 10 or 12
Thread: Blue
Extended abdomen: A cord made of twisted blue Z-lon, which is then twisted back on itself
Wings: Two long, light blue dun hackles curv-ing away from one another
Thorax: Blue deer body hair, spun and trimmed to shape
Legs: Blue thread, coated with Flexament
Eyes: Melted monofilament, colored black, or similar

BURK'S BUG EYE DAMSEL

Hook: Nymph, size 12 or 14
Thread: Olive
Underbody: Lead wire (optional)
Tail: Olive marabou, wrapped to the end of the extended abdomen and cemented
Extended abdomen: Light olive Ultra Chenille
Thorax: Olive seal fur substitute, dubbed full
Legs: Dubbing from the thorax, picked out
Wingcase: Gray ostrich
Eyes: Melted monofilament painted black

Like several other tiers, Burk feels strongly that imitating the prominent eyes of the natural is worth the extra tying time required.

DAVE'S DAMSEL NYMPH, GREEN

Hook: Streamer, 3X long, size 8 to 12
Thread: Olive
Underbody: Lead wire wrapped over the thorax
Tail: Olive marabou or 3 fine ostrich herl tips
Abdomen: Dubbed light olive-green sparkle yarn
Rib: Gold wire
Thorax: Same as abdomen, but fuller
Legs: A speckled hen or grouse body feather, tied flat over the thorax
Eyes: Black beads on monofilament or similar
Wingcase and head: Olive nylon raffia, pulled between the eyes

EMERGENT DAMSEL CRIPPLE

Hook: Dry fly, size 10 to 12
Thread: Light green
Extended body: Mixed strands of pale olive buck-tail and fluorescent lime crystal flash, secured with rib of pale olive thread
Wing: Thin crinkle Mylar, Zing or similar
Hackle: Soft light dun, wrapped parachute style around a "post" formed by the deer hair butt ends of the body
Wingcase: Carefully pull the deer hair post forward, trying not to distort the hackle too much, and tie down

A crippled damselfly, struggling on the surface, must be irresistible to cruising trout.

EMERGENT DAMSEL NYMPH

Hook: Nymph, 3X long, size 12 or 14
Thread: Pale yellow
Tail: Creamy light olive fur, teased out
Abdomen: Creamy olive fur
Rib: Dark olive thread
Thorax: Same as abdomen, tied full and teased out

The color of some emerging damselfly nymphs is pale olive to almost cream. Tied with fur, they can be dressed with floatant and manipulated on the surface to imitate a struggling nymph.

FLUFFY DAMSEL

Hook: Nymph, 2X or 3X long, size 8 to 14
Thread: Olive
Tail: Grizzly marabou, dyed olive
Abdomen: Olive yarn or fur, originally Fluffy Lead
Rib: Pearl Flashabou
Thorax: Olive yarn or fur, applied heavily, over which is short grizzly marabou dyed olive

Borrowing from the theory of Charlie Brooks, this nymph is tied "in the round," so that it provides the same silhouette when viewed from different angles.

FOAM DAMSEL

Hook: Dry fly size 12 or 14
Thread: Blue or black
Extended abdomen: Blue Livebody foam cylinder
Thorax and wings: Several grizzly hackles, wrapped and trimmed on the top and bottom, leaving enough barbs on the sides to look like spent wings

Wingcase: Blue foam cylinder, doubled and pulled forward over the wings and tied off to also form a head
Note: Float Foam can be trimmed with a razor and heated carefully over a flame and molded some with your fingers before it sets

Tied by Dick Stewart

GREEN DAMSEL

Hook: Nymph, 3X long, size 6 or 8
Thread: Light olive
Tail: Light golden-olive marabou
Abdomen: Olive-green yarn

Thorax: Olive-green yarn, short and built up
Rib: Light olive thread
Legs: Teal flank dyed olive
Wingcase: Light golden-olive marabou

Polly Rosborough, who developed this pattern, says that it should be fished rapidly with short one inch "jerks of the rod tip and line."

Tied by Gerry James

JANSSEN'S DAMSEL

Hook: Streamer hook, 4X long, size 10 to 14
Thread: Olive
Tail: Light golden-olive marabou
Abdomen: Medium grayish-olive fur
Rib: Light olive thread

Abdomen: Light olive chenille
Legs: Brown or cree hackle, clipped short and flush on the top and bottom
Wingcase: Brown mottled turkey wing quill section

Tied by Umpqua Feather Merchants

MARABOU DAMSEL

Hook: Dry fly, size 10 to 14
Thread: Olive
Butt: Dubbed ball of pale olive marabou
Tail: Pale olive marabou over which is brown marabou, both very sparse and broken off to length

Underbody: Lead wire over the front half
Abdomen: Mixed brown and pale olive marabou, dubbed
Thorax: Same as abdomen with pale olive guard hair mixed in and teased for legs
Wingcase: Peacock herl

The Marabou Damsel has worked so well, Borger hasn't needed to change it since he developed it.

Tied by Gary Borger

MARABOU DAMSEL, KAUFMANN'S

Hook: Nymph, 3X long, size 10 to 14
Thread: Olive
Tail: Light olive marabou
Body: Light olive marabou, a single plume tied in by the tip, twisted slightly and

wound forward like a piece of chenille
Rib: Copper wire or olive thread
Wingcase: Bunch of light olive marabou, torn off to the length shown

Randall Kaufmann's entire nymph is tied with a single material, olive marabou, and really looks alive in the water.

Tied by Kaufmann's Streamborn

STALCUP'S DAMSEL

Hook: Dry fly, size 12 to 14
Thread: Blue
Extended abdomen: Thin strip of blue closed cell foam; leave enough untrimmed to later fold forward and form the wingcase

Legs and antennae: Monofilament
Wing: Clear Z-lon, very short
Eyes: Monofilament Nymph Eyes
Thorax: Blue Furry Foam
Wingcase: Foam left over from the abdomen

It's impossible to ignore the fact that closed-cell floating foams are ideally suited for tying large floating flies with extended bodies.

Tied by Umpqua Feather Merchants

Scuds, Shrimp & Sowbugs

Aquatic sowbugs (also known as cressbugs because they are commonly found among watercress plants), scuds, and shrimp are all crustaceans which are significant to the trout fisherman. Of the many species of scuds, a few grow quite large, but most are small. They are sometimes mistakenly called freshwater shrimp. Scuds spend most of their lives in shallow water, rarely venturing deeper then several feet. They feed mainly in weed beds, or by scavenging over shallow gravel in lakes, or the calmer stretches of a stream. They are crawlers as well as swimmers and move easily forward and backward. Scuds are flat from *side to side*, and their legs extend on the bottom. Sowbugs are similar in size to many scuds, but are flat from *top to bottom*, with legs sticking out on each side. Sowbugs are crawlers and are virtually helpless when dislodged and set adrift in the current. They are most abundant in vegetation common to rich limestone spring creeks.

Tied by Kaufmann Streamborn

BIG HORN SHRIMP, PINK

Hook:	Wet fly or nymph, 1X or 2X long, size 10 to 16	Shellback:	Clear strip cut from a plastic bag
Thread:	Pink	Rib:	Clear or dyed pink monofilament
Tail:	Pink hackle barbs	Forelegs:	Pink hackle barbs
Body:	Pink dyed Antron dubbing or any fine, seal-like, synthetic fur	Note:	The Big Horn Shrimp is also commonly tied in orange.

Tied by John Shewey

GIANT PIGGY BACK SCUD

Top fly:	Tie a Giant Super Scud (which see), break off the hook at the bend and omit the wire rib.	Body:	Pink to orange dubbing
		Rib:	Fine gold wire. When the bottom fly is finished, secure it to the underside of the top fly with wraps of 6 lb. monofilament.
Bottom fly:	Hook: Standard wet fly, two or three sizes smaller than the top fly		

Although it hardly seems sporting, when scuds are mating they're extremely vulnerable and the trout take advantage.

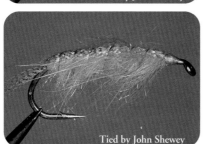

Tied by John Shewey

GIANT SUPER SCUD

Hook:	Nymph, 3X long, size 4 or 6	Shellback:	Barbs of woodduck flank combined with olive crystal flash
Thread:	Cream		
Body:	Olive tan Haretron (a blend of natural rabbit fur and Antron) mixed with a little orange fur	Rib:	Fine gold or copper wire
		Legs:	Body dubbing fibers picked out as shown

John Shewey ties this fly in many shades to mimic the giant scuds that are "common to many fertile Western reservoirs . . . and measure from ¾ of an inch to 1 inch long."

Tied by Dick Stewart

HAIR LEG SCUD

Hook:	Wet fly, size 12 to 18		bing loop; include lots of guard hairs
Thread:	Tan	Legs:	Guard hair from the dubbing
Underbody:	Lead wire	Shellback:	Natural cream latex
Body:	Creamy-tan fur blended with the same color sparkle yarn, applied with a dub-	Rib:	Copper wire

Gary Borger's design is tied in gray, tan, olive, orange, pink or red.

Tied by Dick Stewart

HAIR LEG SOWBUG (CRESSBUG)

Hook:	Wet fly, size 12 to 18		and applied with a dubbing loop
Thread:	Gray	Rib:	Silver wire (optional)
Body:	Gray fur with a lot of guard hair included, blended with gray sparkle yarn	Legs:	Guard hair from the dubbing, trimmed flat on the top and bottom

It's important to trim the guard hairs from the top and bottom of this fly so it will have the flattened appearance of the natural. Sowbug, pillbug and cressbug are different names sometimes given to this little crustacean that lives in weed and cress beds.

MYSIS SHRIMP

Hook:	Nymph, 2X or 3X long, size 16 to 20	Legs:	White ostrich herl, palmered over the body
Thread:	White		
Tail:	White hackle barbs cut short, over which is a slightly longer strand of pearl Flashabou	Rib:	Pearl Flashabou
		Eyes:	Black monofilament Nymph Eyes or melted monofilament painted black
Body:	White dubbing, very slender		

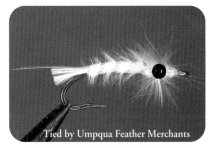

Tied by Umpqua Feather Merchants

SHENK'S CRESSBUG

Hook:	Wet fly or nymph, size 16 to 22	fur spun into a chenille-like rope, wrapped and trimmed flat on the bottom and rounded slightly on top
Thread:	Gray or light olive	
Body:	Natural gray muskrat, mink, or otter	

Ed Shenk developed this imitation in the late 1950s. Many of the spring creeks in his home state of Pennsylvania contain thick beds of watercress, a natural home for the cressbug, and Shenk has great success with this simple imitation.

Tied by Ed Shenk

TROTH SHRIMP, OLIVE

Hook:	Wet fly or nymph, size 10 to 18		plastic bag
Thread:	Olive	Rib:	Clear monofilament or wire
Tail:	Cream hackle barbs	Legs:	Picked out dubbing
Body:	Olive dubbing	Forelegs:	Cream hackle barbs
Shellback:	Strip of clear plastic film cut from a		

Al Troth also ties this pattern in gray. As an alternative, you can use crystal flash or Flashabou to make the shellback, and add a little flash and sparkle to your dressing.

Tied by Dan Bailey's Fly Shop

WERNER SHRIMP

Hook:	Wet fly or nymph, size 8 to 12	Legs:	Brown hackle, palmered over the body and pulled down
Thread:	Olive		
Tail:	Natural deer body hair	Shellback:	Natural deer body hair
Body:	Olive seal fur or similar		

Kelvin McKay of Cowichan Fly and Tackle in Vancouver, British Columbia, tied this fly originated by Mary Stewart of Vancouver. It's become the "most popular shrimp imitation for their interior lakes."

Tied by Kelvin Mckay

YELLOWSTONE SCUD

Hook:	Wet fly or caddis nymph, size 8 to 20		stitute dubbing
Thread:	Orange	Shellback:	Clear strip from a poly bag
Body:	Medium pinkish orange seal fur or similar; blended Antron is a good sub-	Rib:	Gold wire
		Legs:	Picked out dubbing

This is one of the best colors to tie this fly, but olive and gray also work well. The important thing is that you always carry a variety of scud imitations in your fly box.

Tied By Montana's Master Angler

Z-LON SHRIMP

Hook:	Nymph, 1X long, size 12 to 18	Legs :	Z-lon, pulled down from the weave
Thread:	White	Body:	Clear Liqui-Lace, or substitute
Antennae and forelegs:	Clear Z-lon marked with black stripes, over which are barbs of woodduck flank	Eyes:	Painted black
		Markings:	Applied with waterproof marking pens as needed
Underbody:	Woven Z-lon		

Michael Tucker of Thornton, Colorado, designed this interesting shrimp imitation using Z-lon and clear Liqui-Lace.

Tied by Michael Tucker

Leeches

Leeches are one of those aquatic invertebrates that most of us would rather not think about too much. Most larger species are blood-suckers and grow up to six inches in length. They're dark - mostly in shades of dingy olive, brown or black - they're slimey, and everyone will agree, unpleasant to look at. Of all the things in the water that you might be curious enough about to pick up and look at more closely, leeches probably won't be at the top of your list. Leeches are reclusive and spend most of their time hiding from the light in dense weed cover and bottom debris. However, they venture out at dawn and dusk, and swim in the open during periods of low light. They are widely distributed throughout most trout lakes, and are one of the most desirable foods for trout. They swim in a steady rhythmic fashion, utilizing their entire bodies. Keep your retrieve smooth and steady to imitate their fluid, undulating swimming style.

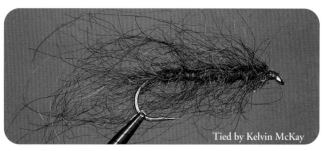

Tied by Kelvin McKay

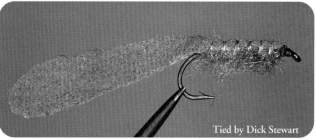

Tied by Dick Stewart

Tied by Redding Fly Shop

Tied by Tony Route

Tied by Redding Fly Shop

CANADIAN BLOOD LEECH

Hook:	Streamer, 3X long, size 6 to 10
Thread:	Black
Body:	A mohair yarn of mixed maroon and black fibers, wrapped and teased out so the long fibers trail out behind and all around the fly

This pattern was developed in the Kamloops region of British Columbia for the remote interior lakes. It has become a popular fly in the U.S. as well.

CHAMOIS LEECH, OLIVE

Hook:	Nymph, 1X or 2X long, size 2 to 8
Thread:	Black or olive
Underbody:	Lead wire (optional)
Body:	Olive sparkle dubbing, picked out
Rib:	Chartreuse Twinkle or a similar braided tinsel
Back and tail:	Olive chamois strip, pulled back and secured with the braided rib

Chamois leeches can be tied in whatever colors suit your needs. Lead eyes are commonly added for weight.

DAVIS LEECH, OLIVE

Hook:	Streamer, 2X or 3X long, size 8 or 10
Thread:	Brown
Tail:	Tip of a large grizzly marabou feather dyed olive, laid flat, curving down
Body:	Olive yarn
Rib:	Gold or copper wire
Wing:	Balance of the feather used to form the tail, secured to the body with the wire rib, Matuka style

This leech is tied in several colors, but olive and black are two of the best.

EGG SUCKING LEECH, BLACK

Hook:	Streamer, 3X long, size 2 to 10
Thread:	Black
Underbody:	Lead wire
Tail:	Black marabou
Body:	Black chenille
Hackle:	Black
Egg:	Pink chenille
Note:	Use any fluorescent color for the "egg" or dark color for the body and hackle

This popular Alaskan pattern has gained wide acceptance elsewhere.

FILOPLUME LEECH

Hook:	Streamer, 3X or 4X long, size 6 to 10
Thread:	Dark brown
Underbody:	Lead wire
Tail:	Two strands of pearl crystal flash over which are several natural gray filoplumes
Body:	Natural gray filoplume, wound up the hook shank
Rib:	Silver wire
Note:	To form the body, it will be neccessary to wrap as many as 6 individual filoplumes, one at a time. Black and olive are both good colors as well as the natural one shown.

GRAY PHEASANT LEECH

Hook:	Nymph or streamer, 3X to 6X long, size 8 or 10		filoplume from a ringneck pheasant
Thread:	Black	Body:	Dark gray-brown yarn or dubbing
Underbody: Lead wire			
Tail:	A dense bunch of gray	Wing:	Same as the tail

Tied by Bob Krumm

RED HAIRY LEECH

Hook:	Streamer, 4X to 6X long, 8 to 12; the front half is bent up slightly		down towards the eye
		Note:	Tease out the fibers on the back half of the body with a fine comb and trim those in front. The Hairy leech can be tied in olive, purple, gray or black
Thread:	Olive		
Body:	Red long fiber mohair yarn, tied far down the hook bend; wrapped thick in back, tapering		

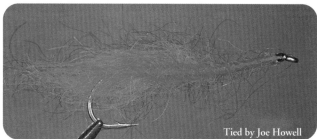

Tied by Joe Howell

LEAD EYE LEECH, BLACK

Hook:	Streamer, 3X or 4X long, size 6 to 10	Hackle:	Black, palmered over the body
Thread:	Black	Eyes:	Chrome plated lead dumbbells
Tail:	Black rabbit strip		
Body:	Black chenille	Head:	Black chenille wrapped around the eyes
Rib:	Oval silver tinsel		

Joe Howell uses this fly when he wants to fish deep.

Tied by Joe Howell

MARABOU LEECH

Hook:	Streamer 3X or 4X long, size 6 to 10	Body:	Butt ends of the marabou tail twisted into rope, and wrapped like chenille, taking care not to mash down the barbs
Thread:	Black		
Underbody: Lead wire (optional)			
Tail:	One or two tips of a black marabou plume		

This is a popular pattern in Alaska where it is usually fished in still water.

Tied by Bill Franke

SHEWEY'S SWIMMING SLEAZE LEECH

Hook:	Salmon dry, size 2 to 6		in front and again at the rear of the body
Tail:	About six strands of black crystal flash		
		Note:	Other effective colors include brown, olive-brown and red-brown.
Body:	Black seal fur or similar		
Wing:	Black rabbit fur strip, tied		

John Shewey likes to fish the Sleaze in lakes, early in the morning or after dark, alternating long smooth pulls with short jerking ones.

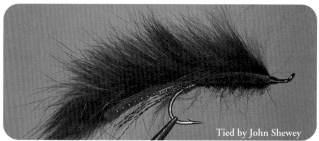

Tied by John Shewey

WHITLOCK'S 'LECTRIC LEECH

Hook:	Salmon fly, size 2 to 10	Body:	Black fur or yarn with the peacock herl and the Flashabou pulled forward
Thread:	Black		
Tail:	Black marabou over which is peacock herl and blue Flashabou on each side; leave enough herl and Flashabou to pull forward later		
		Hackle:	Black, over the herl and Flashabou
		Head:	Black with a wraps of Blue Flashabou in back
Underbody: Lead wire			

Tied by Umpqua Feather Merchants

Backswimmers &
Water Boatmen

Both water boatmen (or corixa) and backswimmers are prolific aquatic bugs common to most trout lakes and ponds. In streams or rivers, they never wander into fast water but stay in the shallows close to shore. To the fisherman, both bugs look the same, act the same, and share identical environments, though backswimmers generally are a little larger and do, in fact, swim on their backs, upside down. One unusual characteristic they share is that they have no gills, so they must paddle to the surface from time to time and take oxygen from the atmosphere, which they carry below as a visible air bubble. They also move about unlike any other insect we're familiar with, awkwardly rowing themselves around on long oar-like legs, continually going to the surface for air and back to the bottom to feed. Between the hatches, and when other conditions are favorable, trout cruise the shallows and forage for these odd bugs.

Tied by Dave Hughes

BACKSWIMMER

Hook:	Wet fly, size 12 to 16	Shellback:	Ringneck pheasant or dark turkey tail
Thread:	Brown		section over which is a strip of clear
Body:	Sandy orange colored fur dubbed full		plastic
Legs:	Ringneck pheasant tail barbs		

When fishing backswimmers, try to imitate the their erratic movements by retrieving your line with short pulls. This is important because the flat water they live in won't impart any movement to your fly.

Tied by Dick Stewart

BACKSWIMMER NYMPH

Hook:	Wet fly, size 12 to 16		and lacquered
Thread:	Brown	Thorax:	Gray rabbit fur
Abdomen:	Mixed gray rabbit and orange wool	Shellback:	Pheasant or turkey tail
Legs:	Brown hackles with the barbs trimmed		

Although it's not a common occurrence, Gary Borger, in his book *Designing Trout Flies,* tells of encountering a flight of backswimmers migrating from one lake to another: "They came buzzing in and splatted on the water, driving their plump bodies through the surface."

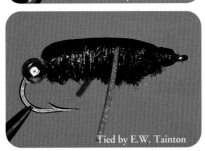

Tied by E.W. Tainton

E.T.'S CORIXA

Hook:	Streamer, 3X to 4X long, size 8 to 12		wraps of lead wire
Thread:	Black	Body:	Peacock herl
Butt:	Silver bead secured with CA cement	Shellback:	Latex strip, colored black
Underbody:	Foam strip, built up over optional	Legs:	Black rubber hackle

Tainton added a silver bead to his water boatmen imitations after collecting the insects in jars and observing that these bugs carried a captured air bubble attached to their rear end.

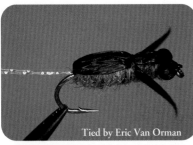

Tied by Eric Van Orman

MONTANA BOATMAN

Hook:	Nymph or dry fly, size 10 to 14	Shellback:	Black nylon raffia in two segments as
Thread:	Tan		shown
Underbody:	Lead wire along each side	Legs:	Black goose biots, angled forward
Tail:	Two long strands of pearl crystal flash	Eyes:	Black beads on monofilament
Body:	Tan poly dubbing		

The crystal flash represents a stream of tiny air bubbles trailing a water boatman as it swims toward the bottom after having surfaced for air.

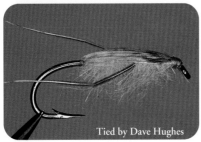

Tied by Dave Hughes

WATER BOATMAN

Hook:	Nymph or wet fly, 1X long, size 12 to 20	Legs:	Ringneck pheasant tail barbs, bent
		Body:	Olive-yellow fur, soft and full
Underbody:	Lead wire (optional)	Shellback:	Natural or dyed olive mottled turkey
Thread:	Light olive		wing quill section

Hughes suggests that water boatmen may be tied effectively in shades of tan, olive and green. Also, when imitating small specimens, size 16 to 20, Hughes finds it unnecessary to include the legs or shellback in his fly.

Crayfish, called crawdads by many, inhabit all types of water: still or fast moving, cold or warm, clear or discolored. They're incredibly prolific throughout North America - one state alone has recorded 29 different species of crayfish within its borders. Crayfish spend most of their time hiding on the stream bottom, only occasionally darting from cover. Many times the only evidence seen is a puff of gravel or sand left behind by a departing crayfish. They're nocturnal creatures, and during daylight many like to hide in tunnels burrowed into sand and soft clay banks. Others don't burrow at all, but hide under rocks and other bottom debris. As darkness approaches, or skies cloud over, most become quite active, leaving their hideouts to scramble about in the open. During these periods they provide an opportunity for trout to intercept them. Often associated with bass fishing, crayfish are sometimes overlooked as a trout food.

BROWN'S CRAYFISH

Hook:	Nymph, 1X or 2X long, size 4 to 10
Thread:	Black
Claws:	Two bunches of red or gray squirrel tail, divided
Body:	Dark brown yarn
Legs:	Brown or dark furnace hackle, palmered and pulled down
Shellback:	Dark brown turkey or goose quill, well lacquered

Don Brown ties this in gray as well, to imitate moulting crayfish. He likes to use this imitation on limestone streams at dusk.

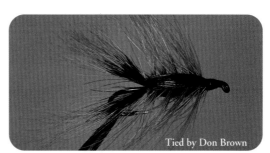

Tied by Don Brown

CLOUSER'S CRAYFISH

Hook:	Nymph, 3X long, size 8 to 12
Thread:	Gray
Underbody:	Lead wire mounted along each side of the hook shank
Antennae:	Fine barbs from a ringneck cock pheasant tail
Pincers:	Hen mallard flank feather barbs, curving in
Body:	Cream to pale green sparkle dubbing
Legs:	Bleached grizzly or light ginger hackle wrapped over the abdomen
Shellback and tail:	A section of medium to dark turkey wing or tail, held in place with a rib of gray 3/0 thread

Tied by Bob Clouser, Jr.

FLEEING CRAYFISH

Hook:	Nymph, 2X long, size 4 to 10
Thread:	Brown
Tail:	Pale olive marabou
Body:	Rusty brown fur spun in a dubbing loop of pale tan thread
Weight:	Chrome-plated lead eyes tied on top of the hook shank
Collar:	Iridescent bronze ringneck pheasant body feather including the fluff at the base
Fur strip:	Rusty brown, impaled on the hook

Borger's imitation was designed to look like a crayfish in flight, swimming backwards.

Tied by Gary Borger

WHITLOCK'S SOFTSHELL CRAYFISH

Hook:	Streamer, 6X long, size 2 to 8
Thread:	Orange
Claws:	Orange hen body feathers
Antennae:	Peccary hair
Mouth:	Orange elk hair
Body:	Rusty orange dubbing
Legs:	Grizzly hackle dyed orange
Rib:	Copper
Carapace and tail:	Orange nylon raffia (Swiss Straw) pulled over the thorax, ribbed over the abdomen with the copper wire and detailed with a black marking pen

Tied by Umpqua Feather Merchants

WONDER BUG

Hook:	Nymph or streamer, 3X or 4X long, size 6 to 10
Thread:	Gray or tan
Claws:	Natural brown bucktail
Body:	Natural gray or brown deer body hair, spun and trimmed to form a long cylindrical body

Al Brewster's Wonder Bug may be dressed in neutral gray-brown or, like most crayfish imitations, whatever color that matches the naturals you're trying to imitate.

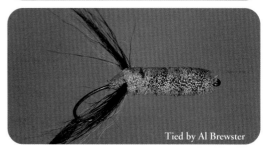

Tied by Al Brewster

Hellgrammites

Hellgrammites are the larval form of dobsonflies, which are one of the largest aquatic insects you're likely encounter along a trout stream. Fully grown, the adult dobsonfly has a wing span of 3" to 4", depending on the species. Mature hellgrammite larvae measure about 3" long. It takes 3 years for the nymph to completely develop into an adult, so hellgrammites of different ages, in various sizes, are available to trout throughout the year. Their bodies are long, flat and well suited to the rapids and cobble-strewn riffles they mostly inhabit. By day they bury themselves under rocks, and unless you go looking for them, they are not readily apparent. Where you do find them they are abundant, and you will find them sharing their habitat with smaller fishfly and alderfly larvae which are similar in appearance. They're nasty, defensive and ill tempered, neither pleasant to look at or hold. If disturbed, they'll either escape downstream or gladly exhibit the use of their strong mandibles. Nonetheless, in areas where hellgrammites exist, trout will always be on the lookout for them.

Tied by Redding Fly Shop

Tied by Farrow Allen

Tied by North Country Angler

Tied by Kaufmann's Streamborn

Tied by Umpqua Feather Merchants

HEARTWELLGRAMMITE

Hook: Streamer, 6X long, size 2 to 8
Thread: Black
Underbody: Lead wire, wrapped
Tail: Divided tufts of soft black hackle
Abdomen: Dark brown yarn
Gills: Black hackle, palmered over the abdomen and trimmed
Thorax: Dark brown yarn
Legs: A black hen feather, cemented and separated into three leg segments per side and pulled flat over the top of the thorax
Wingcase: Dark turkey tail, treated with vinyl cement
Mandibles: Brown dyed goose biots with the tips cut off

HELLGRAMMITE, ALLEN

Hook: Streamer, 6X long, size 2 to 8, bent as shown
Thread: Black
Underbody: Lead wire along each side
Tail: Natural black hackle barbs
Abdomen: Black and dark brown fur
Rib: Black floss followed by gold wire
Gills: Black schlappen palmered and trimmed flush on the top and bottom, short on the sides
Thorax: Same as the abdomen
Legs: Natural black schlappen, trimmed on the top and bottom
Wingcase: Black goose wing quill section, coated with vinyl cement
Mandibles: Black goose biots

HELLGRAMMITE, COSGRO

Hook: Streamer, 6X long, size 2 to 10
Thread: Black
Underbody: Lead wire along the sides, wrapped with dark brown floss
Tail: Strips of dark brown Swannundaze, trimmed to a point
Abdomen: Transparent black Swannundaze
Gills: Black ostrich herl, wrapped between the wraps of Swannundaze
Thorax: Black seal fur substitute
Legs: Black hen hackle
Wingcase: Dark turkey tail
Mandibles: Same as tail

HELLGRAMMITE, KAUFMANN

Hook: Streamer, 6X long, size 2 to 8
Thread: Brown
Underbody: Lead wire along the sides
Tail: Brown dyed goose biots
Abdomen: Brown dyed Antron or similar, picked out on the sides
Thorax: Same as abdomen but fuller
Legs: Speckled hen body feather tied flat over the thorax
Back and wingcase: Ringneck pheasant tail segment, pulled forward over the abdomen and thorax
Rib: Copper wire
Head: Same as abdomen and thorax
Mandibles: Brown goose biots
Note: Tied in shades of brown to black

HELLGRAMMITE, WHITLOCK'S

Hook: Streamer, straight eye, 6X long, size 4 to 8, bent as shown and tied point up
Thread: Black
Tail: Goose biots dyed brown
Abdomen: Dark gray fur
Back: Dark gray nylon raffia or Swiss Straw
Rib: Copper wire
Thorax: Dark gray fur
Legs: Dark speckled hen feather
Wingcase: Dark gray nylon raffia or Swiss Straw
Antennae: Goose biots dyed brown

BUNNY FLY, GINGER

Hook:	Streamer, 3X long, size 2 to 6		strip
Thread:	Tan	Body:	Ginger colored rabbit fur strip,
Tail:	Short ginger colored rabbit fur		palmered over the hook shank

Flesh flies, like the Bunny Fly, are tied to resemble bits of fish flesh. On some rivers in the Pacific Northwest and Alaska, pieces of decaying salmon flesh drift in the current, providing a steady supply of food for the resident trout. When this occurs, these flies are important.

Tied by Tony Route

FISHFLY

Hook:	Dry fly, 2X or 3X long, size 8		squirrel, tied in such a way that
Thread:	Black		the white portion of the gray
Tail:	Black squirrel tail		squirrel tail is about midway
Body:	Black fur or synthetic dubbing		down the wing
Wing:	Gray squirrel over which is black	Hackle:	Black

Relatives of the dobsonfly and alderfly, fishflies are an occasional trout food.

Tied by Dick Stewart

HAIR LEG WOOLY WORM, BLACK

Hook:	Streamer, 3X long, size 2 to 12	Rib:	Copper wire
Thread:	Black	Legs:	Black calftail, applied with a
Underbody: Lead wire over the front half			dubbing loop
	of the hook	Note:	Hair legs may be applied over
Tail:	Black calftail		the entire body or the thorax
Body:	Black mohair yarn or dubbing		only

Designed by Gary Borger to imitate large nymphs like riffle beetle larvae.

Tied by Dick Stewart

JUDGE PALMER

Hook:	Streamer, 4X to 6X long, size 6	Body:	Brown or black wool, cigar
	to 10		shaped
Thread:	Black	Rib:	Black hackle, trimmed
Tail:	Black hackle barbs, on each side	Collar:	Black hackle
	of which is a short section of	Antennae:	Two peacock herls the same
	peacock herl		length as the tail, divided

Tied by Dick Stewart

SAN JUAN WORM

Hook:	Caddis nymph, size 4 to 8	Rib:	Gold or copper wire (optional)
Thread:	Red	Girdle:	White thread, lacquered (op-
Body:	Red Swannundaze, Larva Lace,		tional)
	chenille or monofilament		

The "Worm" developed on the San Juan River in New Mexico. The San Juan has a cold tailwater fishery where the trout feed on the abundant aquatic worms that are present.

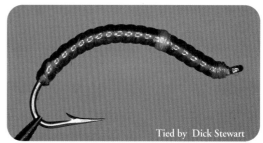

Tied by Dick Stewart

SAN JUAN WORM, VERNILLE

Hook:	Wet or dry fly, size 12 to 16		cured to the hook in two places
Thread:	Orange or brown		and singed with a flame on
Body:	Rusty orange, red, or tan		both ends
	Vernille or Ultra Chenille, se-		

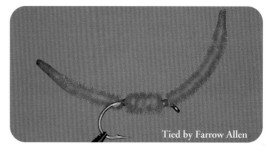

Tied by Farrow Allen

Other Aquatics

Tied by John Shewey

Tied by Dick Stewart

Tied by Farrow Allen

Tied by Farrow Allen

Tied by Karl Svendsen

Tied by Karl Svendsen

SNAIL, FLOATING

Hook:	Nymph, 2X long, size 8 to 14	Hackle:	One turn of partridge hackle or similar
Thread:	Black		
Weight:	A few wraps of light wire at the rear	Head or foot:	Piece of white closed-cell foam, colored with a black marking pen, extending over the eye of the hook
Body:	Dark olive or gray chenille, built up and tapered		

Experiment with the lead wire and foam to get the tail down and the head afloat.

SNAIL, PEACOCK

Hook:	Wet fly, size 10 to 14	Body:	Several peacock herls, twisted together with copper wire and wrapped full
Thread:	Olive, brown or black		
Underbody:	Lead wire		
Rib:	Fine copper wire	Hackle:	Brown

Gary Borger suggests that the peacock herl body and copper rib provides the brownish iridescent look of a snail's shell. The hackle, which is often tied fore and aft, suggests the snails "foot" and should be of dry fly grade.

SNAIL, TAYLOR

Hook:	Wet fly, size 10 to 14	Body:	Dark olive chenille, built up
Thread:	Olive	Collar:	Soft olive hackle

Marv Taylor also ties his snail in shades of brown and gray-green. Because snails lie mostly in weedy areas, Taylor says that presenting the fly in such dense cover presents more of a challenge than that of tying this simple imitation.

TADPOLE

Hook:	Wet fly, size 4 to 10		dark deer body hair, spun and trimmed to shape
Thread:	Olive		
Tail:	Four grizzly variant hackles dyed dirty olive brown	Note:	Small black plastic bead chain eyes may be included if you like.
Head and collar:	Mixed olive and natural		

Although tadpoles are not a major part of a trout's diet, during the Spring they congregate in the shallows, where trout will eat them.

WOOLY WORM, BLACK

Hook:	Nymph, 2X to 4X long, size 2 to 12	Tail:	Red wool, short
		Body:	Black chenille
Thread:	Black	Hackle:	Grizzly
Underbody:	Lead wire (optional)		

Wooly worms are tied in as many colors as you can imagine, but brown and olive are two of the more popular ones, along with the black and yellow.

WOOLY WORM, YELLOW

Hook:	Nymph, 2X to 4X long, size 2 to 12	Tail:	Red wool, short
		Body:	Yellow chenille
Thread:	Black or yellow	Hackle:	Brown or grizzly
Underbody:	Lead wire (optional)		

They don't neccessarily imitate anything specific, but when rolled along the bottom through a riffle, these flies surely must look like something good to eat.

Ants are of value to the fly fisher simply because of their sheer numbers and their availability to trout throughout the year. Before, after and all the time between hatches, are times to consider fishing an ant. Both the wingless and winged adult stages are important to anglers. Throughout the day ants occupy their time scurrying about, gathering food and sundry building materials. Wherever vegetation meets the water's edge, ants will tumble into the water on a regular basis. Dead trees are usually covered with crawling ants, and an opportunistic angler should never wade past one that's fallen half into the water without casting an ant pattern to it. During a mating flight, swarms of spent ants fall to the surface and create remarkable feeding frenzies, when even the most unsophisticated backcountry trout will be highly selective to the size and color of the spent naturals.

BETTS' RED FLYING ANT

Hook: Dry fly, straight eye, size 12 to 18
Thread: White
Abdomen: White closed-cell foam, colored red with a waterproof marking pen
Wing: Zing wing material
Legs: Heavy sewing thread
Thorax: Same as abdomen

John Betts' ant may be tied with or without wings, and in any size or color you choose. Closed cell floating foams have provided the fly tier an easy-to-use material for ant bodies

Tied by John Betts

BLACK FOAM ANT

Hook: Dry fly, size 14 to 18
Thread: Black
Abdomen: Black closed cell foam
Legs: Black hackle
Thorax: Black closed-cell foam

Most experienced fly fishermen would agree that when constructing an ant imitation it's quite important to maintain a realistic silhouette by tying the body in two distinctive parts. The abdomen (or gaster) is separated from the thorax by a thin waist.

Tied by Dick Stewart

BLACK FUR ANT

Hook: Dry fly, size 14 to 20
Thread: Black
Abdomen: Black fur
Legs: One or two turns of black hackle,
optionally trimmed on the top and bottom
Thorax: Black fur

Of all the ant patterns, this may be the one most commonly used.

Tied by Dick Stewart

CALCATERRA ANT

Hook: Dry fly, size 12 to 20
Thread: Black
Abdomen: Black deer body hair secured to the shank, pulled forward and tied down
Legs: Three hairs pulled out on each side
Thorax and head: Pull the balance of black deer body hair forward, tie it down as shown, trim the butt ends to form a head, and lacquer

This deer -hair construction results in a pattern which is the ant equivalent of the Crowe Beetle (which see).

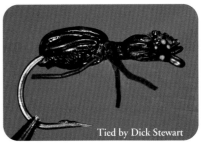

Tied by Dick Stewart

CARPENTER ANT

Hook: Dry fly, size 10 or 12
Thread: Black
Abdomen: Cylinder of closed-cell foam colored brown-black with a marking pen, extending beyond the bend of the hook
Wing: Zing wing material, tied tent style and colored amber with a marking pen
Legs: One turn of dark brown hackle
Abdomen: Black fur
Head: Black fur

Carpenter ants are quite large and mate in swarms during the Spring. They are extremely clumsy fliers and often end up in the water, providing a sizable meal for trout.

Tied by Dick Stewart

Tied by Dick Stewart

CINNAMON ANT, SPENT-WING

Hook: Dry fly, size 14 to 24
Thread: Red, orange or brown
Abdomen: Red, orange or brown thread, built
up and lacquered
Wing: White Z-lon, tied spent
Thorax: Same as abdomen

"Cinnamon" colored ants are tied in hues ranging from bright red to light brown and nearly every shade of orange. It's always a good practice to carry some spent-wing ant imitations in a variety of colors.

Tied by Dick Stewart

E-Z SIGHT ANT

Hook: Dry fly, size 12 to 20
Thread: Black
Abdomen: Black fur
Visual aid: Tuft of fluorescent synthetic hair tied
as an upright wing
Legs: Black hackle wrapped parachute style around the base of the fluorescent hair
Thorax: Black fur

Without the addition of some kind of visual aid it's all but impossible to see a small black ant on broken water surfaces.

Tied by Andrew Gennaro

GRAY ANT

Hook: Dry fly, size 14 to 18
Thread: Black
Abdomen: Gray fur or synthetic dubbing
Legs: Black hackle, wrapped criss-cross and trimmed on the top and bottom
Head: Black fur or synthetic dubbing

Andrew Gennaro developed the Gray Ant as his imitation of a "black" ant after observing that although they may appear black, upon closer inspection he found ". . . the abdomen is covered with a fine grayish fuzz"

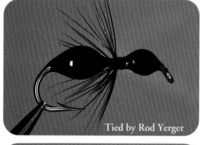

Tied by Rod Yerger

HARD-BODY BLACK ANT

Hook: Nymph, 1X long, size 14 to 22
Thread: Black
Abdomen: Built up with wraps of black thread that are covered with epoxy colored
black
Legs: Several turns of black hackle
Thorax: Same as abdomen

This is Rod Yerger's basic wet ant; it's an old pattern that he now makes using epoxy in place of lacquer. He states that if he were "limited to one fly pattern for trout fishing, this would be it."

Tied by Bill Skilton

HARD SHELL FOAM ANT

Hook: Dry fly, size 10 to 18
Thread: Black
Abdomen: Hard Shell foam, black
Legs: Ant Leg material, black
Thorax: Hard Shell foam, black

Hard Shell foam is a closed-cell floating foam that available in strips. The top side of the strip is shiny and hard looking. It resembles the exoskeleton of a natural ant .

Tied by Bill Skilton

HARD SHELL FOAM FLYING ANT

Hook: Dry fly, size 10 to 18
Thread: Brown
Abdomen: Hard Shell foam, brown
Legs: Ant Leg material, brown
Wing: Two sections cut from a sheet of
transluscent Wasp Wing material (pearlescent Mylar) tied flat over the abdomen
Thorax: Hard Shell foam, brown

Wasp Wing material is similar to the pearlescent Mylar sheets used for gift wrap.

HI-VIZ FOAM ANT

Hook: Dry fly, size 12 to 20
Thread: Black
Abdomen and thorax: Hi-Viz foam cylinder, secured to the middle of the hook with thread forming a waist and two distinct body parts
Legs: Black hackle, several wraps

These two-color foam ant-body cylinders can be purchased in several colors and sizes from fly-tying material suppliers.

Tied by Bill Skilton

MAGIC WING FLYING ANT

Hook: Dry fly, size 14 to 22
Thread: Black
Abdomen: Black closed-cell foam
Wing: Strands of white Magic Wing, or organza
Legs: Several wraps of black hackle, trimmed on the top and bottom
Thorax: Black closed-cell foam

This is a flying ant pattern that's popular in the Rockies. When swarms of flying ants are about the trout can be very selective and you better have a matching fly in your arsenal.

Tied by Ray Cotnoir

McMURRAY ANT, RED

Hook: Dry fly, size 14 to 20
Thread: Red
Abdomen and thorax: Pre-formed, balsa wood cylanders, connected by monofilament and bound to the hook. Lacquered red
Legs: Several turns of red hackle

McMurray ant bodies were developed by Ed Sutryn and are available in several ready-made colors and sizes. You can probably make them up yourself if you have a lot of time on your hands.

Tied by Redding Fly Shop

PARA-ANT, BLACK

Hook: Dry fly, size 12 to 24
Thread: Black
Abdomen: Blended black fur and black sparkle yarn, on top of the hook
Thorax: Same as the abdomen
Legs: Black hackle, wound parachute style around the base of the ball of fur forming the thorax

To form the fur balls for the body, and to keep them on the top of the hook shank, Borger forms a compressed ball of dubbed fur on the thread and slides it into place on top of the hook. He then reinforces each ball with wraps of thread, in front and behind, and several turns around the base.

Tied by Gary Borger

RED FUR FLYING ANT

Hook: Dry fly, size 10 to 18
Thread: Black
Abdomen: Red fur
Outriggers: Black moose or elk hair, one hair on each side
Wing: Section of gray duck wing quill tied flat on top over the abdomen, treated with vinyl cement
Legs: Dark dun hackle
Thorax: Red fur

This style of ant, with hair outriggers to help flotation, was apparantly developed by Western fisherman for some of the Montana and Idaho waters.

Tied by Dick Stewart

ROD'S BLACK ANT

Hook: Dry fly, size 12 to 22
Thread: Black
Abdomen: Shaped balsa wood lacquered black and connected by monofilament
Legs: Black deer body hair
Thorax and head: Two balls of spun dyed black deer body hair, trimmed and lacquered black

Rod Yerger of Lawrence, Pennsylvania, developed this extremely realistic pattern and ties it to his leader whenever fish refuse a McMurray or standard Fur Ant. Yerger says "they always work on the toughest fish."

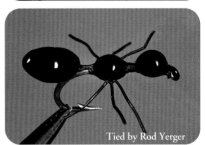
Tied by Rod Yerger

Grasshoppers

It has been often said that about the only thing that will bring a large trout to the surface in bright summer sunlight is a large hopper. Grasshopper imitations are the ideal summertime lure for anyone interested in catching large trout on dries. They are members of the family Orthoptera, which includes crickets as well as lowly cockroaches. In early summer grasshoppers are likely to be quite small, growing larger as the season progresses. Their colors will vary considerably from place to place, between species, and depending on their maturity. It seems that the larger grasshoppers grow, the clumsier they become, and the more likely they are to crash land into your favorite trout stream. Only occasionally found in heavily wooded areas, hoppers are most plentiful in open grassland and meadows. They are most active during the heat of the day. During low temperature periods of early morning, and late evening, they become inactive. Fortunately, this often occurs at about the same time that summer fly hatches begin. At this time, too, the grasshopper's cousins, the crickets, begin their nocturnal activity.

Tied by John Betts

Tied By James Bowen

Tied by Harrison Steeves

Tied by Umpqua Feather Merchants

Tied by Dick Stewart

BETTS' YELLOW HOPPER

Hook: Dry fly, straight eye, size 8 or 10
Legs: 30lb. braided Dacron, colored with waterproof marking pens
Abdomen and thighs: Brown over yellow poly yarn, fused at the ends
Eyes: Black glass beads
Wings: Zing wing material
Thorax: Yellow Furry Foam
Head: Yellow and brown poly yarn pulled over Furry Foam
Antennae: 12lb. braided Dacron, colored with waterproof marking pens

BING'S HOPPER

Hook: Dry fly, size 8 to 14
Thread: Tan
Extended body: Narrow strip of tan Ace Bandage wrapped over a base of synthetic hair
Rib: Flat gold tinsel
Legs: Ringneck pheasant tail barbs, dyed yellow and knotted
Wing: Sparse red calftail over which is a mallard or woodduck flank feather, coated with vinyl cement and cut to shape
Collar: Light antelope hair, spun and trimmed flat on the bottom and slightly rounded on the top
Forelegs: Fine dark elk hair

CINNAMON HOPPER

Hook: Dry fly, size 8 to 14
Thread: Dark brown
Underbody: Copper metallic braid
Extended abdomen: Braided brown macrame cord
Legs: Brown-orange deer body hair extending on the sides like outriggers
Wing: Dark mottled turkey tail segment or similar, laquered and applied tent wing style
Bullet head and collar: Natural brown elk or deer body hair

DAVE'S HOPPER

Hook: Dry fly, 2X long, size 6 to 14
Thread: Tan
Tail: Dyed red deer body hair or hackle
Body: Pale yellow yarn including a loop extending over the red tail
Hackle: Brown, palmered over the yarn and trimmed short
Wing: Yellow deer body hair over which is a tent wing of mottled turkey quill, coated with vinyl cement
Legs: Stripped grizzly hackle stems or mottled wing quill barbs dyed yellow and knotted as shown
Head and collar: Natural brown deer body hair dyed yellow, spun and trimmed as shown

FLEX HOPPER

Hook: Articulated Flex-Hook
Head and collar (tied on to the front portion of the two-part Flex-Hook): Bright yellow and brown deer body hair dyed yellow, spun and trimmed as shown, or painted cork
Body (tied onto the rear articulated hook): Dubbed yellow sparkle yarn
Rib: Light to dark ginger hackle, clipped short
Legs: Knotted yellow rubber hackle
Wing: Brown bucktail dyed yellow over which is mottled turkey wing quill, tied flat

GARTSIDE PHEASANT HOPPER

Hook: Dry fly , 2X long, size 8 to 14
Thread: Light olive or yellow
Tail: Dark moose hair
Body: Yellow poly yarn
Rib: Brown or furnace hackle trimmed as shown
Underwing: Natural deer body hair extending half the length of the tail

Wing: Ringneck pheasant "church window" shoulder feather coated with varnish and tied tent style
Collar: Dark deer body hair, on the sides only
Head: Spun gray deer body hair, trimmed as shown

Tied by Jack Gartside

IMMATURE HOPPER

Hook: Dry fly, size 14 to 20
Thread: Black or tan
Body: Yellow fur
Legs: Knotted pheasant tail barbs
Collar: Light antelope hair, spun and

trimmed flat on the bottom and slightly rounded on the top as shown
Forelegs: Light elk hair

This is a variation of Bing's Hopper, but is tied in small sizes for early season fishing.

Tied by James Bowen

JAY-DAVE'S HOPPER

Hook: Dry fly, 2X or 3X long, size 6 to 12
Thread: Tan, cream or yellow
Tail: Deer body hair or hackle barbs dyed red
Body: Cream, yellow or green poly yarn
Hackle: Brown, trimmed as shown
Underwing: Yellow or natural gray deer

body hair (optional)
Wing: Mottled turkey wing segment, coated with vinyl cement
Legs: Golden pheasant tail barbs or similar, knotted and coated with vinyl cement
Head and collar: Spun deer body hair, trimmed as shown

Tied by Ray Cotnoir

JOE'S HOPPER

Hook: Dry fly, 2X long, size 6 to 12
Thread: Brown or black
Tail: Red hackle barbs
Body: Yellow poly yarn, including a loop extending over the tail

Rib: Brown hackle, clipped short
Wing: Matched sections of mottled turkey wing quill, coated with vinyl cement
Hackle: Mixed grizzly and brown

Joe Brooks popularized this pattern, and for many years it was about the only "hopper" that was tied commercially. It's also known as the Michigan Hopper.

Tied by Umpqua Feather Merchants

LAWSON'S HENRY'S FORK HOPPER

Hook: Dry fly, 2X long, size 6 to 14
Thread: Yellow
Body: Light elk hair, extended past the bend, ribbed with thread then reversed forward and secured with more wraps of tying thread
Wing: Yellow dyed elk hair over which

is a brown hen body feather or similar, coated with vinyl cement, stroked into shape and tied tent style
Bullethead and collar: Natural brown elk hair
Legs: Yellow rubber hackle

Tied by Mike Lawson

LETORT HOPPER

Hook: Dry fly, 1X or 2X long, size 8 to 16
Thread: Yellow
Body: Yellow fur
Wing: Mottled brown turkey wing quill

section, rounded at the tip
Head: Natural deer body hair, trimmed leaving a few hairs unclipped, over the wing and along each side

Ed Shenk developed the Letort Hopper around 1960 and it's been fooling trout ever since. It is usually most effective in smaller sizes.

Tied by Ed Shenk

Beetles

Beetles come in many sizes, shapes and colors as well as temperaments. They range from bright-spotted ladybugs to swarms of plant-devouring Japanese beetles to primitive scarab-like carnivores that prowl at night feeding on ants, smaller beetles and various larvae. There are well over 25,000 varieties of true North American beetles that make up the order Coleoptera. Most beetle larvae (grubs) live in the ground, rotten trees or other forms of decaying woodland debris where they are unavailable to trout, but some species are aquatic. Throughout the summer these larvae hatch into a variety of full-grown beetles that seem to share the same clumsiness. They are constanly flying into things or dropping from a feeding perch for no apperent reason. From about May until October beetles provide a major source of food for opportunistic trout so the angler should never be without a good supply of beetle imitations, particularly in areas with overhanging trees.

Tied by Umpqua Feather Merchants

CDC PEACOCK BEETLE

Hook:	Dry fly, size 12 to 18
Thread:	Black
Abdomen:	Peacock herl
Legs:	Clumps of black CDC, extending on each side, about ¾ up the body in front of the abdomen
Thorax:	Peacock herl
Shellback:	Black CDC
Head:	Tuft of CDC from the shellback clipped short extending over the hook eye

This beetle was designed at the House of Harrop by Bonnie and René Harrop.

Tied by Dick Stewart

CROWE BEETLE

Hook:	Dry fly, size 12 to 20
Thread:	Black
Body:	Black thread wrapped over black deer body hair. Dubbing may be applied to the body if a wide silhouette is desired
Shellback:	Black deer body hair
Legs:	Three black hairs from the shellback, pulled out on each side
Head:	Balance of deer hair cut square over the eye of the hook

This is a versatile beetle imitation that can be modified in size and color as needed. While somewhat fragile, its adherents claim the more ragged it becomes, the better it fishes.

Tied by Harrison Steeves

FLOATING JAPANESE BEETLE

Hook:	Dry fly, size 10 to 14
Thread:	Black
Body:	Peacock herl
Legs:	Unraveled mallard green metalic braid
Shellback:	Black closed cell foam, over which is a section of orange nylon raffia (Swiss Straw), both pulled forward
Head:	Black foam and Swiss Straw, cut off square in front of the legs

This is one of several innovative patterns that Harrison Steeves of Blacksburg, Virginia, ties using some of the new metallic braids and ribbons from Kreinik Manufacturing.

Tied by Bill Skilton

HARD SHELL BEETLE

Hook:	Dry fly, size 12 to 18
Thread:	Brown
Legs:	Beetle Leg material, green
Body:	Peacock herl
Back:	Hard Shell foam, brown

One side of the special Hard Shell foam used for the back of this beetle is glossy, and results in a very convincing imitation. Skilton's Hard Shell foam and his Beetle Leg material are commercially available.

Tied by George Kesel

HARVEY'S BEETLE

Hook:	Dry fly, size 6 to 12
Thread:	Black
Body:	Spun black deer body hair, trimmed round and flat
Waist:	Black thread over the deer body hair
Legs:	Black goose biots, one on each side with the tip facing to the rear
Back:	Jungle cock, well cemented
Head:	Spun black deer body hair, trimmed

This beetle was designed by George Harvey, author of *Techniques of Trout Fishing and Fly Tying*. Harvey spent most of his life in Pennsylvania teaching others how to fish and tie flies, but as his eyesight diminished he began designing flies with higher visibility.

HI-VIZ BEETLE

Hook: Dry fly size, size 12 to 18
Thread: Brown, covering the hook shank
Legs: Beetle Leg material, brown
Back: Dark brown foam with a spot of fluo-
rescent orange lacquer
Head: Foam from the back, trimmed to ex-
tend over the hook eye

You can make these Hi-Viz foam bodies yourself, or purchase ready-made foam bodies with the fluorescent spots in place. Low profile beetles are usually difficult to see on broken water and the fluorescent paint is a great benefit to the angler.

Tied by Bill Skilton

JASSID

Hook: Dry fly, size 18 to 22
Thread: Black
Body: Black hackle palmered over black thread
and trimmed top and bottom
Wing: Jungle cock eye tied flat over the body
and lacquered

Vince Marinaro introduced this fragile but very appealing leafhopper (or beetle) imitation in his book *A Modern Dry Fly Code.* The scarcity of jungle cock feathers have made this fly less common.

Tied by Dick Stewart

LADYBUG

Hook: Dry fly, size 16 or 18
Body: Peacock herl
Legs: Black hackle, palmered over the body
and trimmed on top
Back: Orange deer body hair, pulled over the
top, painted with black spots and lacquered

Although ladybugs never seem to get blown onto rivers in significant numbers, this little fly is easy to see and can be very effective during the dog days of summer.

Tied by Dick Stewart

LADYBUG, ROD'S

Hook: Dry fly; size 16 or 18
Thread: Olive
Body: Peacock herl
Legs: Grizzly hackle, palmered and trimmed
on the top and bottom
Shell: Shaped balsa wood, painted with red
and black lacquer, and connected by a
section of monofilament glued into the
balsa and tied to the hook

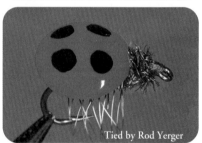

Tied by Rod Yerger

MEGA BEETLE

Hook: Swimming nymph hook, 3X long,
size 6 to 10
Thread: Brown, covering the hook shank
Legs: Beetle Leg material, brown
Body: Hard Shell foam, brown, tied at the
waist to form front and rear sections

The use of new foams makes it simple to tie a large, convincing beetle imitation that floats easily.

Tied by Bill Skilton

THOMPSON'S BLACK FOAM BEETLE

Hook: Dry fly, size 8 to 22
Thread: Black
Body: Blended black fur and sparkle yarn
Legs: Black hackle, slightly undersize and
trimmed on the bottom
Back: Strip of black closed-cell foam
Head: Black closed-cell foam, clipped short

This beetle design of Ken Thompson's may be tied in a variety of colors and sizes. The foam is durable and easy to color with a marking pen.

Tied by Dick Stewart

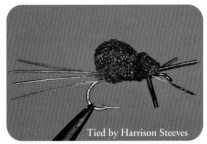

Tied by Harrison Steeves

BARKING SPIDER

Hook: Dry fly, size 12 to 16
Thread: Black, covering the length of the shank
Legs: Four barbs from a ringneck or golden pheasant tail, tied so the black bars extend in front of the body
Body and head: Black closed cell foam tied back, pulled forward and tied off forming the head

This is a simple and effective spider imitation that may be tied in several other colors. An all-yellow version seems to work well.

Tied by Umpqua Feather Merchants

CICADA, STALCUP'S

Hook: Dry fly, 2X long, size 8
Thread: Black
Body: Black poly yarn or similar
Wing: Pearl crystal flash over which is white calf tail over which is squirrel tail dyed orange
Bullethead and collar: Black deer body hair tied reversed
Legs: Black rubber hackle

Although cicadas are found throughout the country, it's in the Southwest where they've been of importance to the trout fisherman.

Tied by Dick Stewart

DEER FLY

Hook: Dry fly, size 12 or 14
Thread: Claret
Body: Peacock herl
Wing: Grizzly hackle tips
Hackle: Brown or dark furnace
Head: Claret dubbing

Deer flies can be found just about everywhere during the summer and are known best for their tenacious inclination to bite any available flesh. They are common around livestock and in wooded areas.

Tied by Harrison Steeves

FLOATING FIREFLY

Hook: Dry fly, 2X long, size 10 to 14
Thread: Black
Butt: Fluorescent green, glow-in-the-dark, Hi Luster braid
Body: Peacock herl
Shellback and head: Black closed cell foam, tied back and pulled forward, over which are strands of Beetle Black Metallic Flash
Wing: Unravelled Mallard Green Hi Luster braid

Tied by David Lucca

FOAM CATERPILLAR

Hook: 4X to 6X long, size 8 to 12
Thread: Yellow
Tail: Peacock herl
Body: Yellow closed-cell foam folded over the shank
Rib: Yellow thread, defining the segments and holding the foam in place
Hackle: Mixed grizzly and brown, palmered
Antennae: Peacock herl

Constructed from closed-cell foam, Lucca's caterpillar imitation is virtually unsinkable.

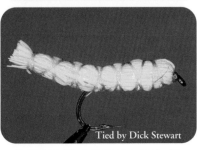

Tied by Dick Stewart

INCHWORM

Hook: Dry fly, size 16 or 14
Thread: Green
Body: Deer body hair dyed chartreuse
Rib: Green thread

During the spring, about the time that fruit trees are in blossom, small green worms can be found hanging from trees by gossamer strands of silk. Some of these trees may be near the bank of a river where trout will lie under them and wait for these little inchworms to spin enough silk to descend to the water.

INCHWORM, SINKING

Hook: Wet fly, size 12 to 16
Thread: Pale yellow, wrapped over the hook shank
Body: Section of chartreuse Vernille, secured at the front and rear of the hook

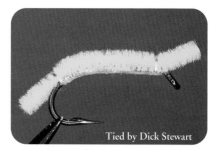

Although many inchworm imitations are tied to float, the worms themselves usually sink after a short struggle.

JUNE BUG

Hook: Dry fly, size 2
Thread: White
Tail: Four red hackle tips curving outward
Wings: Four red hackles tips, two on each side
Body: Alternating bands of red and white deer body hair, spun and trimmed flat on the bottom as shown and tapering up to the head

This large fly imitates one of those monsters that flies around at night banging on your windows while you try to sleep. Brewster ties them in bright colors because in the dark the trout don't care, and he can see them better.

Tied by Al Brewster

ROD'S LEAF HOPPER

Hook: Dry fly, size 18 to 24
Thread: Yellow
Body: Chartreuse fur
Wings: Chartreuse dyed wing quill sections tied tent style
Hackle: Light ginger

Leaf hoppers are generally small, but they're active throughout the summer months, particularly along streambanks with heavy vegetation.

SPRUCE MOTH

Hook: Dry fly, size 12 or 14
Thread: Orange
Body: Cream fur dubbing
Wing: Cream colored elk hair
Head: Butt ends of the cream colored elk hair wing, trimmed short

Tied by Dick Stewart

Spruce moth infestations occur in cyclical patterns. When they reach a peak, the fishing in affected areas is usually spectacular.

SWANNUNDAZE MAGGOT

Hook: Nymph, slightly bent, size 10 to 14
Thread: Tan
Body: White chenille
Rib: White or transparent Swannundaze

In Alaska, the carcasses of spawned-out salmon attract flies that lay their eggs in the rotting flesh. The resulting larvae (maggots) wash into the river during periods of high water, and the trout feed on them.

TENNESSEE BEE

Hook: Dry fly, size 10 to 14
Thread: Black
Body: Yellow poly dubbing
Rib: Black floss, soaked in vinyl cement and
permitted to dry before winding
Wing: Light elk hair
Hackle: Light ginger or ginger grizzly
Head: Yellow poly dubbing

Tied by Brad Weeks

Brad Weeks, an attorney from eastern Tennessee, developed this imitation of a yellow jacket that works just about anywhere.

Mice

Live mice have long been considered an attractive live bait for large predatory fish, particularly bass and pike. It's unusual to find anyone who regularly traps live mice for trout fishing, even though large trout would be hard pressed to pass up a small mouse struggling in the shallows. Fly tiers discovered that the color and texture of clipped natural spun deer body hair is perfectly suited for creating a realistic mouse imitation. In Alaska and Northern Canada mice, shrews, lemmings or voles may enter the water, sometimes as they migrate great distances. When this occurs, large rainbow trout act like largemouth bass and gulp down these helpless creatures as they swim across rivers. Outside of Alaska, grassy banks offer one obvious location where the odd field mouse might stumble into the water. Although it's unlikely that most trout actually see all that many mice in the course of a season, the rare sight of a nearly exhausted mouse swimming desperately back to shore must be an irresistible sight to larger trout.

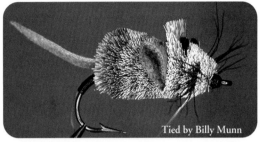

Tied by Billy Munn

Tied by Gary Borger

Tied by Umpqua Feather Merchants

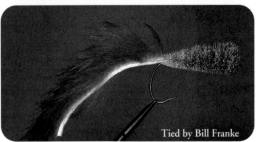

Tied by Bill Franke

Tied by Umpqua Feather Merchants

DEER HAIR MOUSE

Hook:	Wide gape, size 2 to 6
Thread:	Black or gray
Tail:	Gray-tan chamois, suede or Ultra Suede strip tapering to a point
Body:	Alternating bands of natural dark and light deer or caribou body hair, spun and trimmed to shape
Ears:	Chamois, suede or Ultra Suede
Eyes:	Tufts of black yarn
Whiskers:	Dark moose hair
Head:	Same as body

This mouse is tied with enough detail to convinvce the most discriminating trout.

DOWN & DIRTY MOUSE

Hook:	Wide gape, 2X long, size 4 to 4/0
Thread:	Brown
Tail:	Four grizzly hackles curving out
Body:	Natural deer body hair applied in bunches along the shank. The tips of each bunch should be held on top and pulled back while the butt ends are allowed to spin. Don't pack the bunches back, and trim the bottom flat

Gary Borger designed his mouse to lie in the surface film, mostly submerged, like any swimming or drifting land-bred animal.

MOUSERAT, WHITLOCK'S

Hook:	Wide gape, straight eye, size 6 to 2/0
Thread:	Gray or cream
Tail:	Brown chamois or leather strip
Body:	Natural dark deer body hair on top with the tips pulled to the rear and left untrimmed, stacked over natural or light gray deer body hair, trimmed close to the shank on the bottom
Ears:	Same as the tail
Head:	Natural gray deer body hair the same color as the body
Eyes:	Black beads or paint
Whiskers:	Two or three black moose hairs or similar on each side

SIMPLE SHREW

Hook:	Wide gape, straight eye, size 2
Thread:	Black
Tail:	Natural gray-brown rabbit fur strip
Body:	Natural gray antelope or deer body hair, spun and trimmed to the tapered shape of a bass bug, flat on the bottom

"You can't come to Alaska without a mouse pattern," writes Tony Route in his book *Flies for Alaska*, "regardless of what time of year you're coming." In Alaska, big rainbow trout never pass up the chance to eat a mouse.

WIGGLE LEMMING, OLCH'S

Rear Hook:	Wide gape, size 2/0 connected to the front hook by a loop of monofilament
Tail:	Muskrat fur strip
Body:	Cross-cut muskrat fur strip, wrapped
Front Hook:	2/0, straight eye, broken off at the bend, connected to the rear hook with a monofilament loop, and cemented
Body:	Cross-cut muskrat fur strip, wrapped
Head and ears:	Gray deer body hair, spun and trimmed to shape
Eyes:	Black paint
Whiskers:	Black monofilament

Salmon and trout eggs represent a valuable bait for trout fishermen. Walk into any well-equipped tackle shop you'll find shelves displaying jars of pickled salmon eggs, in all sorts of bright and fluorescent colors. Some skillful bait fishermen use nothing but eggs and take trout all year long. In rivers that support spawning runs of Pacific salmon, drifting eggs are of major importance to resident trout. Until recently only a small handful of flies, mostly from the Pacific Northwest, were tied to represent eggs. However, with the developing steelhead fishery in the Great Lakes, and the accessibility of more Alaskan waters, fly tiers began experimenting with more realistic egg imitations. Materials and yarns are now manufactured specifically for tying egg flies, and tiers have responded by devising more ambitious and realistic patterns. Trout fisherman who ignore the importance of these patterns in Alaska, British Columbia, and the Great Lakes area are making a big mistake.

ALASKAN OMLETTE

Hook:	Wet fly, short shank, or offset bend bait hook, size 2 to 6	Body:	Orange Glo Bug yarn, tied as an egg
		Wing:	White fur strip
Thread:	Orange	Hackle:	Sparse salmon pink marabou

Mike Mercer, of the Fly Shop in Redding, California, developed this uniquely constructed Glo Bug variation for Alaskan rainbow trout.

Tied by Mike Mercer

GLO BUG

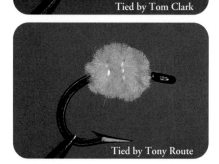

Hook:	Wet fly, short shank, heavy wire, size 6 to 10		around the middle of the hook shank, pulled up as a single bunch and clipped to shape
Thread:	Heavy fluorescent, to match yarn color		
Body:	3 to 6 pieces of Glo Bug yarn secured	Note:	Glo Bug yarn is sold in many colors

You may use a single color yarn, or mix colors to achieve a mottled appearence. Some Glo Bugs are tied all one color except for a single piece of contrasting yarn which creates a spot in the center of the egg. Take care to not let the completed egg interfere with the hook gape.

Tied by Tom Clark

ILIAMNA PINKY

Hook:	Wet fly, short shank, heavy wire, size 6 to 10	Thread:	White
		Body:	Light fluorescent pink chenille wrapped into the shape of an egg
Underbody:	Lead wire		

Tony Route, author of *Flies for Alaska,* says the Iliamna Pinky ". . . is is my hands-down favorite, and I have caught more fish with it than all other egg patterns combined." While other egg flies are tied in your choice of color, the Iliamna Pinky is always pink.

Tied by Tony Route

POLAR SHRIMP, HOT PINK

Hook:	Salmom fly, or wet fly, size 2 to 10	Body:	Fluorescent pink chenille
Thread:	Fluorescent red or orange	Hackle:	Fluorescent pink, applied as a collar
Tail:	Fluorescent pink hackle barbs	Wing:	White calftail
Underbody:	Lead wire (optional)		

The original Polar Shrimp was an all-orange fly with a white wing that was developed in Northern California for steelhead. In its many variations it's a perennial favorite.

Tied by Farrow Allen

TWO EGG SPERM FLY

Hook:	Salmon fly or wet fly, size 4 to 10		orange chenille divided by several wraps of flat gold tinsel
Thread:	Fluorescent orange		
Tag:	Flat gold tinsel	Collar:	Fluorescent orange hackle
Tail:	Golden pheasant crest	Wing:	White marabou
Underbody:	Lead wire (optional)	Note:	May be tied in and color you like or even as a single egg.
Body:	Two balls built up from fluorescent		

Dave Whitlock introduced this fly in the 1960s to give the impression of several eggs rolling downstream along the river bottom. It's also called a Double Egg Sperm Fly.

Tied by Tom Clark

Muddlers

In 1937 Don Gapen of Anoka, Minnesota tied the first Muddler Minnow during an excursion into Northern Ontario in pursuit of big brook trout. The fly was designed to imitate what the local Indians called a Cockatoosh Minnow, a type of flat-headed, sculpin-like darter that played prominently in the food chain of the Nipigon River watershed. It's hard to know if Gapen had any idea of the influence the Muddler Minnow would ultimately have although he clearly had some thoughts on its versatility when he wrote that "... fished under water it represents a minnow ... fished very slowly it represents a nymph. In the grasshopper season you can float them to represent this trout food." It sounds like a cliche, but if fly fishermen had to pick a single fly to fish with for the rest of their lives, it's certain that many would choose a Muddler Minnow. The diversity of flies on these pages offers some idea of the importance of the Muddler. But as you look at modern grasshoppers, crickets and sculpins, and into bass and saltwater flies, you may begin to get a feeling for the impression Don Gapen's fly made on fly design.

Tied by George Kesel

Tied by George Kesel

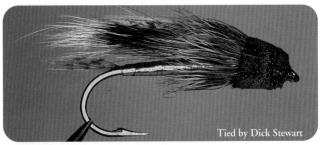
Tied by Dick Stewart

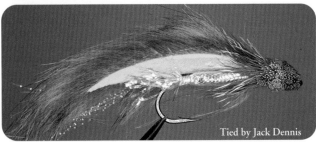
Tied by Jack Dennis

Tied by Kaufmann Streamborn

BUCKTAIL MUDDLER

Hook: Keel, size 4 to 12
Thread: White
Body: Pearl crystal flash, polyflash, diamond braid or similar
Wing: Brown bucktail over which is pearl crystal flash and black bucktail over which is a large bunch of peacock herl
Head and collar: Natural gray deer body hair, spun and trimmed as shown
Note: The wing protects the hook and makes this fly nearly weedless.

COTTONTAIL MUDDLER

Hook: Streamer, 3X long or up eye salmon, size 8 to 14
Thread: Tan
Tail: Brown cottontail rabbit fur with some of the underfur left in
Body: Flat gold tinsel over lead wire
Wing: Same as the tail
Collar: Cottontail rabbit fur and guard hair, applied with a spinning loop and wrapped like wet hackle, the fibers stroked to the rear
Head: A ball of dubbed cottontail rabbit underfur

EPOXY MUDDLER MINNOW

Hook: Streamer, 3X or 4X long, size 2 to 12
Thread: Brown or gray
Tail: Mottled turkey wing quill sections
Body: Flat gold tinsel over lead wire
Wing: Gray squirrel tail over which are mottled turkey wing quill sections
Head and collar: Natural deer body hair, spun and trimmed and coated with epoxy

KIWI MUDDLER

Hook: Streamer, 3X or 4X long, size 2 to 10
Underbody: Lead wire
Body: Pearlescent Mylar tubing, secured at the rear with white thread
Tail: Unraveled pearlescent Mylar
Wing: A broad diamond shape rabbit fur strip, tapering to a point at the back over which are a few strands of pearl crystal flash
Head and collar: Spun natural and olive dyed deer body hair, trimmed broad, flat on the top and bottom

KRYSTAL FLASH MUDDLER, OLIVE

Hook: Salmon, up turned eye or streamer, 3X long, size 2 to 10
Thread: Olive
Body: Green Krystal Flash or Diamond Braid
Throat: Red wool or dubbing
Wing: Gray squirrel tail over which is chartreuse or pearl Krystal Flash over which are dark mottled turkey wing quill sections or similar dark mottled feather
Head and collar: Spun olive brown deer body hair, trimmed slightly flat on the top and bottom

MARABOU MUDDLER, WHITE

Hook: Streamer, 3X or 4X long, size 2 to 14
Thread: White
Tail: Red hackle barbs
Body: Silver tinsel chenille, oval or braided silver tinsel
Wing: White marabou over which are several strands of peacock herl
Head and collar: Natural deer body hair, spun and trimmed
Olive, yellow, black or brown marabou are also commonly used.

Tied by Bill Franke

MIZZOLIAN SPOOK

Hook: Streamer, 3X or 4X long, size 6 to 14
Tail: Light mottled turkey wing quill sections
Butt: Red chenille
Body: White yarn
Rib: Flat gold tinsel
Wing: Barred teal flank over which is light mottled turkey wing
Collar: Natural gray deer body hair on top and white underneath
Head: White deer body hair, spun and trimmed to shape

Tied by Dick Stewart

MUDDLER MINNOW

Hook: Streamer, 3X or 4X long, size 2 to 16
Thread: Brown or gray
Tail: Mottled turkey wing quill sections
Body: Flat gold tinsel
Wing: Gray squirrel tail over which are mottled turkey wing quills sections
Head and collar: Natural deer body hair, spun and clipped as shown
This is the basic Muddler designed in 1937 by Don Gapen.

Tied by Bill Franke

ROLLED MUDDLER

Hook: Nymph, 2X to 3X long, size 6 to 10
Thread: Fluorescent orange
Tail: Mallard flank
Body: Flat silver tinsel; several wraps of thread showing at the rear
Rib: Oval silver tinsel
Wing: Mallard flank, rolled
Eyes: Pearlescent plastic bead chain with a painted black pupils
Head: Spun deer body hair trimmed as shown

Tied by Tom Murray

THIEF

Hook: Streamer, 3X or 4X long, size 2 to 12
Thread: Black
Tail: Red duck or goose quill sections
Body: Flat silver tinsel
Rib: Oval silver tinsel (optional)
Wing: Gray squirrel tail over which are sections of dark turkey tail
Head: Black chenille
The chenille head distinguishes this muddler-like fly from Dan Gapen.

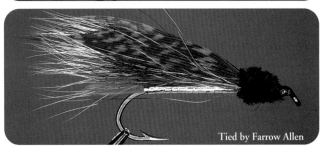

Tied by Farrow Allen

WHITLOCK'S MULTICOLOR MARABOU

Hook: Streamer, 4X long, size 2 to 12
Thread: Red
Body: Braided silver Mylar tubing
Wing: White marabou, gold and lime Flashabou over which is yellow marabou, peacock herl and olive marabou on top
Head and collar: White deer body hair on the bottom, yellow on the sides and olive and black on the top. The head is trimmed rounded and slightly flat on the bottom and top
Whitlock's Multicolor Marabou Muddler is tied using many color variations.

Tied by Umpqua Feather Merchants

Sculpins

Sculpins are small bottom-dwelling fish which, unlike shiners and smelt that travel in schools, are solitary by nature. They are subdued in color and assume the coloration of the river bottom, where they spend most of their life. Over a sandy riverbed sculpins may be light tan while in an environment of dark peat or moss covered debris they'll be dark, even olive-green to black. As sculpins dart from the cover of one rock to another, they are easy prey for trout. Trout usually intercept sculpins between rocks, or flush them out of hiding places, rarely having to pursue them into open water . Sculpins are not streamlined, but are blunt and stubby with broad flat heads designed for hugging the bottom and poking under rocks. Their dorsal and pectoral fins are pronounced and mottled, as most imitations reflect. Flies are usually weighted in order to keep them on the bottom where they belong. Wool and epoxy heads have become popular because they sink better than the spun deer-hair heads of earlier flies.

Tied by Lenny Moffo

Tied by Dick Stewart

Tied by Montana's Master Angler Fly Shop

Tied by Umpqua Feather Merchants

Tied by Blue Ribbon Flies

EPOXY SCULPIN

Hook:　　Streamer, size 2 to 10
Thread:　Black
Tail:　　Two grouse, partridge or speckled hen body feathers curving in
Body:　　Flat gold tinsel over lead wire
Wing:　　Brown marabou
Pectoral fins: Same as tail, but feathers should curve outward
Head:　　Black crystal chenille wrapped around solid plastic eyes, saturated and covered with epoxy

HENBACK SCULPIN

Hook:　　Streamer, 3X or 4X long, size 2 to 10
Thread:　Brown
Body:　　Creamy tan fuzzy yarn or dubbing
Rib:　　　Heavy oval gold tinsel
Throat:　Red yarn or dubbing
Wing and tail: 2 or more speckled brown hen back (body) feathers tied matuka style using the oval gold tinsel
Head:　　Brown lamb's wool stacked over a little white, trimmed to shape

SPUDDLER

Hook:　　Streamer, 3X or 4X long, size 2 to 10
Thread:　Brown
Tail:　　Brown calftail
Body:　　Creamy yellow mohair yarn, dubbing or similar
Throat:　Red yarn
Wing:　　Brown calftail over which are webby grizzly hackles dyed brown
Collar:　Red squirrel tail over the top and sides of the wing
Head:　　Brown dyed deer body hair, or antelope, spun and trimmed flat

WHITLOCK'S MATUKA SCULPIN

Hook:　　Streamer, 4X to 6X long, size 2 to 8
Thread:　Olive
Body:　　Olive yarn or dubbing over lead wire ribbed with oval gold tinsel
Throat:　Red yarn or dubbing
Wing and tail: Four to six olive dyed grizzly hackles tied matuka style
Pectoral fins: Speckled hen body feather or similar, dyed olive
Collar:　Olive deer body hair over the top half of the fly
Head:　　Olive with stripes of black spun deer body hair

WOOLHEAD SCULPIN, GRAY

Hook:　　Streamer, 3X or 4X long, size 2 to 10
Thread:　Gray
Body:　　Red yarn
Rib:　　　Gold wire
Wing:　　Natural gray rabbit fur strip, matuka style using the gold wire
Pectoral fins: Small gray body feather
Head:　　Spun gray and brown lambs wool, trimmed flat and sculpin-like, leaving a short collar on top

As you can see from the flies on this page, the "bugger" family is quite diverse and colorful. The original was the Woolly Bugger and it, together with most of its descendants are here to stay. Tied in a range of colors, bugger variations make convincing imitations of minnows and leeches as well as some large swimming nymphs and possibly crayfish. Tied with some of the new flashy chenilles, fluorescent and pearlescent Crystal Buggers and Jig-A-Buggers are fly designs that excite trout and draw them from the deepest holes. Perhaps the key to the universal success of these Woolly Buggers may be the texture of their marabou tails, which never stop moving. Even if you tried to hold your rod perfectly still, the marabou is so sensitive to every minor current variation, that it dances about unceasingly. You can add lead wire or chrome dumbbell eyes, rubber legs and anything else you can find, and the buggers are among the easiest flies you can tie - and they sure catch trout!

BOW RIVER BUGGER

Hook: Streamer, 4X to 6X long, size 2 to 6
Thread: Black
Tail: Black marabou
Body: Dark olive chenille
Rib: Oval gold tinsel
Hackle: Brown or furnace hackle
Head and collar: Natural light gray deer body hair spun and trimmed as shown

CRYSTAL BUGGER, OLIVE

Hook: Streamer, 3X to 6X long, size 2 to 14
Thread: Olive
Underbody: Lead wire (optional)
Tail: Olive marabou
Body: Olive crystal chenille
Hackle: Olive dyed grizzly hackle
Note: This pattern is tied in many colors and has several names including Flashy Bugger and Crystal Chenille Woolly Bugger.

GIRDLE BUGGER, ORANGE BELLY

Hook: Streamer, 3X long, size 2 to 8
Thread: Black
Tail: Black marabou
Legs: Three sets of white rubber hackle
Body: Black chenille and a single strand of fluorescent orange chenille pulled forward underneath, ribbed with clear monofilament
Wing: Black marabou
Collar: Black hackle

JIG-A-BUGGER, ORANGE

Hook: Streamer, 3X or 4X long, size 4 to 8
Tail: Orange marabou, outside of which is orange crystal flash
Body: Orange crystal or estaz chenille
Hackle: Orange, palmered over the body with a couple of turns in front of the eyes forming a webby collar
Eyes: Chrome lead dumbbells

WOOLLY BUGGER, TAN

Hook: Streamer, 3X or 4X long, size 2 to 14
Thread: Tan
Underbody: Lead wire (optional)
Tail: Tan marabou
Body: Tan chenille
Hackle: Bleached grizzly, or natural ginger-grizzly variant

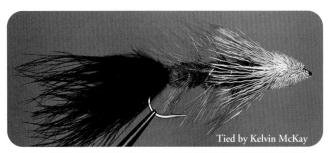
Tied by Kelvin McKay

Tied by Karl Svendsen

Tied by Tom Travis

Tied by Farrow Allen

Tied by Karl Svendsen

Match-the-Minnow Streamers

As new synthetic materials became available and began to replace the dwindling supplies of traditional components, inquisitive fly tiers began experimenting with their potential applications to flies. Cements, epoxies, super glues and other bonding materials found their way into our fly tying kits. When Dave Whitlock originated his Match-the-Minnow series, he began to discover what could be done with a roll of reflective tape, a few yards of braided Mylar tubing, some acrylic paint and C.A. glue. Nearly any minnow you can imagine can be replicated using this style. Note that all these flies are tied with white thread on various sizes of straight-eye streamer hooks with bronze, gold or silver finishes. The metallic or plastic tape is folded over the hook shank, shaped and secured before applying the body tubing. The wings are separated around the hook point and carefully cemented to the very top of the Mylar body, taking care to not cement the barbs on the top side of the wing.

Tied by Umpqua Feather Merchants

Tied by Umpqua Feather Merchants

Tied by Umpqua Feather Merchants

Tied by Umpqua Feather Merchants

Tied by Umpqua Feather Merchants

BLACK NOSE DACE

Underbody: Aluminum, lead or Mylar tape
Body: Pearlescent Mylar tubing; secured at the rear with white thread and pearlescent lacquer
Wing: One light blue and one grass green dyed badger hackle, outside of which are two natural golden badger hackles
Shoulders: Small mallard breast feather
Eyes: Solid plastic
Head: White or pearl, painted olive on top

BROOK SMELT

Underbody: Aluminum, lead or Mylar tape
Body: Pearlescent Mylar tubing; secured at the rear with white thread and pearlescent lacquer
Wing: Two grizzly hackles dyed golden olive, split around the hook point and cemented along the top of the body
Eyes: Solid plastic
Head: White or pearl, painted olive on top

GOLDEN SHINER

Underbody: Aluminum, lead or Mylar tape
Body: Pearlescent Mylar tubing painted as shown
Wing: Two or four dark badger hackles, split around the hook point and cemented along the top of the body
Shoulders: Small ringneck pheasant body feather
Eyes: Solid plastic
Head: White or pearl, painted brown on top

THREADFIN SHAD

Underbody: Aluminum, lead or Mylar tape
Body: Pearlescent Mylar tubing with a painted fluorescent red anal spot
Wing: Two badger hackles dyed golden olive outside of which are two silver badger hackles
Shoulders: Mallard breast feather with a painted black spot
Eyes: Solid plastic
Head: White or pearl, painted black on top

TROUT-SALMON PARR

Underbody: Aluminum, lead or Mylar tape cut to shape, folded, stuck together and secured over the hook shank
Body: Pearlescent Mylar tubing, decorated with parr markings as shown
Wing: Two grizzly variant hackles dyed golden olive
Shoulders: Small ringneck pheasant body feather
Eyes: Solid plastic
Head: White or pearl, painted olive brown on top

Thunder Creek Streamers

In the early 1970s Keith Fulsher introduced the Thunder Creek streamers in his book *Tying and Fishing the Thunder Creek Series*. These new dressings represented the culmination of years of studying minnows and how to imitate them. Although Fulsher was not the first to experiment with reverse-wing bucktails, he was the one to develop and refine the style through a series of useful and accurate baitfish imitations. As early as 1940 both Carrie Stevens and George Grant had tied some reverse-wing streamers, but neither perfected the slim, streamlined appearance that distinguishes Fulsher's designs. Fulsher found that by utilizing this style he could he could imitate all of the important features of the baitfish on which trout regularly feed. Thunder Creek flies have proven to be most effective when tied very sparse.

BLACK NOSE DACE

Hook:	Streamer, straight eye, size 6 to 12
Thread:	White
Body:	Embossd silver tinsel
Throat:	White bucktail
Wing:	Black bucktail, two sparse bunches on either side, over which is brown bucktail
Gills:	Red paint
Eyes:	Cream lacquer with black pupils

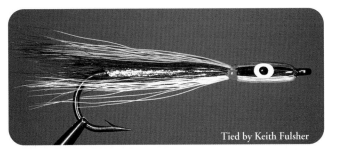

Tied by Keith Fulsher

EMERALD SHINER

Hook:	Streamer, straight eye, size 6 to 12
Thread:	White
Body:	Pearlescent green Mylar tubing
Throat:	White bucktail
Wing:	Brown bucktail dyed olive
Gills:	Red paint
Eyes:	Cream lacquer with black pupils

Tied by Keith Fulsher

RAINBOW TROUT

Hook:	Streamer, straight eye, size 6 to 12
Thread:	White
Body:	Embossd silver tinsel
Throat:	White bucktail
Wing:	Pink bucktail over which is olive brown bucktail
Gills:	Red paint
Eyes:	Cream lacquer with black pupils

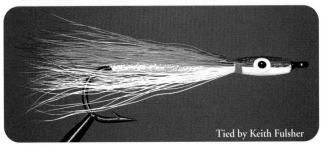

Tied by Keith Fulsher

SILVER SHINER, MARABOU

Hook:	Streamer, straight eye, size 6 to 12
Thread:	White
Body:	Embossd silver tinsel
Throat:	White marabou
Wing:	Olive marabou
Gills:	Red paint
Eyes:	Cream lacquer with black pupils

Tied by Keith Fulsher

SWAMP DARTER

Hook:	Streamer, straight eye, size 6 to 12
Thread:	White
Body:	Embossd silver tinsel
Throat:	White bucktail
Wing:	Grizzly hackle over which is brown bucktail
Gills:	Red paint
Eyes:	Cream lacquer with black pupils

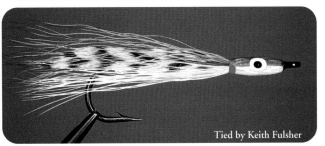

Tied by Keith Fulsher

Trout
107

Streamers

In Joseph Bates' 1979 edition of *Streamers and Bucktails*, he sub-titled his book *The Big Fish Flies*, for indeed they are. It's never been a secret that big fish eat little fish and that all things being equal, given the choice between a big minnow dinner and a little mayfly snack, the trout will take the minnow. Of course "all things" are never equal in fly fishing, and that's part of the charm of our pastime. Nonetheless, if you're interested in catching large fish you often need more than a small insect to get their attention. Many of the the streamers in the following pages have originated in Maine, where trout and salmon feed heavily on smelt, and where streamer-fly tying is practiced like an art. Some patterns might be better labeled as "baitfish imitations," tied to imitate various forage fish, while others are bright and flashy and designed to excite a predatory response. These are often called "attractor" flies. Fly tiers love streamers because they're attractive, and fun to tie.

Tied by Redding Fly Shop

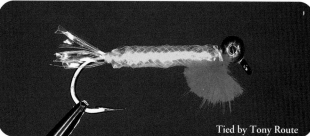
Tied by Tony Route

Tied by Eric Leiser

Tied by Mike Martinek

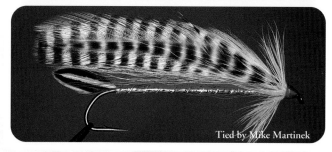
Tied by Mike Martinek

ALASKA SALMON SMOLT

Hook: Streamer, 3X or 4X long, size 6
Tail: Flesh colored marabou and unravelled ends of Mylar from body
Body: Pearlescent Mylar tubing
Wing: Flesh colored marabou over which is yellow marabou
Eyes: Lead dumbbells painted orange with black pupils
Throat or egg sac: Orange lamb's wool
Head: Pale olive lamb's wool, spun and trimmed to shape

ALEVIN

Hook: Stainless steel wet fly, 2X or 3X long, size 6 to 10
Thread: White
Tail: Unravelled pearlescent Mylar tubing
Body: Pearlescent Mylar tubing
Throat or egg sac: Short tuft of orange marabou
Eyes: Small silver bead chain
Alevins are immature salmon fry, still carrying their egg sac. They are abundant in many Alaskan rivers during the spring.

ANGUS, BLACK

Hook: Streamer, 4X long, size 2 to 4
Thread: Black
Tail: Four black hackles curving out
Underbody: Lead wire, double wrapped over the front half of the hook
Body: Black floss
Hackle: Several black marabou plumes palmered over the floss
Head and collar: Black deer body hair spun and trimmed in a wedge
Eric Leiser designed this fly for Alaskan rainbow trout.

BALLOU SPECIAL

Hook: Streamer, 4X to 8X long single, size 2 to 8, or tandem
Thread: Black
Tail: Golden pheasant crest, curving down
Body: Flat silver tinsel
Wing: Sparse red bucktail over which are two white marabou plumes tied flat over which is a large bunch of peacock herl
Cheeks: Jungle cock
This was possibly the first marabou streamer of record.

BARNES SPECIAL

Hook: Streamer, 4X to 8X long single, size 2 to 8, or tandem
Thread: Red
Tail: Short jungle cock body feathers
Body: Flat silver tinsel, ribbed with oval silver tinsel
Wing: Sparse red bucktail over which is white bucktail over which are two yellow hackles flanked by two grizzly hackles
Collar: White hackle
This fly was developed for trolling in Maine's Lake Sebago, and it's a favorite when a bright fly is desired.

BEADY EYE, BLACK NOSE DACE

Hook: Streamer, straight eye, 6X long, size 4 to 10
Thread: Black, wrapped along the shank to represent the lateral line
Tail: Light tan synthetic hair
Eyes: Split brass bead, painted with a black pupil
Body: Silver Mylar tubing pulled back top and bottom and tied off
Throat: White synthetic hair
Wing: Tan over which is very sparse dark brown synthetic hair
Gills: Fluorescent red thread; epoxy head and gills area

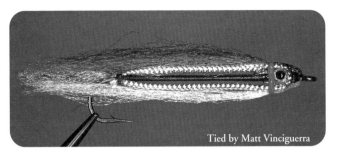

Tied by Matt Vinciguerra

BETTS' BULL-IT HEAD

Hook: Kinked shank popper hook
Diving lip: .010 clear Mylar, trimmed to shape and secured to the hook
Tail: Black marabou
Body: Strip of closed-cell foam tied at the head and pulled back along each side, tied off at the rear and colored with waterproof marking pens as shown
Eyes: Black-headed dressmaker pins pushed into the body
Weight: .025 lead wire wrapped and cemented to the hook as shown

Tied by John Betts

BETTS' Z-LON BROOK TROUT FRY

Hook: Streamer, straight eye, 6X long, size 4 to 12
Thread: Olive
Body: Red and blue Z-lon
Eyes: Black beads on monofilament, figure-8 wrapped in place
Wing: Z-lon: light blue, over which is light olive, over which is dark dun
Throat and belly: Orange Z-lon
Tail: Orange, light blue, light olive and dark dun Z-lon, pulled back and secured at the rear with olive thread

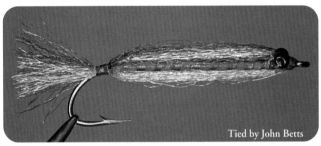

Tied by John Betts

BLACK GHOST

Hook: Streamer, 4X to 8X, size 2 to 12, or tandem
Thread: Black
Tail: Yellow hackle barbs
Body: Black floss or wool
Rib: Flat silver tinsel
Throat: Yellow hackle
Wing: Four white hackles (marabou or bucktail optional)
Cheeks: Jungle cock

Tied by Farrow Allen

BLACK NOSE DACE

Hook: Streamer, 3X to 4X long, size 4 to 12
Thread: Black
Tail: Red yarn
Body: Flat silver tinsel
Rib: Oval silver tinsel (optional)
Wing: White bucktail over which is black bear hair followed by natural brown bucktail

Art Flick designed this bucktail to imitate a common river dace.

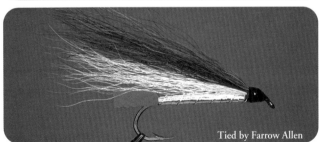

Tied by Farrow Allen

BLUE SMELT

Hook: Streamer, 6X to 8X long, sizes 2 to 6, or tandem
Thread: Black
Body: Flat silver tinsel
Wing: White bucktail over which is blue bucktail over which are several strands of peacock herl
Cheeks: Jungle cock

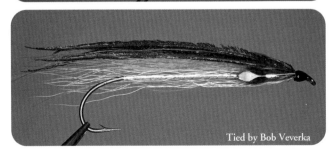

Tied by Bob Veverka

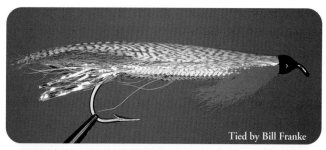

Tied by Bill Franke

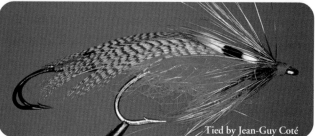

Tied by Jean-Guy Coté

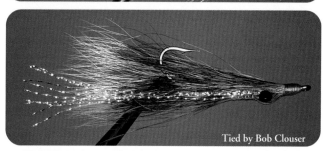

Tied by Bob Clouser

Tied by Bob Clouser

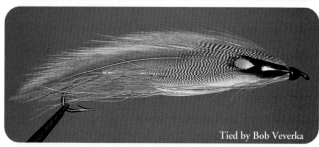

Tied by Bob Veverka

Tied by Larry Dahlberg

BLUE SMOLT

Hook: Streamer, 4X long, size 2 to 8
Thread: White
Underbody: Lead wire
Body: Silver Mylar tubing secured in the rear with red thread
Tail: Unravelled Mylar tubing
Throat: Red calftail, full
Wing: White bucktail over which is blue bucktail over which is a mallard flank feather tied flat

BRANCHU

Hook: Streamer, 4X or 6X long, size 4 to 8, or tandem
Thread: Red
Tail: Golden pheasant tippet
Body: Bright orange seal fur or substitute, teased
Wing: A symmetrical woodduck flank feather tied flat over the body
Cheeks: One jungle cock eye, split, with half on each side
Collar: Cree hackle
Note: When tied as a tandem the rear hook is covered with red thread

CLOUSER DEEP MINNOW, REDD FINN

Hook: Streamer, 2X or 3X long, size 4 to 10
Thread: Gray
Eyes: Lead dumbell eyes painted red with black pupils
Throat: Orange dyed squirrel tail
Wing: Silver crystal flash over which is natural gray squirrel tail
Note: Bob Clouser's Deep Minnow series has developed a strong reputation for catching fish everywhere.

CLOUSER MINNOW, FOXEE REDD

Hook: Streamer, 2X to 3X long, size 4 to 10
Thread: Tan
Eyes: Lead dumbbell eyes painted red with black pupils
Throat: Cream colored red fox tail guard hair
Wing: Mixed strands of gold crystal flash and bronze Flashabou, over which is black-tipped red fox tail guard hair showing a little of the dark gray butts

COUNTERFEITER

Hook: Streamer, 6X to 8X long, size 2 to 6, or tandem
Thread: Black
Body: Flat silver tinsel
Wing: Mixed pink and lavender bucktail over which are dun hackles
Throat: Bright orange bucktail next to the body, then white bucktail, then a shorter golden pheasant crest feather
Shoulders: Pintail duck flank and jungle cock
Topping: Black crest feather from a silver pheasant (optional)

DAHLBERG DIVER

Hook: Wet fly, straight eye, wide gape, size 2 to 8
Thread: White
Wing: A few sparse black marabou barbs over which is gold Flashabou and two orange dyed grizzly hackles curving out, over which is orange marabou
Collar and head: Orange deer body hair, spun and trimmed as shown; the underside of the head should be well lacquered

DOWN EAST SMELT

Hook: Tandem or streamer, 4X to 8X long, size 1 to 8
Thread: Black
Body: Flat silver tinsel
Wing: White bucktail over which are two light badger hackles dyed gray
Shoulders: Mallard breast feathers dyed gray
Eyes: Painted yellow with black pupils

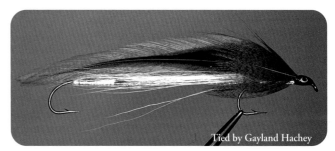

Tied by Gayland Hachey

EDSON TIGER, DARK

Hook: Streamer, 6 X long, size 6 to 14
Head: Lacquered yellow
Tag: Flat gold tinsel
Tail: Two yellow hackle tips
Body: Yellow chenille, dressed slim
Throat: Two red hackle tips
Wing: Brown bucktail dyed yellow
Cheeks: Jungle cock, very short

Tied by Mike Martinek

EDSON TIGER, LIGHT

Hook: Streamer, 6X long, size 6 to 14
Head: Lacquered yellow
Tag: Flat gold tinsel
Tail: White tipped woodduck
Body: Peacock herl, twisted together with black thread
Wing: Yellow bucktail over which is a short section of red goose quill or two red hackle tips
Cheeks: Jungle cock, very short

Tied by Mike Martinek

ERSKINE

Hook: Streamer, size 2 to 10
Thread: White
Body: White floss
Rib: Oval silver tinsel (optional)
Throat: White calftail
Eyes: Solid glass taxidermy eyes on wire stems
Wing: Light badger, tied tent style
Head: Black, in front of the eyes

Tied by Dick Stewart

FLAGG'S MAGNUM RAINBOW TROUT

Hooks: Two wet fly hooks tied in tandem, size 2 to 6
Thread: White
Tail: Two mallard flank feathers trimmed and painted olive with black spots
Body: White cardboard cut to shape, folded over the tandem hook set up, and secured with white thread in the front and back and saturated with lacquer; when dry, painted as shown and coated with epoxy

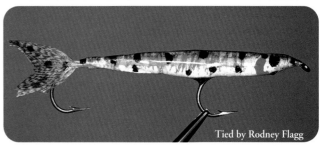

Tied by Rodney Flagg

FLAGG'S MINI-MAG SMELT

Hook: Streamer, size 4 to12
Thread: White
Tail: Two mallard flank feathers trimmed into a fishtail shape
Body: White cardboard cut to shape, folded over the hook, and secured with thread in the front and back and saturated with lacquer; when dry, fold and secure a piece of pearlescent prism tape over the cardboard, paint as shown and coat with epoxy

Tied by Rodney Flagg

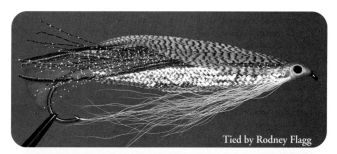

Tied by Rodney Flagg

Tied by Bill Hunter

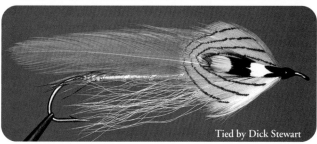

Tied by Dick Stewart

Tied by Mike Martinek

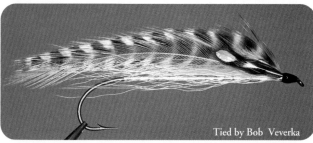

Tied by Bob Veverka

Tied by Bill Thompson

FLAGG'S SMELT

Hook: Streamer, 6X or 8X long, size 2 to 6
Tail: Red yarn
Underbody: Built up to a "minnow form"
Body: Silver Mylar tubing secured at the rear with red thread
Throat: White bucktail
Wing: Crystal flash: blue, over which is pink, over which is blue; over this are two peacock herls and a single mallard flank feather
Head: White with yellow eyes and black pupils

GOLDEN DEMON

Hook: Streamer, 3X to 6X long, size 6 to 10
Tail: Golden pheasant crest
Body: Flat gold tinsel, or yellow floss ribbed with flat gold tinsel
Wing: Bronze mallard
Cheeks: Jungle cock
Throat: Orange hackle

GRAY GHOST

Hook: Streamer, 6X to 8X long, size 2 to 6, or tandem
Thread: Black
Body: Golden-yellow floss ribbed with flat or embossed silver tinsel
Wing: Peacock herl over which is a golden pheasant crest curving down and four gray hackles
Throat: Sparse white bucktail and a short golden pheasant crest
Shoulders: Silver pheasant body feather
Cheeks: Jungle cock

GREEN GHOST

Hook: Streamer, 6X to 8X long, sizes 2 to 6, or tandem
Thread: Black
Body: Orange floss ribbed with flat silver tinsel
Wing: Peacock herl over which is a golden pheasant crest curving down and four green hackles
Throat: Sparse white bucktail and a short golden pheasant crest
Shoulders: Silver pheasant body feather
Cheeks: Jungle cock

GREEN KING

Hook: Streamer, 6X to 8X long, size 2 to 6, or tandem
Thread: Black
Body: Flat silver tinsel
Wing: Sparse white bucktail over which are two grizzly hackles flanked by two grass-green hackles. The two green hackles should be set slightly lower than the grizzly hackles
Cheeks: Jungle cock

HARRIS SPECIAL

Hook: Streamer, 6X long, size 6 to 12
Thread: Black
Tail: Golden pheasant tippit
Body: Flat gold tinsel
Throat: Red hackle barbs
Wing: Sparse white bucktail over which is a narrow, symmetrical woodduck flank feather tied flat

HORNBERG SPECIAL

Hook: Streamer, 2X or 3X long, size 6 to 14
Thread: Black
Body: Silver tinsel
Underwing: Yellow calf or bucktail or a pair of yellow hackle tips
Wing: A pair of matched gray mallard breast or flank feathers, one on each side, cupped together over the body and underwing
Cheeks: Jungle cock lacquered to the wing
Collar: Grizzly hackle

Tied by Farrow Allen

HUMPY RAINBOW TROUT FRY

Hook: Streamer, 3X long, size 2 to 12
Thread: Red
Body: White and pink Z-lon over which is pink crystal flash, pulled back together and tied along the shank; over is pale olive Z-lon, tied reversed, pulled back and secured with spiral thread wraps and striped with a marking pen
Eyes: Silver bead chain with painted black pupils; cover eyes and body with 3 coats of epoxy or Plasti-dip, with glitter flakes mixed in

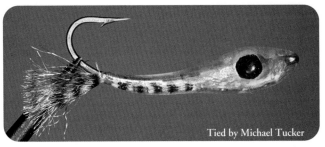

Tied by Michael Tucker

JANSSEN MINNOW

Hook: Streamer, 3X or 4X long, size 4 to 10
Thread: White
Tail: Marabou
Underbody: Lead tape or similar folded to the shape of a minnow
Body: Silver Mylar tubing, slipped over the underbody, secured in the front and back and painted appropriately
Eyes: Painted, with black pupils
Note: Colors are selected to match the natural baitfish.

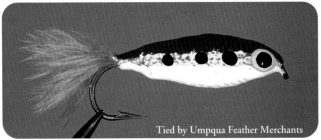

Tied by Umpqua Feather Merchants

JOE'S SMELT

Hook: Streamer, 6X long, size 2 to 6
Thread: Black
Tail: Short red hackle barbs
Body: Silver Mylar tubing secured in back with red thread
Throat: Red lacquer painted over the Mylar tubing
Wing: Pintail or canvasback duck flank tied flat over the top
Head: Black with a painted yellow eye and black pupil
Note: A similar fly, Jerry's Smelt, uses pearlescent Mylar for the body.

Tied by Bill Thompson

KEEL FLY STREAMER

Hook: Keel Fly, size 2 to 10, tied hook point up
Thread: Red
Tail: Two red hackle tips outside of which are two yellow hackle tips, veiled by natural deer hair from the body
Body: Deer body hair, secured with cross wraps of heavy red thread
Wing: Gray squirrel tail over which is deer body hair from the head
Head: Natural deer body hair, spun and trimmed as shown

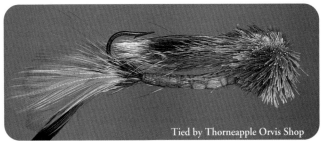

Tied by Thorneapple Orvis Shop

KNUCKLEHEAD

Hook: Streamer, 3X or 4X long, size 2 to 8
Wing: Two short webby grizzly hackles, natural or dyed olive, tied to include some of the fluff at the base of each hackle
Pectoral fins: Chartreuse pearlescent Flashabou
Collar: Several wraps of soft grizzly hackle, natural or dyed olive
Weight: Heavy lead wire, secured with hot glue in the area of the head
Head: Olive yarn wrapped over the lead wire and coated with gap-filling super glue

Tied by Sandy Pittendrigh

Tied by Bill Peabody

Tied by Lenny Moffo

Tied by Bill Thompson

Tied by Bill Thompson

Tied by Bill Thompson

Tied by Dick Stewart

KUKONEN SMELT

Hook: Streamer, 6X to 8X long, size 2 to 10
Thread: Fluorescent red
Body: Pearlescent Mylar tubing wrapped over the shank and ribbed with fluorescent red thread; sections of tubing pulled over the top and underneath as well, secured and coated with epoxy
Throat: Bleached gray squirrel tail (a substitute for polar bear hair)
Wing: Dark dun hackle
Cheeks: Jungle cock

LENNY'S EPOXY HEAD MINNOW

Hook: Salmon, up eye, size 2 to 8
Thread: Yellow
Body: Flat gold Mylar tinsel or braid, built up and tapered
Wing: Yellow fur strip, tied in at the head, pulled back and secured at the rear with yellow thread
Eyes: Solid plastic
Head: Yellow tinted epoxy

This is a freshwater version of his Lenny's Sea Bunny, a saltwater fly.

LITTLE BROOK TROUT

Hook: Streamer, 4X to 6X long, size 4 to 12
Thread: Black
Tail: Sparse bright green bucktail over which is red floss
Body: Cream spun fur ribbed with flat silver tinsel
Throat: Sparse orange bucktail
Wing: Sparse white bucktail over which is orange and bright green bucktail, over which is sparse badger hair or gray squirrel tail
Cheeks: Jungle cock

LITTLE BROWN TROUT

Hook: Streamer, 4X to 6X long, size 4 to 12
Thread: Black
Tail: Small bronze ringneck pheasant breast feather curving up
Body: White spun fur ribbed with copper wire or flat gold tinsel
Wing: Sparse bunches of yellow bucktail over which is orange bucktail over which is gray squirrel tail over which is dark red squirrel tail
Cheeks: Jungle cock

LITTLE RAINBOW TROUT

Hook: Streamer, 4X to 6X long, size 4 to 12
Thread: Black
Tail: Bright green bucktail
Body: Pale pink spun fur ribbed with flat silver tinsel
Wing: Sparse bunches of white bucktail over which is pink and bright green bucktail over which is badger hair or gray squirrel tail
Cheeks: Jungle cock

The Little Trout series was designed by Sam Slaymaker.

LLAMA

Hook: Streamer, size 4 to 12
Thread: Black
Tail: Grizzly hen hackle barbs
Body: Red floss ribbed with oval gold tinsel
Wing: Woodchuck guard hair including the underfur
Collar: Soft grizzly hackle tied back

Eric Leiser, who popularized the Llama, says that the unique use of underfur makes the wing breathe and pulsate. A painted white eye, with black pupil, is optional.

MAGOG SMELT

Hook:	Streamer, 6X to 8X long, size 2 to 6, or tandem
Thread:	Black
Tail:	Teal flank feather barbs (optional)
Body:	Flat silver tinsel
Wing:	White over which is yellow over which is lavender bucktail topped by strands of peacock herl
Throat:	Red hackle barbs
Shoulders:	Teal flank

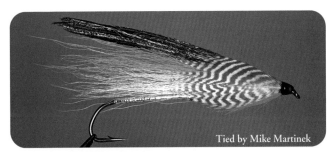

Tied by Mike Martinek

MARABOU STREAMER, BLACK

Hook:	Streamer, 4X to 6X long, size 2 to 12
Thread:	Black and red
Body :	Gold Mylar tubing secured at the rear with red thread
Wing:	Two golden pheasant crest feathers tied flat curving down over the body, over which is black marabou and strands of peacock herl

Tied by Farrow Allen

MATUKA, MARABOU

Hook:	Streamer, 3X to 6X long, size 2 to 12
Thread:	Primrose yellow
Body:	Golden yellow yarn
Throat:	Red wool or dubbing
Rib:	Heavy oval gold tinsel or gold wire
Wing:	Olive marabou, secured to the body with even wraps of oval gold tinsel, matuka style

Tied by Farrow Allen

MATUKA, OLIVE

Hook:	Streamer, 3X or 4X long, size 2 to 12
Thread:	Black
Body:	Olive chenille, yarn or dubbing
Throat:	Red yarn or dubbing
Rib:	Oval silver tinsel or wire
Wing:	Four webby badger or grizzly hackles, dyed olive and secured with oval silver tinsel, matuka style
Collar:	Webby badger or grizzly hackle, dyed olive

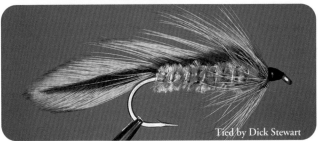

Tied by Dick Stewart

MICKEY FINN

Hook:	Streamer, 3X to 6X long, size 2 to 12
Thread:	Black
Body:	Flat silver tinsel ribbed with oval silver tinsel
Wing:	Small bunch of yellow bucktail over which is an equal amount of red bucktail over which is a larger bunch of yellow bucktail equal in size to the first two combined
Cheeks:	Jungle cock (optional)

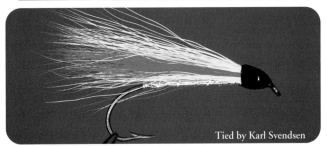

Tied by Karl Svendsen

MISS SHARON

Hook:	Streamer, 6X to 8X long, size 2 to 6, or tandem
Thread:	Black
Body:	Red floss
Rib:	Flat silver tinsel
Wing:	Very sparse, red bucktail over which is white bucktail, then orange bucktail and finally black bucktail

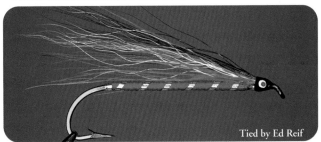

Tied by Ed Reif

Tied by Danny Legere

Tied by Bill Thompson

Tied by Bill Thompson

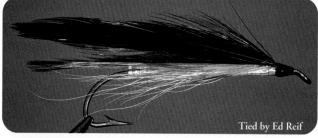

Tied by Ed Reif

Tied by Bob Veverka

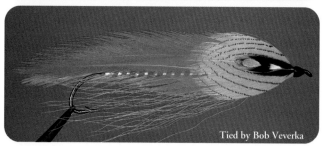

Tied by Bob Veverka

MITCHELL CREEK MARABOU

Hook:	Streamer, 6X long, size 4 to 10
Thread:	Red
Body:	Silver Mylar tubing
Wing:	Gray marabou
Throat:	White marabou
Head:	Gray and white marabou tied Thunder Creek style
Throat:	Red thread
Eyes:	Painted yellow with a black pupil

MOE BUCKTAIL SMELT

Hook:	Two wet fly hooks tied in tandem as shown and connected by plastic coated wire, size 2 to 6
Thread:	White and red
Throat:	White bucktail
Wing:	Green over which is blue bucktail; outside is pearl crystal flash
Body:	Pearlescent Mylar tubing, built up as needed and coated with epoxy
Note:	Eyes, gills, and lateral line are drawn with waterproof pens.

MONTREAL WHORE

Hook:	Streamer, 6X to 8X long, size 2 to 6
Thread:	Black
Body:	Fluorescent orange yarn, dressed thin
Wing:	Sparse blue bucktail over which is sparse white bucktail and red bucktail over which is white marabou
Note:	Like its namesake, this fly has flash, form and lots of action.

NINE-THREE

Hook:	Streamer, 4X to 8X long, size 2 to 6, or tandem
Thread:	Black
Body:	Flat silver tinsel
Wing:	Sparse white bucktail over which are two green hackles tied flat and two black hackles tied conventionally on top of the flat green ones

This unique wing construction provides for a lot of movement in the water, although many tiers today tend to dress the wing conventionally

OUANANICHE SUNSET

Hook:	Streamer, 6X to 8X long, size 2 to 6
Thread:	Black
Body:	Flat gold tinsel
Veiling:	Two golden pheasant crests, one above and one below
Wing:	Two yellow outside of which are 2 orange and 2 purple hackles
Throat:	Red schlappen next to the body, then purple schlappen
Cheeks:	Jungle cock
Note:	In Canada the landlocked salmon is known as a Ounananiche.

PINK GHOST

Hook:	Streamer, 6X to 8X long, sizes 2 to 6, or tandem
Thread:	Black
Body:	Red floss
Rib:	Flat silver tinsel
Wing:	Pink saddle hackles
Throat:	White bucktail
Shoulders:	Silver pheasant body feathers
Cheeks:	Jungle cock

PURPLE JOE

Hook: Streamer or salmon, size 4 to 10
Thread: Black
Tail: Red hackle barbs, cocked up slightly
Butt: Fluorescent orange yarn
Body: Purple chenille ribbed with silver tinsel
Wing: Light badger hackles, curving out
Collar: Light badger hackle
This popular fly was designed for sea-run cutthroat trout.

Tied by Dave Hughes

RAINBOW GHOST

Hook: Tandem or streamer, 6X to 8X long, size 2 to 8
Thread: Black
Body: Yellow floss ribbed with wide flat silver tinsel
Wing: Pink crystal flash, over which are two medium blue dun hackles
Throat: White bucktail
Shoulders: Silver pheasant body feathers
Eyes: Yellow with green pupils
A good new smelt from Ernest "Moose" Bodine of Houlton, Maine.

Tied by Ernest Bodine

RED & WHITE BUCKTAIL

Hook: Streamer, size 2 to 12
Thread: Black or red
Body: Flat silver tinsel
Rib: Oval silver tinsel
Wing: Equal bunches of white bucktail over which is red bucktail over which is white bucktail or peacock herl

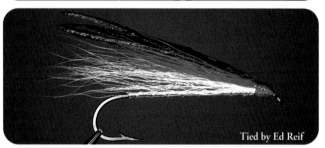

Tied by Ed Reif

RED-GRAY GHOST

Hook: Streamer, 6X to 8X long or tandem, size 2 to 8
Thread: Black
Body: Red floss ribbed with flat silver tinsel
Wing: Peacock herl over which are medium to dark blue dun hackles
Throat: Red bucktail next to hook then a golden pheasant crest and red hackle barbs
Shoulders: Silver pheasant body feathers
Cheeks: Jungle cock

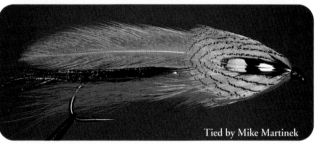

Tied by Mike Martinek

SANDBAR SMELT

Hook: Streamer, 6X to 8X long, size 2 to 6
Body: Light orange floss ribbed with flat silver tinsel
Wing: Peacock herl over which are four white hackles and outside of which are two slightly shorter olive-yellow hackles
Throat: Sparse yellow bucktail next to the hook, then white bucktail, and a small bunch of yellow hackle barbs
Shoulders: Woodduck flank
Cheeks: Jungle cock

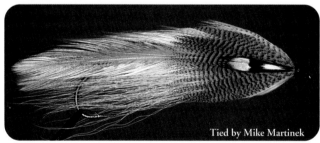

Tied by Mike Martinek

SOCKEYE SHINER

Hook: Jig hook or straight eye streamer, size 4 to 10, bent to shape
Thread: Red
Head weight: Double wrapped lead wire secured with hot glue
Underwing: Sparse red and purple marabou
Head and wing: Pearl Flashabou, secured with hot glue and reversed to form a bullet head
Throat: Red thread securing the head
This jig-like imitation of a shiner sinks to where the fish are. Hot glue keeps the lead wire and Flashabou from spinning around the hook.

Tied by Sandy Pittendrigh

Tied by Jack Gartside

Tied by Joe Howell

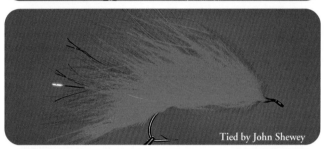

Tied by John Shewey

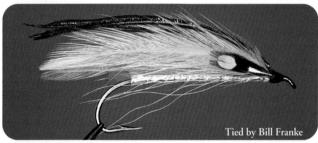

Tied by Bill Franke

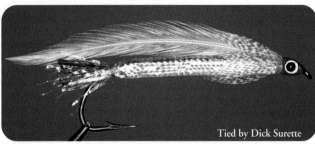

Tied by Dick Surette

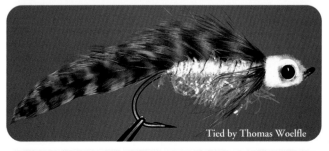

Tied by Thomas Woelfle

SOFT HACKLE STREAMER, OLIVE

Hook: Wet fly, straight eye, size 2 to 10
Underwing: Several strands of pearlescent Flashabou
Wing: Olive marabou blood feather tied in by the butt and wound so the barbs lie back
Collar: Mallard flank dyed light olive, folded back
Note: It's very important that you tie in the marabou by the butt, and not the tip, if this fly is to swim properly.

SPRUCE, DARK

Hook: Streamer, 3X or 4X long, size 2 to 12
Thread: Black
Tail: Peacock sword feathers
Body: Red floss in back and peacock herl in front
Rib: Silver wire (optional)
Wing: Dark furnace hackles, curving out
Collar: Dark furnace hackle
The original was tied with badger hackle, and is called the Light Spruce.

SUPER STREAKER

Hook: Streamer, 6X long, size 2/0 to 2
Tail: Red marabou over which are a few strands of red Flashabou
Wing: Two or three bunches of red marabou evenly spaced at intervals along the hook shank
Note: Color variations are limitless, but all flies should be sparse and at least three to 6 inches in length
Designed for lake fishing by John Shewey, the Super Streaker should be retrieved as fast as possible.

SUPERVISOR

Hook: Streamer, 6X to 8X long, sizes 2 to 6, or tandem
Thread: Black
Tail: Red wool, short
Body: Flat silver tinsel, ribbed with oval silver tinsel
Wing: Sparse white bucktail over which are four light blue hackles topped by several peacock herl
Shoulders: Pale green hackles about ⅔ the length of the wing
Cheeks: Jungle cock

SURE SMELT

Hook: Streamer, 6X to 8X long, size 2 to 8
Thread: Gray
Tail: Peacock herl and unravelled braided Mylar from the body
Body: Pearlescent Mylar tubing, colored on top with a green marking pen, lacquered and squeezed flat
Throat: A few wraps of red thread
Wing: Two light blue dun hackles and mallard flank shoulders
Eyes: Painted white with black pupils

TOM'S BANDIT

Hook: Streamer or up eye salmon, size 2 to 10
Underbody: Furry Foam, for bulk
Body: Pearlescent crystal chenille, trimmed to shape if desired
Rib: Gold wire
Wing: Two grizzly hackles outside of which are two grizzly hackles dyed olive, secured matuka style with the gold wire
Collar: Grizzly hackle dyed olive
Eyes: Solid plastic
Head: White chenille

TROTH BULLHEAD

Hook: Salmon, up eye, size 2 to 10
Thread: Brown
Underbody: Lead wire
Tail: White bucktail over which is black marabou and peacock herl
Body: White yarn
Shellback: Black marabou and peacock herl left over from the tail
Head and collar: Dark deer body hair spun and trimmed; the top of the
                head may be darkened with a marking pen

Tied by George Kesel

WARDEN'S WORRY

Hook: Streamer, 3X to 6X long, size 4 to 12
Thread: Black
Tag: Flat gold tinsel
Tail: Red duck wing quill sections
Body: Orange-yellow fuzzy yarn or dubbing
Rib: Oval or flat gold tinsel
Throat: Yellow hackle
Wing: Natural tan bucktail

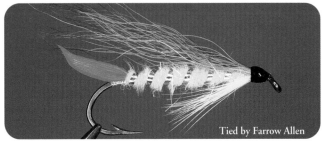

Tied by Farrow Allen

WINNIPESAUKEE SMELT

Hook: Streamer, 6X to 8X long, size 2 to 6, or tandem
Thread: Black
Body: Flat silver tinsel
Wing: Sparse white bucktail over which are a few narrow strands of
                peacock herl over which is sparse lavender bucktail, white
                marabou, and one or two natural black silver pheasant crests
Head: Black with pearlescent eyes with black pupils

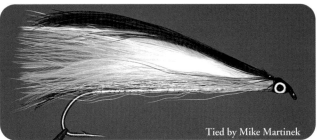

Tied by Mike Martinek

WOOD SPECIAL

Hook: Streamer, 3X to 6X long, size 4 to 12
Thread: Black
Tail: Golden pheasant tippet
Body: Fluorescent orange chenille ribbed with flat silver tinsel
Throat: Brown hackle barbs, sparse
Wing: A narrow woodduck flank feather tied flat
Cheek: Jungle cock
Collar: Soft grizzly hackle

Tied by Bill Thompson

YELLOW PERCH

Hook: Streamer, 4X to 6 X long, size 2 to 10
Thread: Hot orange
Underbody: Bright yellow yarn
Body: Chartreuse pearlescent Mylar tubing
Throat: Orange hackle
Wing: Two natural grizzly hackles flanked by two yellow dyed grizzly
                hackles over which is peacock herl
Cheeks: Jungle cock

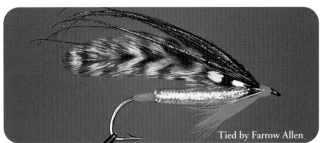

Tied by Farrow Allen

ZONKER

Hook: Streamer, straight or down eye, size 2 to 8
Thread: Black and red
Underbody: Lead or aluminum tape, folded over and trimmed to a
                minnow shape
Body: Silver Mylar tubing
Tail: Unravelled Mylar from the body
Hackle: Soft grizzly
Wing: Rabbit fur strip secured at the head, pulled back over the body
                and tied down with red thread and a little red dubbing

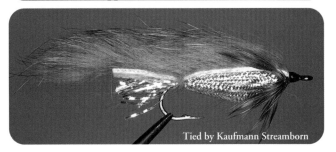

Tied by Kaufmann Streamborn

SELECT BIBLIOGRAPHY

BOOKS

Alaska Flyfishers. 1983. *Fly patterns of Alaska*. Portland, Ore.: Frank Amato Publications.

Atherton, John. [1951] 1971. *Fly and the fish*. Rockville Centre, N.Y.: Freshet Press.

Bates, Joseph D., Jr. 1979. *Streamers & bucktails*. New York: Alfred A. Knopf.

_____. 1950. *Streamer fly tying and fishing*. Harrisburg: Stackpole Books.

Bay, Kenneth E., ed. 1979. *American fly tyer's handbook*. New York: Winchester Press.

Betters, Fran. 1986. *Fran Betters' fly fishing - fly tying and pattern guide*. Wilmington, N.Y.: Adirondack Sports Publ.

Borger, Gary A. 1991. *Designing trout flies*. Wausau, Wis.: Tomorrow River Press.

Boyle, Robert H. and Dave Whitlock, eds. 1975. *Fly-tyer's almanac*. New York: Crown Publishers.

_____. 1978. *Second fly-tyer's almanac*. Philadelphia & New York: J.B. Lippincott.

Brooks, Charles E. 1976. *Nymph fishing for larger trout*. New York: Crown Publishers.

Caucci, Al and Bob Nastasi. 1986. *Hatches II*. Piscataway, N.J.: New Century Publishers.

Clarke, Brian and John Goddard. *1980. Trout and the fly*. New York: Lyons & Burford.

Dennis, Jack. 1974. *Western trout fly tying manual*. Jackson Hole, Wyo.: Snake River Books.

_____. 1980. *Western trout fly tying manual*. Vol. II. Jackson Hole, Wyo.: Snake River Books.

Flick, Art, ed. 1972. *Master fly-tying guide*. New York: Crown Publishers.

_____. [1969] 1972. *New streamside guide*. New York: Crown Publishers.

Fulsher, Keith. 1973. *Tying and fishing the Thunder Creek series*. Rockville Center, N.Y.: Freshet Press.

Hanley, Ken. 1991. *California fly tying & fishing guide*. Portland, Ore.: Frank Amato Publications.

Helleckson, Terry. [1976] 1981. *Popular fly patterns*. Salt Lake City: Gibbs M. Smith, Inc.

Inland Empire Fly Fishing Club. 1986. *Flies of the northwest*. Spokane, Wash.

Iwamasa, Ken. 1988. *Iwamasa flies*. Boulder, Colo.: Pruett Publishing.

Juracek, John and Craig Mathews. 1992. *Fishing Yellowstone hatches*. West Yellowstone, Mont.: Blue Ribbon Flies.

Kaufmann, Randall. 1986. *Fly tyers nymph manual*. Portland, Ore.: Western Fishermen's Press.

_____. 1991. *Tying dry flies*. Portland, Ore.: Western Fishermen's Press.

Koch, Ed. [1972] 1988. *Fishing the midge*. Harrisburg: Stackpole Books.

LaFontaine, Gary. 1990. *Dry fly*. Helena, Mont.: Greycliff Publishing.

_____. 1981. *Caddisflies*. Piscataway, N.J.: New Century Publishers.

Leisenring, James E. [1941] 1971. *Art of tying the wet fly*. New York: Crown Publishers.

Leiser, Eric. 1987. *The book of fly patterns*. New York: Alfred A. Knopf.

_____ and Robert H. Boyle. 1982. *Stoneflies for the angler*. New York: Alfred A. Knopf.

Marinaro, Vincent. [1950] 1970. *Modern dry-fly code*. New York: Crown Publishers.

Mathews, Craig and John Juracek. 1987. *Fly patterns of Yellowstone*. West Yellowstone, Mont.: Blue Ribbon Flies.

McCafferty, W. Patrick. 1981. *Aquatic entomology*. Boston: Science Books International.

McClane, A. J., ed. 1965. *McClane's new standard fishing encyclopedia*. New York: Holt, Rinehart and Winston.

Migel, J. Michael and Leonard M. Wright, Jr., eds. 1979. *Masters on the nymph*. New York: Doubleday.

Richards, Carl and Doug Swisher and Fred Arbona, Jr. 1980. *Stoneflies*. Tulsa, Okla.: Winchester Press.

Rosborough, E. H. "Polly." [1965] 1988. *Tying and fishing the fuzzy nymphs*. Harrisburg: Stackpole Books.

Route, Anthony J. 1991. *Flies for Alaska*. Boulder, Colo.: Johnson Books.

Schwiebert, Ernest G. Jr. [1955] 1988. *Matching the hatch*. South Hackensack, N.J.: Stoeger Publishing.

Solomon, Larry and Eric Leiser. 1977. *Caddis and the angler*. Harrisburg: Stackpole Books.

Staples, Bruce. 1991. *Snake River country flies and waters*. Portland, Ore.: Frank Amato Publications.

Stetzer, Randle Scott. 1992. *Flies: the best one thousand*. Portland, Ore.: Frank Amato Publications.

Stewart, Dick. 1979. *Universal fly tying guide*. Brattleboro, Vt.: Stephen Greene Press.

_____ and Farrow Allen. 1992. *Flies for bass & panfish*. Intervale, N.H.: Northland Press.

_____ and Farrow Allen. 1992. *Flies for steelhead*. Intervale, N.H.: Northland Press.

_____ and Bob Leeman. 1982. *Trolling flies for trout & salmon*. Brattleboro, Vt.: Stephen Greene Press.

Surette, Dick, ed. 1985. *Fly Tyer pattern bible*. North Conway, N.H.: Saco River Publishing.

Swisher, Doug and Carl Richards. 1971. *Selective trout*. Piscataway, N.J.: New Century Publishers.

Taylor, Marv. 1979. *Float-tubes, fly rods and other essays*. Boise, Idaho.: Marv Taylor Enterprises.

Whitlock, Dave. 1982. *Guide to aquatic trout foods*. New York: Lyons & Burford.

Wright, Leonard M., Jr. 1972. *Fishing the dry fly as a living insect*. New York: E. P. Dutton.

PERIODICALS

American Angler. various dates 1990 - 1992. Intervale, N.H.: Northland Press.

American Angler & Fly Tyer. various dates 1988 - 1990. Intervale, N.H.: Northland Press.

American Fly Tyer. various dates 1986 - 1987. Intervale, N.H.: Northland Press.

Flyfishing. various dates 1988 - 1992. Portland, Ore.: Frank Amato Publications.

Fly Fisherman. various dates 1984 - 1992. Harrisburg, Pa.: Cowles Magazines.

Fly Fishing Quarterly. various dates 1988 - 1992. Shrewsbury, N.J.: Aqua-Field Publishing.

Fly Rod & Reel. various dates 1989 - 1992. Camden, Maine: Down East Enterprise.

Fly Tyer. various dates 1978 - 1986. North Conway, N.H.: Fly Tyer, Inc.

INDEX TO FLY DRESSINGS

ABOUT THE AUTHORS

Dick Stewart (left) and Farrow Allen

Dick Stewart has been tying flies since the age of fourteen and has been professionally involved in the fly-fishing industry for the past twenty years. He has authored or co-authored nine books, including the best-selling *Universal Fly Tying Guide*. His trout fishing experience began in Pennsylvania and has since included fly fishing throughout the northeast and most of the rocky mountain states. Formerly editor and publisher of *American Angler* magazine, Dick has settled in the White Mountains area of New Hampshire.

Farrow Allen moved from New York City to Vermont where for twelve years he owned a fly-fishing shop in the Burlington area. During this time he co-authored a book *Vermont Trout Streams*. A long time fly tier, Farrow has fished extensively for trout throughout the northeast, and has ventured as far as Washington state. He has been associated with *American Angler* magazine and now resides in New Hampshire.

ABOUT THIS BOOK

This is the last book in a series of five which cover the majority of recognized fly patterns in use in the United States and Canada. The series is entitled *Fishing Flies of North America* and the individual titles are as follows:

Flies for Atlantic Salmon
Flies for Steelhead
Flies for Bass & Panfish
Flies for Saltwater
Flies for Trout